ESSENTIALS OF EXPORTING AND IMPORTING
U.S. Trade Policies, Procedures, and Practices

ESSENTIALS OF EXPORTING AND IMPORTING
U.S. Trade Policies, Procedures, and Practices

Harvey R. Shoemack
Illinois Institute of Art—Chicago
Oakton Community College

Patricia Mink Rath
International Academy of Design and Technology—Chicago

Fairchild Books | New York

EXECUTIVE EDITOR: Olga T. Kontzias

ASSISTANT ACQUISITIONS EDITOR: Amanda Breccia

EDITORIAL DEVELOPMENT DIRECTOR: Jennifer Crane

SENIOR DEVELOPMENT EDITOR: Joseph Miranda

ASSOCIATE ART DIRECTOR: Erin Fitzsimmons

PRODUCTION DIRECTOR: Ginger Hillman

PRODUCTION EDITOR: Jessica Rozler

ANCILLARIES EDITOR: Noah Schwartzberg

COVER AND TEXT DESIGN: Alisha Neumaier

COVER ART: Jerry Driendl/Getty Images (top); Eric Remann/STOCK 4B/Getty Images (bottom);
Courtesy of Fairchild Publications, Inc. (back cover).

PAGE COMPOSITION: Alisha Neumaier and SR Desktop Services, Ridge, NY

DIRECTOR, SALES & MARKETING: Brian Normoyle

LIBRARY OF CONGRESS CATALOG CARD NUMBER: 2008943317

ISBN: 978-1-56367-573-7   GST R 133004424

Printed in the United States of America

TP13

Contents

Extended Contents

Introduction

GLOBALIZATION AND THE BENEFITS OF TRADE

When the authors began the research for this textbook, the U.S. economy, the world's largest, was experiencing one of the strongest growth periods in recent history. Gross Domestic Product was at an all-time high, estimated at $13 trillion, constituting 21 percent of the gross world product. Total U.S. international trade for 2007 was at record levels, with exports of goods and services at 1.6 trillion dollars and imports at 2.3 billion dollars. U.S. exports of foods, feeds, and beverages ($84 billion); industrial supplies and materials ($315 billion); and consumer goods ($146 billion) were all records. Exports grew 12.2 percent over 2006, while the growth rate of imports was 5.9 percent—all good news for the overall U.S. trade deficit, which showed the first year-to-year decrease since 2000–2001.

The climate for U.S. export-import trade was favorable going into 2008. American companies such as Coca-Cola, McDonald's, and Disney claimed footprints worldwide. Fashion goods marketers like Ralph Lauren, Guess, Calvin Klein, Gap, and others were well-established in Europe and Asia, and American consumers could choose from global brands such as Chanel, H&M, Zara, Prada, and Burberry.

Domestically, the picture seemed really rosy. With personal income at record levels and enticingly generous mortgages available, the American dream of owning a home was within reach even for the less-than-average wage-earner. Sub-prime mortgages were wholesaled by banks across the country, as government policy encouraged lending for new homeowners. As individual stock portfolios and personal wealth expanded for millions of Americans, few could have anticipated—or believed—the bursting of the housing and financial bubbles in the second half of 2008. As a result, Wall Street investment bankers and stockbrokers went from receiving multimillion dollar bonuses at the end of 2007 to pink slips in 2008.

According to the Bureau of Economic Analysis at the U.S. Department of Commerce in its February 27, 2009, report, real **Gross Domestic Product (GDP)**—the output of goods and services produced by labor and property located in the United States—contracted at an annual rate of 6.3 percent during the fourth quarter of 2008, the sharpest decline in GDP in more than two decades. U.S. GDP for the first half of 2009 recorded further declines in growth as the nation slumped further into recession. The decrease in real GDP in the first half of 2009 primarily reflected negative contributions from exports, personal consumption expenditures, equipment and software, and residential fixed investments that were partly offset by a positive contribution from federal government spending. Imports, which are a subtraction in the calculation of GDP, decreased as well in the first half of 2009.

"The U.S. economy in 2008 suffered its biggest decline since 2001, ushering in what may be the worst recession in a quarter century. Unemployment was at a five-year high of 6.1 percent," according to Jan Hatzius, chief economist at Goldman Sachs in New York, and actually rose to 10.2 percent by the end of the year.

A narrower trade deficit at the start of 2009—primarily due to a weak U.S. dollar, which made exports less expensive for foreign buyers and reduced demand for imports as America consumers cut back on overall consumption—was the lone bright spot for the U.S. economy. It became dim, however, as declining consumer demand spread worldwide, coupled with a deepening global credit crunch.

Global trade volume dropped in 2008—the first decline since 1982, according to economists at the World Bank. Over the past decade, annual increases in global trade averaged five to ten percent. The current lack of credit has been a shock to the entire global trade economy. International business trade was second, after the banks, to feel the effects of the global economic crisis. Of the 13.6 trillion dollars of goods traded worldwide, 90 percent rely on letters of credit or related forms of financing and guarantees such as credit insurance, according to the World Trade Organization (WTO). For centuries, letters of credit have been used to allow buyers in one country to trade with sellers in another country thousands of miles away. The buyer or importing country would have its bank issue the letter, guaranteeing payment to the exporting company. "When banks don't trust each other, as seen in the current economic crisis, they are unwilling to accept a letter of credit as proof that payment for the traded goods is coming," an analyst for Moody's Economy.com wrote in an October 23, 2008 report. "The whole global trade production line relies on letters of credit. No letters of credit, no transaction—and no transactions mean no international trade," the report concluded.

According to Gulfnews.com, on October 30, 2008, "U.S. and global suppliers of oil, coal, grains, and consumer products are losing sales as the credit crisis spreads beyond financial institutions, with banks refusing financing or increasing fees they charge buyers."

Hopefully, such dire predictions will not create a modern-day collapse of international trade, as free trade is one antidote to a sick global economy. As nations attempt to shield the domestic economy, some people believe that by imposing trade barriers on imports, demand will increase for domestically produced goods and services. They see this action as a way to protect American jobs and also as an opportunity to raise revenue from tariffs, or taxes, on imported goods.

Historically, this thinking resulted in economic disaster, as when, in June 1930, the Smoot-Hawley Tariff Act raised tariffs on imports, some up to 50 percent. Naturally, sales tumbled, and unfortunately, the drop in imports created unemployment in nations trading with the United States. The nations then responded with protectionism that created more unemployment here. To the dismay of the protectionists, the sharp rise in tariff rates caused imports to decline so much that resulting revenues actually dropped by almost 50 percent over the next two years. And tax revenues were lost from domestic unemployment indirectly caused by the tariffs.

The loss of international trade in the 1930s had devastating global economic effects, similar to that of the bank failures. It is widely believed that the U.S. protectionist policies of the 1930s led to the collapse of world trade and, as such, to the global depression. It is the hope of these authors that today's world government and financial leaders will recall the lessons learned from Smoot-Hawley and the Great Depression of the 1930s, and use protectionist policies sparingly, if at all, while simultaneously striving for fair trade. Both free trade (the open exchange of goods, services, and information among nations with few or no protectionist barriers), and fair trade, (working to create a level playing field, meaning creating more equitable trading relationships between developed and less-developed countries) should be used as often as possible.

Fair trade practices focus on alleviating poverty, enhancing gender equality, improving working conditions, protecting the environment, and promoting equality and justice among all peoples of the world. Free trade proponents believe that free trade will create the environment for fair trade to exist, as the markets will solve the issues of equilibrium, a goal that unfortunately has yet to eliminate the economic and social barriers between industrialized and emerging nations. After all, the goal, whether through free trade and/or fair trade, should be the well-being of people everywhere.

This textbook, *Essentials of Exporting and Importing: U.S. Trade Policies, Procedures, and Practices*, is not intended to be a thorough analysis of U.S. or global trade policy. Instead, the authors offer a basic, step-by-step approach for the novice student or trader whose career path includes potential ventures into the dynamic world of exporting American-designed goods and services, or of sourcing imports from countries all over the world in response to American customers' needs and wants. Exporting and importing fashion goods are emerging occupational fields offering opportunities full of adventure, challenges, risks, and rewards. In writing this text, the authors, through their years of international business management, teaching, writing, and marketing experience, hope to alert you to the opportunities and spare you the pitfalls so frequently encountered by the uninitiated. We wish you an enjoyable reading and successful ventures!

Preface

E ssentials of Exporting and Importing: U.S. Trade Policies, Procedures, and Practices was written for those students and businesses interested in learning about exporting and/or importing, whether through formal college courses or independent study. It is based on the facts that the world is shrinking, and that consumer demand and global trade will expand in the coming years. For people contemplating marketing careers, the export/import fields offer a variety of opportunities to connect with customers everywhere. For businesses planning expansion, global trade offers vast new market opportunities.

Typically suitable for business people and for college-level students enrolled in International Marketing and Export/Import classes, the text provides examples of global trade in terms of fashion (currently popular designed goods and services), but is representative of a range of businesses concerned with market-driven products, services, and ideas. These factors make studying export/import relevant for students and entrepreneurs today:

* Through vast communications networks, the world today is smaller, allowing businesses global opportunities for sourcing and marketing a wide variety of products
* Many students seeking careers from among the various fashion fields which appeal to them can expand their horizons by learning about opportunities in export-import marketing
* By discovering the appropriate steps to take, thus avoiding many pitfalls, readers can encounter less risk and more successfully navigate the routes of export/import trade

This text was developed by an experienced export/import business practitioner who, after extensive experience in international trade, applied his expertise to college teaching and, over the years, created a series of several college-level and adult courses which became the foundation for Essentials of Exporting and Importing: U.S. Trade Policies, Practices, and Procedures. The co-author, an international traveler and experienced business text author and specialist in fashion marketing and consumer behavior, contributes a specific fashion focus to this work.

While this text was developed for college students and business professionals, anyone interested in the export/import business will find it useful, as its organization and contents reveal.

Organization of the Text

Essentials of Exporting and Importing: U.S. Trade Policies, Practices, and Procedures is divided into three main parts: Part I, Globalization and the U.S. Export-Import Business; Part II, U.S. Exporting Policies and Procedures; Part III, Importing into the United States; and Part IV, Rewards and Challenges of Export-Import Trade.

PART I: Globalization and the U.S. Export-Import Business. Chapter 1 offers an overview of global business today; Chapter 2 tells how globalization and trade liberalization came about; and Chapter 3 explains the role of the U.S. in global trade and cites major trade agreements in effect today.

PART II: U.S. Exporting Policies and Procedures. Chapter 4 describes the basics of exporting step-by-step; Chapter 5 covers government export controls and procedures.

PART III: Importing into the United States. Chapter 6 covers the basics of importing into the United States; Chapter 7 describes ways of entering the import business; while Chapter 8 points out relevant government controls on imports.

PART IV: Rewards and Challenges of Export-Import Trade. Chapter 9 gives extensive examples of successful fashion goods export businesses of all sizes; while Chapter 10 explains the procedures for getting paid or paying for exports and imports.

Features of the Text

Each chapter contains current examples of relevant export/import activities. Included within the chapters are two types of boxed features: Spotlight on Global Trade, which explains current practices in international trade such as a day in the life of the Customs agency; and International Fashion Focus, that describes special aspects of certain fashion businesses, such as how the celebrity Bono participates in global fashion marketing.

The chapters are packed with current illustrations and tables. Each chapter's relevant vocabulary terms appear in bold print in the chapter and are immediately defined in context. At the end of each chapter a Summary reviews that chapter's major points, followed by a listing of the chapter's vocabulary as Key Terms. Review Questions cover the major chapter topics, and Discussion Questions and Activities offer opportunities for further application of the chapter content. A Glossary and Appendices at the end of Chapters 4 and 5 provide additional resources. A PowerPoint lecture series and an Instructor's Guide offer useful information for teachers, such as chapter outlines, answers to review questions, and examinations, and serve as sources for enriched classroom instruction and activities.

Acknowledgments

The enthusiasm and direction on the part of the Fairchild organization gave the authors the impetus to complete this text. In particular, the authors are grateful to: Olga Kontzias, Joseph Miranda, Amanda Breccia, Erin Fitzsimmons, Noah Schwartzberg, and Jessica Rozler.

The authors are also indebted to the following individuals and organizations for their contributions to this effort:

Alliance Française de Chicago, French Decorative Arts Symposium
Evy J. Alsaker, Past President, Rotary Club of Chicago
Paul S. Anderson, Partner, Sonnenberg & Anderson, Attorneys at Law, Chicago, and
    Honorary Consul General, Honorary Royal Norwegian Consulate General, Chicago
Susan Cisco, Chair, Global Business Studies Program, Oakton Community College,
    Des Plaines, Illinois
Foreign Policy Association, New York, *Great Decisions 2009*
Ric Frantz, CEO, LR International, Wood Dale, Illinois
Karen Janko, Program Director of Fashion Marketing & Management, The Illinois
    Institute of Art-Chicago
Kathryn Kerrigan, owner, Kathryn Kerrigan, Inc., Libertyville, IL
Robin F. Mugford, International Trade Specialist, U. S. Commercial Service,
    U. S. Department of Commerce
Laura Welmers, Director of Information Technology and Facilities, International
    Academy of Design and Technology, Chicago

Harvey Shoemack is very thankful to Patricia Mink Rath for encouraging him to put into an actual textbook his practical and popular study guide on the basics of exporting and importing. He also greatly appreciates her fashion-focused inputs that make this text much more readable and enjoyable, while also teaching students the importance of U.S. global trade policies, procedures and practices. He also acknowledges the encouragement and patience of his wife Frieda and his family, friends, and colleagues who will be happy to hear that, yes, the book is finally finished.

Patricia Mink Rath is grateful to Harvey Shoemack for inviting her to participate in the preparation of this text. She deeply appreciates the love, humor, and patience of her husband Philip Balsamo in the development of this work and others; the encouragement of son Eric Rath, his wife Kiyomi, and daughter Dana, who are constant inspirations; and the dedication of son Nicholas Balsamo and his son Brian in firmly placing her in the world of twenty-first century technology. To cousin Jim Strom she is grateful for photographs and international marketing data. Finally, she remains indebted to colleague, former co-author, and friend Dr. Ralph E. Mason, for his counsel over the years, stemming from the opportunity, a while back and ten publications ago, to write text materials enriching student learning, a practice that energizes and inspires beyond today.

Globalization and the U.S. Export-Import Business

Part I

Figure 1.1
The fabric and
production of
fashionable
jeans draw
from resources
throughout
the world.

......

1

The Italian washing machines beat up the denim jeans by rubbing them with pumice, but this time the process works, unlike the earlier one using river stones which destroyed both the garments and the washers. Artificially aging denim fabric is a global fashion practice involving businesses throughout the world because customers are demanding denim apparel with some kind of processing, be it distressed looks, embroidery, sequins, or even holes. Fashions don't always have to look new to be successful and profitable, but producing the right fashion looks today may often be a global undertaking, as up to five countries may be involved in the creation of one apparel item.

onsider the northern Italian firm, Martelli Lavorazioni Tessili (Martelli Textile Washers). Working with jeans bearing European design influences and international brand names like Diesel, Seven for All Mankind, and Levi's manufactured perhaps in Romania, Turkey, or Morocco, Martelli employees—many of them legal Chinese immigrants—produce faded, creased, and distressed jeans often with holes or other ornamentation.

In four factories, the company turns out 120,000 garments every day. While some of these are premium jeans offered worldwide in department and specialty stores for $60 and more, others are elite quality, selling in boutiques for $130 and more. Martelli creates still other denim garments for clients such as Armani, Calvin Klein, and Yves Saint Laurent. The demand is versatile—Galliano first created formal wear in denim—and long-term, and so Martelli is looking to expand its capabilities, next seeking ventures in the United States and China.[1]

Just as Martelli is exploring ways to grow its business, other companies are on the lookout for profitable opportunities in new locations. Influencing business expansion is the worldwide rise of terrorism. In particular September 11, 2001, has permanently altered ways of conducting business. Recent changes in the world's economic, political, legal, technological, and socio-cultural environments have made it both easier and more difficult for companies of any size, in any country, to conduct international trade. More efficient production results in better products, lower prices, and more choices for their customers—all key to more sales and larger profits. But why do most countries promote and engage in global business?

BENEFITS OF TRADE

The intellectual benefits of free trade are well-known (to economists). Nations benefit by specializing in the production of goods and services that they can produce and market most efficiently. Ideally, they exchange these for the goods and services that other countries produce at higher quality or lower cost.

Globalization, the increasing interdependency and interaction of nations, economies, and businesses all over the world, has had a profound effect on both markets and production. Lowering or eliminating government barriers to export-import trade allows individuals or firms access to the world's vast offerings of food, clothing, and other manufactured goods, and for the services that form the infrastructure of the modern economy. These services range from finance to telecommunications and from transportation to education. Companies can also benefit from foreign manufacturing, or **outsourcing**, that is, shifting factory production or services such as call centers, to less-developed, cheaper labor countries in virtually any part of the world, as long as government barriers to investment and production do not prevail.

Figure 1.2 As the world's largest market, the United States encourages foreign trade to enhance its economy.

• • • • • • • •

Why are globalization and export-import trade so important to the United States? As a free and democratic nation, the United States is dedicated to world peace and security that come from increasing integration of economies around the world. Since the United States is the world's largest economy and a large exporter and importer, trade is critical to America's prosperity—fueling economic growth and supporting jobs at home. The United States engages in trade to obtain goods and services that some other countries can produce at relatively lower costs. Most nations try to exchange goods or services that they produce most efficiently. These actions help raise living standards and provide families with affordable goods and services. The U.S. economy continues to grow and is the model for the free world. But foreign governments often restrict U.S. exported goods, such as domestic farm products and services that face numerous barriers. Reducing global trade barriers will give farmers, ranchers, manufacturers, and service providers better access to the 95 percent of the world's customers living outside U.S. borders.

In just the last 10 years, freer trade has helped raise U.S. **Gross Domestic Product (GDP)**—a nation's total output of domestically-produced goods and services within a one year period—by nearly 40 percent. Over the same period, the United States has added over 16 million jobs, according to a July 2006 release from the Office of the U.S. Trade Representative.

Christina R. Sevilla, former deputy assistant U.S. trade representative for intergovernmental affairs and public liaison, wrote in the January 2007 edition of eJournal USA, an electronic journal of the U.S. Department of State:

> Developing and developed countries alike face an important choice in the direction of their trade policy. In a rapidly shifting global economy, policy-makers may be tempted to shield their domestic markets from competition and erect new barriers [protectionism] that advantage a relatively small group at the expense of the vast majority of producers, workers, and consumers. Theory and empirical evidence counsel a wiser path. Openness to trade has been the foundation for economic growth, prosperity, rising standards of living, and a better life for countless millions in countries around the world.

When the United States engages in global trade, the real purchasing power of its consumers rises. Incomes stretch further when individuals can obtain necessary goods and services at a lower cost. A nation can create a higher GDP from its **factors of production** (land, labor, and capital) because it is not using them to produce outputs other countries can, at lower prices.

Figure 1.3 About half of the global benefits from freer trade in goods would go to people in developing countries, such as this Angolan fruit trader.

·······

Figure 1.4 American-designed fashion goods are marketed throughout the world.

·······

WHAT MAKES UP GLOBAL BUSINESS?

All commercial transactions—private and governmental—among governments or enterprises of two or more countries are considered **global business**. A segment of global business, trade between businesses or governments in two or more countries, is known as **international trade**. For study purposes, two primary components or activities of global business can be identified as foreign investment and export-import trade, as you can see in Table 1.1.

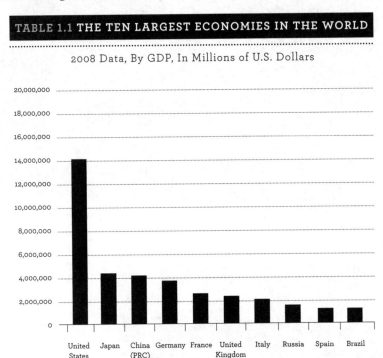

TABLE 1.1 THE TEN LARGEST ECONOMIES IN THE WORLD

2008 Data, By GDP, In Millions of U.S. Dollars

Sources: 2008 listings from IMF; the World Bank; and the *CIA World Factbook*.

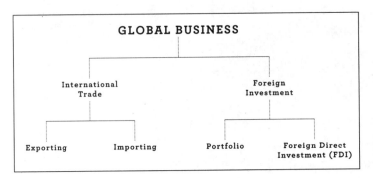

GLOBAL BUSINESS

International Trade

Foreign Investment

Exporting   Importing

Portfolio   Foreign Direct Investment (FDI)

Figure 1.5
International trade is one of two primary components of global business; the other is foreign investment.

....

Source: Harvey R. Shoemack.

Foreign Investment

Financial transactions involving loans or ownership of international enterprises and institutions, known as **foreign investment**, take place daily. When Abercrombie & Fitch opens a store in Madrid, a Japanese firm purchases an interest in a Korean factory, or a lawyer in Canada buys shares of stock in a foreign company, each is participating in foreign investment. There are two types of foreign investments: foreign direct investment and portfolio investment of assets in a foreign country.

Foreign Direct Investment

Foreign direct investment (FDI) occurs when an investor, an individual, a company, or a government organization, gains an **equity** or *ownership*, interest in a foreign operation. Recently, in its global expansion, specialty retailer Banana Republic opened a store in Singapore, part of the parent company Gap's expansion into Indonesia, South Korea, Turkey, and Saudi Arabia; these branches, along with Gap's other overseas stores are examples of foreign direct investment.[2]

Figure 1.6 This Banana Republic store in Singapore is part of Gap's plan for global expansion.
. . . .

Figure 1.7 Barneys New York, a well-known U.S. fashion retailer, was acquired in 2007 by Istithmar, a Dubai-based firm.

....

Mergers and Acquisitions (M & As)

Much foreign direct investment occurs through mergers and acquisitions (M&As). An **acquisition** takes place when one company buys another. If one of the companies is headquartered in a foreign country, that acquisition becomes another example of foreign investment. Not long ago, after heavy bidding from competitors, Istithmar, a Dubai-based private equity firm acquired the prestigious Barneys New York fashion retail chain from the U.S. firm Jones Apparel Group. A **merger** occurs when two firms join together as owners for a specific purpose, each participating company retaining a portion of control over the new (merged) organization. Recently, two major Japanese department stores, Isetan Co., Ltd. and Mitsukoshi Ltd., decided to merge, forming Japan's largest department store group, Isetan Mitsukoshi Holdings Ltd.[3] Note the combined names; this arrangement differs from an acquisition where the purchasing company remains dominant.

Joint Venture

One form of merger is a **joint venture**, a direct investment in which two or more partners share ownership. In India, Wal-Mart Stores, Inc. and India's Bharti Enterprises negotiated an agreement, a 50-50 joint venture for a wholesale operation permitting the new organization to gather goods from Indian manufacturers and farmers which would then be sold in Bharti's wholly-owned subsidiary, Bharti retail stores. India's laws protect its merchants, for they do not permit foreign multibrand retailers to sell to consumers, although they do allow wholesaling.[4] In another situation, Polo Ralph Lauren along with the Swiss luxury goods group Compagnie Financière Richemont formed a 50-50 joint venture under the name The Polo Ralph Lauren Watch and Jewelry Company, S.A.R.L., to design and market luxury watches and fine jewelry to Ralph Lauren boutiques and independent jewelry stores throughout the world.[5]

Mixed Ventures

A **mixed venture** represents a commercial operation in which ownership is shared by a government and a business. In China, joint ventures with foreign companies include partnership with a Chinese government agency or company partially owed by the government. Forming joint ventures in China always involves the government. The challenge begins with the search for a potential partner. Even firms that are comfortable in global expansion elsewhere may find themselves struggling in China. Market research is in its infancy, and government statistics are not very reliable. Moreover, China has set a limit on how many joint ventures it wants per industry and the maximum per district. "The accepted wisdom is that without *Guanxi* (connections usually referring to government contacts and influence) outsiders have no chance of penetrating the Chinese bureaucracy. Yet, some have managed with no *Guanxi* other than the China Phone Book, found in most hotel bedrooms in that country."[6]

Mixed Ventures in China: The Gillette Story

While many U.S. companies seek out ventures in China, Gillette was pursued by the Chinese. Gillette's then international affairs vice president was contacted by MACHIMPEX, a Chinese agency-business cooperative, while he was accompanying the Boston Symphony Orchestra, of which Gillette is a sponsor, on a tour of China. He told the Chinese that Gillette never sells its proprietary, made-in-house equipment but that it was interested in exploring other ways of working together.

During his visit, he toured China's four small razor blade factories as well as 20 plants potentially capable of making other Gillette items. Gillette's product range includes White Rain shampoo, Dry Idea deodorant, Paper Mate pens, Liquid Paper typewriter correction fluid, and Braun appliances. Ultimately, Gillette settled on razor blades for its joint venture because they are comparatively simple to make and were considered most suitable for China in its early stages of modernization.

Gillette preferred Shanghai as a site but quickly lost interest because the local manufacturer was only agreeable to spinning off part of its business. It wanted to retain the rest, and this would have made it a competitor to the joint venture. Also, the Chinese government was eager for Gillette to locate elsewhere, since Shanghai already had plenty of light industry. The Chinese never stated that Gillette would not otherwise gain entry, but they did promote as a site Shenyang in northeast China, which at that time had no joint ventures. One hour by plane from Beijing, Shenyang is China's fourth largest city.

Foreign investors were avoiding Shenyang because the winters are very cold and grittily dusty in the spring. There is nothing of sightseeing interest nearby, or much in the way of evening entertainment. The Chinese believed that if world-famous Gillette were to select Shenyang, other foreign investors would follow. This has been the case.

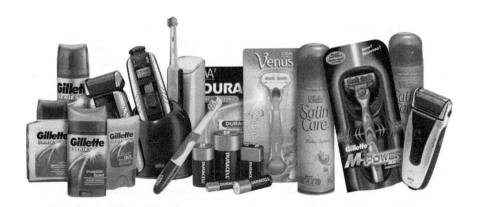

Figure 1.8 The Gillette story in China shows how business and government cooperate in building international trade.

. . . .

China was so eager to establish this venture that it allowed Gillette several unusual concessions. Of most significance to Gillette is that although it shares ownership 50-50, the Chinese agreed that Gillette could make most of the operations decisions and run the venture—Shenmei Daily Use Products Company ("Shen" for Shenyang, "mei" for America)— "in Western style."

The factory that Shenmei Daily Use Products took over had 260 employees. At that time, Chinese authorities still firmly espoused their theory of jobs for life, identical salaries, equality of workers, and respect for seniority. Gillette believed the factory had too many employees to be profitable. It insisted that the Chinese lay off personnel and keep only 60 or there would be no deal. The Chinese gave way. Shenmei's workforce has since grown to 104 people, but that number covers three shifts and is enough to handle expansion in production.[7]

The working relationship of government officials and foreign joint ventures cannot be overlooked when contemplating business ventures in China.

Licensing Agreements

Other forms of foreign direct investment can include licensing agreements. A **licensing agreement** is an arrangement between a company with a well-known name and a manufacturer who pays a royalty to create goods using that name. Fashion designers and organizations use licensing extensively to market their goods throughout the world; a few of these are Christian Dior, Pierre Cardin, Marc Jacobs, Ralph Lauren, and Martha Stewart. Accessories such as sunglasses, shoes, handbags, and scarves bearing the Liz Claiborne label are all produced under licensing agreements with manufacturers (many in foreign countries) specializing in that particular accessory line.

A form of licensing sometimes referred to as a franchise, is an agreement between a company such as Polo Ralph Lauren and a foreign organization to set up and operate Ralph Lauren retail stores in foreign countries. For example, in a 2007 agreement with the Russian distribution organization Mercury, Ralph Lauren opened up two stores in Moscow. One store, in a prestigious downtown shopping area, offers its highest luxury brands, the Purple and Black Labels. The other store, on the edge of the city, sells more sportswear. Earlier in the year, Polo Ralph Lauren stores opened in Tokyo and Milan, and two stores in Paris the following year.[8]

While the Moscow stores were the company's first venture in Russia, the company has maintained a presence in Europe for a number of years. The Lauren organization got its start in Europe and Asia through licensing agreements which minimized the company's financial investment in each project. Now, however, the company is interested in acquiring greater direct control over local operations, and is in the process of buying out these licenses.[9] As of 2007, nearly 70 percent of Polo Ralph Lauren sales came from within the United States, the rest came from Europe (16 percent), Japan (9 percent), Korea and Pacific Rim countries (4 percent), and the balance from Australia, South America, and Canada. Since management sees its future major growth stemming from overseas operations, closer supervision over these businesses is in its best interest.[10] (See Chapter 9.)

Figure 1.9 The Polo Ralph Lauren stores in Moscow offer Russian consumers access to American luxury brands.

....

Portfolio Investment

The second major component of foreign investment, **portfolio investment**, is a non-controlling interest in a venture made in the form of either debt or equity. American individuals, companies, associations—even governments—can buy stocks or bonds of publicly-traded foreign corporations, and they can invest in American firms. An example of portfolio investment occurs when an individual investor purchases shares of ownership in a mutual fund that invests in foreign corporations. In another example, China, Germany, and Great Britain's purchase of U.S. government bonds are financing our national debt, as well as enhancing their investment portfolios. All of which makes the United States a debtor nation, not necessarily a bad thing if the economy is stable.

TABLE 1.2 INTERBRAND'S TOP GLOBAL FASHION BRANDS

Rank in Top 100	Fashion Brand	Brand Value[1]
17.	LOUIS VUITTON	$20.3M
29.	NIKE	$12.0M
46.	GUCCI	$7.7M
58.	CHANEL	$5.8M
61.	GAP	$5.5M
64.	ZARA	$5.2M
69.	ADIDAS	$4.8M
71.	ROLEX	$4.6M
73.	HERMÈS	$4.3M
79.	TIFFANY & CO.	$4.0M
83.	CARTIER	$3.9M
94.	PRADA	$3.3M
95.	BURBERRY	$3.2M
95.	POLO RALPH LAUREN	$3.2M

[1] The amount of a corporation's market capitalization attributable to a brand's contribution to net revenue, influence over consumer purchases, and customer retention.

Source: Valerie Seckler, "Vuitton Top-Ranked Among Fashion Brands," *Women's Wear Daily*, July 27, 2007, p. 12.

Export-Import Trade

Export-import trade, the marketing and physical distribution of goods, services, technologies or ideas to countries other than their origin, is the second major division of global business. Export-import trade may seem to be complex, requiring extensive physical and financial resources, as well as language skills and extensive cross-cultural training. Fortunately, for tens of thousands of successful companies, this is not entirely true. The benefits of expanded markets and higher profit margins frequently outweigh the possible risks to export-import trade.

SPOTLIGHT ON GLOBAL TRADE 1.1:
Mitumba Trade: Where Do All the Used T-Shirts Go?

What do you do with your old clothing? Give the jacket to your niece or nephew? Turn the T-shirt into a dust rag? Bundle everything and send it off to a charity? And what does your favorite organization do then, say, with your used T-Shirt? The items it cannot use are sold to be offered as *mitumba*—castoff apparel from Americans and Europeans destined for markets in African nations such as Tanzania, Benin, Togo, and the Republic of Congo. Because of global entrepreneurs, many Africans, for small pocket change, can outfit themselves well—not as copies of Americans or Europeans, but with their own keen sense of local fashion. And for these consumers, shopping at the mitumba market is fun, providing the thrill of locating a treasure perhaps in the right Nike T-shirt much as an American maven's finding a jewel of a dress at Target.

When a consumer in the United States gives used clothing to, say, a non profit organization such as the Salvation Army, the goods it cannot use are picked up by an organization which sorts and bales clothing and ships it off to African nations such as Tanzania; in fact, the largest U.S. export to that country, by far, is used clothing. While some African nations such as Botswana and South Africa ban importing used clothing, other nations such as Tanzania and Zambia find that it provides jobs as well as consumer goods. The bales of garments coming from the United States and Europe are often 2,000 pounds in weight and need further sorting; those entering Tanzania go to a warehouse, operated by the local conglomerate METL, where they are further sorted, cleaned, pressed, and sometimes altered. They are then bundled into smaller bales and offered to individual entrepreneurs to sell in their stalls at mitumba markets. In these situations, exporting, importing, and individual entrepreneurship work hand-in-hand to provide goods in great demand.

Source: Pietra Rivoli. *The Travels of a T-Shirt in the Global Economy: An Economist Examines the Markets, Power, and Politics of World Trade.* Hoboken, John Wiley & Sons, 2005.

Exports represent the *sales* of goods and services that flow *out* of a country, as when the U.S. handbag company Coach, or the cosmetics firm Estée Lauder, offers its goods for retail sale to foreign stores such as Bon Marché in Paris or Takashimaya in Japan. **Imports** are purchases of goods and services that come *into* a country, as when U.S. retailers purchase goods from Chanel, Gucci, or Aquascutum. However, to be officially counted as a country's exports or imports, they must be distributed across national boundaries for the purpose of re-selling them. Therefore, products brought home from a foreign vacation for personal use or as gifts for friends or relatives do not count toward a nation's **balance of trade**, the difference between a country's total imports and exports. If exports exceed imports, a favorable balance of trade, or a **trade surplus** exists; if imports are higher than exports, a **trade deficit** exists. When a country imports more than it exports, as the United States has since the early 1970s, its currency loses value (known as currency devaluation), inflation rises, and consumers pay more not only for imports, but also for domestic goods.

Trade balances are customarily measured bilaterally; the United States has experienced large trade deficits with both Japan and China over the past five years. A nation's **balance of payments** is a record of all export-import trade and other financial transactions including investments and gold, with the rest of the world, during a one-year period. It provides a snapshot of a nation's economic health used by government institutions, banks, and other agencies to maintain economic stability.

Figure 1.10 **Web sites such as this give consumers all over the world access to fashion goods.**

. . . .

RECENT CHANGES IN U.S. EXPORT-IMPORT TRADE POLICIES AND PROCEDURES

Here are some of the recent changes that have occurred in United States export-import procedures. The goal of many of these changes, as you can tell, is to encourage and protect trade throughout the world:

> **Globalization** of both markets and production enables firms or individual entrepreneurs opportunities to safely market or produce goods and services in the vast majority of countries around the world. The interdependency that has resulted from globalization allows consumers or manufacturers to source products from virtually any country or to sell their goods and services to targeted audiences on a global basis via eBay, or millions of B2B (business-to-business) or B2C (business-to-consumer) Web sites.

> **Recent elimination** or major reductions of tariffs and other trade barriers provide our exports increased access to most foreign markets. The Multifiber Agreement to remove textile and apparel **quotas** (limits on the amount of certain categories of goods allowed to be imported from specific countries over a period of time, usually one year), on a world-wide basis became effective January 1, 2005, gives U.S. manufacturers access to previously blocked foreign textile and apparel markets.

> **Improved information** technologies in the form of home computers and small business networks have resulted in better informed consumers who now demand higher-quality, innovative, and more cost-competitive imported products. Most households now have computers that can access product information to ensure greater choices and lower prices for commodities, fashions, even purchases of new homes or automobiles.

Some of the changes after the World Trade Center attacks have added further challenges for exporters and importers; these include:

> an environment of concern over international terrorism;
> higher international transportation security taxes, and
> more complex distribution procedures for business.

On the import side, enhanced communications and information technologies contribute to anti-terrorism and defense programs. Newly required software is used for import documentation for companies to track shipments, and it is used by U.S. government agencies to know what is coming into the country, from which country, and the identity of the shipper.

Figure 1.11 After the World Trade Center attack, the U.S. government
added trade and transportation regulations to increase the security of consumers.
....

TECHNOLOGY ENERGIZES GLOBALIZATION

While the United States continues to negotiate more liberalized international trade policies and procedures, new technologies are easing the implementation of those agreements and are energizing globalization. These include:

Electronic Technologies

> electronic technologies adapted by most businesses;
> new information resources added to the Web daily;
> communications breakthroughs—wireless communication around the globe, and
> supply chain (distribution) management/innovation.

Thanks to computer technologies, it is easier, faster, and less expensive to research potential export markets or import sources, and to move information, products, services, people, and ideas around the world. The microprocessor has enabled developments in communications and information processing technology—especially the Internet and World Wide Web—so companies can conduct research before investing in the people, time, energy, and money necessary for a successful import or export effort.

Once the decision has been made for a company to globalize, computer networks can link all their components, from manufacturing to distribution to retail, into an efficient, sophisticated operation. For example, due to advanced technology, a fashion business like Talbot's or Forever 21 can create a garment design in its U.S. office, send the specifications to Asia to be produced, and have the outfit for sale in its U.S. stores in a matter of weeks, a task that formerly took several months to complete.

New Information Resources

Information—from both internal and external sides—is one key to satisfying today's customers who want the right product, at the best price, distributed where and when they want them.

Figure 1.12
Popular American household products, such as Tide, command prominent shelf space in Asian supermarkets.
....

Sam Walton, founder of Wal-Mart—the world's largest retailer, a global corporation with more than 1.8 million employees and nearly 6,500 stores and wholesales clubs across 14 countries—attributed his company's retailing success to "giving the customer what they want . . . a wide assortment of good quality merchandise; the lowest possible prices; guaranteed satisfaction . . . a pleasant shopping experience." The firm acknowledges information technology as playing an important role in helping Wal-Mart stay customer focused:

> Wal-Mart invented the practice of sharing sales data via computer with major suppliers, such as Proctor & Gamble. Every time a box of Tide is rung up at the cash register, Wal-Mart . . . takes note and knows when it is time to alert P&G to replenish a particular store.

In addition to internal **management information systems (MIS)**, a combination of customized computer technologies and processes that provide information for management decision-making, Wal-Mart and other global businesses use external information resources concerning foreign country economies, demographics, and psychographics to provide a steady stream of data on market changes and opportunities for exporters or new sources of products or raw materials for importers.

Communications Breakthroughs

The way in which we communicate has also energized globalization. Previously, long-distance telephone communications were expensive, often unreliable, and had to compensate for language competencies. The introduction of first the facsimile (fax) machine and then global e-mail communications were big steps toward using technology to link companies, their customers, and suppliers worldwide. Printed words, photos, technical drawings, or even contracts could be transmitted globally for the first time, at a low cost, and with less time than telephone calls. Although the fax is still used by businesses today, the majority of international communications now take place via e-mail. Through the use of mobile technology, it is now possible for individuals, corporations—even government officials—to be accessible virtually anywhere in the world, at any time—24/7—for a telephone call or e-mail message.

Supply Chain Management

Supply chain management—coordinating supply sources with market demands to ensure production and delivery meet customer needs—is the last example of technological help for American exporters and importers. For retailers, such as Wal-Mart and Macy's, who import fashion goods, their suppliers—foreign manufacturers as well as distributors—are an integral part of the **data warehouse concept**, which is monitoring retail sales in order to fill in-store inventory swiftly. After gleaning information from the data warehouse, the actual replenishment of popular items while still in style is called **Quick Response**. As a result, Wal-Mart and many other retailers who practice state-of-the-art supply chain management rarely run out of stock of popular items.

These positive and negative changes are destined to be an integral part of global trade—exporting and importing—for the foreseeable future.

CHALLENGES TO GLOBALIZATION

Globalization has its critics. They point to unequal sharing of benefits among all nations of the world, with a disregard for human rights and exploitation in developing nations as cause for economic and social unrest that may result in the eventual breakdown of a fragile global economic system.

INTERNATIONAL FASHION FOCUS 1.1:
Two Guys Market Scents Internationally

Many companies, from huge detergent and cosmetics manufacturers to tiny enterprises, create and market fragrances (in the form of lotions, oils, scented candles, and sprays for home use) to sell to department stores, supermarkets, specialty shops, and even farmers' markets. But few entrepreneurs have as unique a point-of-view as that of Fabrice Penot and Edouard Roschi, the founders of Le Labo. Here is their story:

After completing a five-year training program with L'Oréal Paris, Fabrice Penot was named a marketing executive for the Giorgio Armani fragrances, Acqua di Gio and Armani Privé. Here, he met Eddie Roschi who came from a large fragrance, flavor, and chemical manufacturer. Every three weeks they would fly to Milan to confer with Giorgio Armani in person on the current marketing campaigns.

As they became friends, Penot and Roschi talked about the fragrance industry and some of its outmoded concepts, such as men will not buy any product with a rose fragrance, and a store in Tokyo will never succeed because Japanese men don't like scents. The two men formed their own ideas about the business of smells and decided to create their own enterprise. They moved to New York, found a few investors interested in their concepts, and after two years of experimenting, came up with 10 fragrances of their own.

They opened Le Labo, a fragrance boutique in New York. With walls of brick, old wood, and a fleur-de-lys-patterned tin wall, the shop has a worn and welcoming aura.

Fragrances come in a variety of sizes and may be combined by a lab-coated assistant to create a custom scent with the owner's name on the bottle. The products are classified for men, women, and unisex. Penot and Roschi have gone a long way in debunking old industry myths: their most popular-selling fragrance for men contains the scent of rose, and their plans include opening other boutiques, one in San Francisco and another in Tokyo.

Source: Mike Albo, "The New Sophisticated Smelling Me." Critical Shopper, *New York Times*, sec. 3, August 16, 2007.

According to Sherrow O. Pinder, at California State University, in the essay, "Globalization and Beyond: The Future of Poor Nations":

> Globalization is proceeding selectively, including and excluding segments of economies and societies in and out of the networks of wealth and power that characterize the new dominant system. There is a new form of colonization/imperialistic domination in place. . . . [Governments of poor countries are] under severe pressures to maximize exploitation of [their] resources and to forgo environmental laws in order to attract foreign investment. As the re-emergence of a new form of colonization unfolds, environmental issues are not the only threats to [these nations.] Other threats include the worsening of poverty and political instability. . . . [While] globalization is proceeding with [an] unrelenting vigor; the inequalities that it reveals will continue to prevail in poor nations. The control of central parts of Guyana's economy, for example, has been handed over to foreign interests, with little or no return to the Guyanese people and little impact on its enormous debt. As such, the government control of the economy is more urgent than ever.[12]

Another anti-globalization argument, often the platform of political campaigns and claims of union officials, is that U.S. global companies create jobs overseas at the expense of domestic jobs. Would American public interest be better served if government policy stopped supporting global companies and focused instead on domestic employment and U.S. competitiveness? Should the United States protect its home markets with higher trade barriers, such as **tariffs** (taxes on specific imports to compensate for cheaper labor costs of our foreign competitors) or quotas? Economists, government leaders, and journalists will be debating globalization for many years to come, as it is a complex matter and simple answers will not satisfy any side. Most do agree that the benefits of increased globalization can be costly to individuals and nations. And that society as a whole—which stands to benefit—should share in the costs of those who may lose.

Many people agree with Robert L. Thompson, visiting scholar, Federal Reserve Bank of Chicago, when he said that globalization through on-going trade negotiations offers opportunities to liberalize trade, bid up wages, and reduce poverty in low-income countries. Thompson believes, "this would make the world a safer and more just place, while creating larger potential markets."[13] Our goal, as authors of this text, is to introduce the steps to international trade—through entrepreneurial export-import activities—that offer the potential of bringing about increased peace and prosperity.

SUMMARY

Globalization, the increasing interdependency of nations and businesses, has a profound effect throughout the world. For the United States, trade with foreign countries can help provide domestic jobs, increase the standard of living by providing a wide assortment of goods and services, and raise the nation's overall production as measured by its Gross Domestic Product (GDP).

International business is made up of two primary components: foreign investment and international trade. There are two types of foreign investment: foreign direct investment and portfolio investment. Foreign direct investment occurs when an individual, organization, or government gains ownership interest, or equity, in a foreign operation. Joint ventures and mixed ventures are examples of foreign direct investment. Portfolio investment is a non-controlling interest in a foreign venture, as through the purchase of stocks or bonds of a foreign company.

International trade is concerned with exporting or importing. Exports are goods or services offered to foreign businesses, as when handbags from the U.S. firm Coach, or cosmetics from Estée Lauder, are offered for retail sale to foreign stores such as the Bon Marché in France or Takashimaya in Japan. Imports are foreign goods that are brought into a country for sale, as when U.S. retailers buy from European vendors such as Chanel, Gucci, and Aquascutum.

The difference between a country's total exports and imports is indicated in its balance of trade. When the value of exports exceeds that of imports, a nation has a balance of trade surplus; when imports exceed exports, it experiences a balance of trade deficit. Typically, trade balances are measured between two nations. For example, today China sells more goods to the United States than it buys, therefore, it has a huge trade surplus, while the United States has a large trade deficit with China. The record of all of a nation's financial transactions with the rest of the world, including exports and imports, investments and gold, makes up its balance of payments.

Export-import trade is important to the United States because it fuels economic growth, maintains domestic employment, tends to raise living standards, and supplies consumers with a wide range of goods and services. The sum total of the goods and services produced within the borders of any country is that country's Gross Domestic Product.

Exporting and importing have become more prevalent due to enhanced communications and technologies, more favorable legislation, increased use of the Internet by businesses and ultimate consumers, and the globalization of markets. Current challenges include the threat to safety, resulting in the need for greater security in product manufacture and distribution, and the advent of more complex legislative procedures.

While globalization has certainly benefited many nations and their citizens, its critics believe the exploitation of the poorer countries must be addressed and eliminated, for the future of world peace and prosperity.

Key Terms

> Acquisitions
> Balance of payments
> Balance of trade
> Data warehouse concept
> Equity
> Export-import trade
> Exports
> Factors of production
> Foreign direct
  investment
> Foreign investment
> Global business
> Globalization
> Gross Domestic
  Product (GDP)
> Guanxi

> Imports
> International trade
> Joint venture
> Licensing agreement
> Management
  Information System
  (MIS)
> Merger
> Mixed venture
> Outsourcing
> Portfolio investment
> Quotas
> Tariffs
> Trade deficit
> Trade surplus

Review Questions

1. Describe three or four benefits of globalization.

2. What are three reasons that globalization and export-import business are important to the United States?

3. Describe the two major components of international business with an example of each.

4. Explain the relationship between a nation's exports and imports and its balance of trade.

5. Cite three or four changes that recent events have brought about to facilitate global trade.

Discussion Questions and Activities

1. From your own experience, provide three examples of foreign direct investment in the United States. Visit your library and, consulting references, identify three foreign-owned companies operating in the United States. Should the United States encourage such investment? If yes, what benefits come from these investments? If no, what drawbacks exist?

2. Using the Internet, locate at least three major mergers or acquisitions between U.S. and foreign corporations over the past five years.

3. The U.S. steel industry was in dire straits in the 1970s until the major Japanese steel companies formed joint ventures with most of the U.S. steel giants. Cite three reasons why you agree or disagree with this idea, considering the strategic importance of the steel industry as the primary supplier of military aircraft, tanks, weapons, and ammunition.

4. Using an Internet search engine, such as AOL, Yahoo, or Google, search "Product Licensing" and determine the world's largest consumer products licensor. Why, at many major domestic trade shows, are vendors of licensed products given increasingly larger amounts of floor space? Cite three licensed products that you own. (Hint: Consider logo products licensed by professional or collegiate sports teams).

5. For more than 25 years, the United States has had a growing trade deficit, with current imports exceeding exports by more than $600 billion. What steps in importing and/or exporting might be taken to reverse this economic dilemma? What are the risks of allowing the trade deficit to grow each year? Research recent literature on the U.S. trade deficit to determine the pros and cons of the growing imbalance of trade.

References

1. John Tagliabue, "Yeah, They Torture Jeans, But It's All for the Sake of Fashion," *The New York Times*, International Business Section, July 12, 2006, Section C, pp.1 and 4.

2. Betsy Lowther, "Banana Republic Opens in Singapore as Part of Global Expansion," *Women's Wear Daily*, August 1, 2007, p. 14.

3. Tsukasa Furukawa, "Isetan, Mitsukoshi Join Forces," *Women's Wear Daily*, August 24, 2007, p. 2.

4. "Wal-Mart signs deal to sell to India," *Chicago Tribune*, August 7, 2007, sec. 3, p. 3.

5. *Polo Ralph Lauren Annual Report*, 2007, p. 77.

6. Danny Chan, "Some Case Histories of Joint Ventures in China," November 7, 2002. Retrieved on October 4, 2007, from www.geocities.com/dannychan/articles/jvcase.html.

7. Ibid.

8. Robert Murphy, "Rendezvous in Russia: Ralph Lauren Launches First Stores in Moscow," *Women's Wear Daily*, May 16, 2007, pp. 1, 12, and 13.

9. *Polo Ralph Lauren Annual Report*, op. cit. p. 76.

10. Ibid., p. 28.

11. Sherrow O. Pinder, "Globalization and Beyond: The Future of Poor Nations," *Globalization*, Icaap.org, Athabasca University, Canada. March 2007. Retrieved on October 4, 2007, from http://globalization.icaap.org/content/special/pinder.html.

12. Robert L. Thompson, "Globalization and the Benefits of Trade," *Chicago Fed Letter*, March 2007, Number 236; The Federal Reserve Bank of Chicago.

Chapter 2

Globalization
and Trade
Liberalization

Figure 2.1
Fashion ideas and goods come from throughout the world. Here is a gown from designer John Galliano's Japanese-inspired collection.

......

2

As the lights dim, fashion enthusiasts delight in the ball gowns floating satin origami, silk obis encircling waists, and precise kimono shapes, all hits of the designer John Galliano's Paris couture showing for Christian Dior. At about the same time and not far away, Giorgio Armani's new boutique on the Avenue Montaigne exudes luxury with its elegant Chinese-style lamps, walls from the Iran-Iraq border, and back-lit floors highlighting the minimal styles of the Italian designer. While artists and designers have traditionally drawn their innovations from across the world's time and culture, recently they seem to be doing so at an increasingly rapid rate.[1] And they are not alone. Just about every country in the world participates, in some way, in the textile and apparel marketplace.

The Dior example is just one of many global businesses that have interconnected ideas and cultures, as well as production and marketing processes in the last 30 years. This concept may be misunderstood as implying that national markets have merged into one giant global marketplace. Fortunately, they have not. Although the participants may have become increasingly interdependent, they still retain their uniqueness and individuality, no matter where they are located.

INTERNATIONAL ALLIANCES

A critical catalyst for U.S. export and import growth has been the liberalization of international trade. Multilateral trade negotiations have brought about significant reductions in tariffs and non-tariff barriers along with international commitments toward future growth in trade.

The first major international trade cooperation began while World War II was still raging. In July 1944, at the **Bretton Woods Conference**, the name commonly given to the United Nations Monetary and Financial Conference, held at Bretton Woods, New Hampshire, 750 delegates from all 44 allied nations, including Russia, met to prepare for rebuilding the post-war international economic system.[2]

Bretton Woods gave birth to the **International Monetary Fund (IMF)**, to promote international monetary cooperation, and to the International Bank for Reconstruction and Development (IBRD), to provide funds for rebuilding war-torn countries, both of which will be discussed presently in depth. Thus began the new era of global alliances and economic cooperation.

Until the early 1970s, the Bretton Woods system was effective in controlling conflict and in achieving the common goals of the leading countries that had created it, especially the United States. A number of developments, however, including the persistent printing of too much money while maintaining a peg to gold; strenuous budget deficit problems; the Vietnam War; and marginal tax rates have been blamed for the collapse of the Bretton Woods monetary system in 1971. It was one result after the United States suspended the convertibility of dollars to gold. Most economists agree that the United States's increasing balance of trade deficit, and the inability of the government to ever reverse it, brought decades of continued economic strain on Bretton Woods.

The International Monetary Fund (IMF)

The IMF is an organization currently consisting of 186 countries, working to foster global monetary cooperation, secure financial stability, facilitate international trade, promote high employment and sustainable economic growth, and reduce poverty.[3]

The World Bank

The International Bank for Reconstruction and Development (IBRD), formally organized in 1945 with only 28 countries, now known as the **World Bank**, is a specialized agency of the United Nations, with headquarters in Washington, D.C. Its goal is to facilitate productive investment, encourage foreign trade, and discharge international debt. Each of the 184 members of the World Bank must belong to the IMF. World Bank assistance tends to be long-term (rather than short-term as is that of the IMF) and is funded both by member country contributions and through bond issuance.[4]

Figure 2.2 The scene of the birth of the International Monetary Fund and the World Bank, today Bretton Woods is a 10,000 acre ski resort in the White Mountains of New Hampshire.

....

Both the IMF and World Bank provide low-interest loans, interest-free credit, and grants to developing countries for projects and programs to, for example, build schools and health centers, provide water and electricity, fight disease, and protect the environment.

The General Agreement on Tariffs and Trade (GATT)

Another one of Bretton Woods' successes, first signed in 1947, was the **General Agreement on Tariffs and Trade (GATT)**, an international agreement to encourage free trade among member states by regulating and reducing barriers to trade, and by providing a common mechanism for resolving trade disputes. Barriers to trade include both *tariffs*, import taxes on traded goods, and *quotas*, limits on the quantities of goods nations may export. Originally, GATT was supposed to become a full international organization like the World Bank or IMF and would be called the International Trade Organization. However, the agreement was not ratified, so GATT simply remained an agreement. While the IMF and the World Bank are still functioning entities, GATT activities have been absorbed by the World Trade Organization.[5]

Figure 2.3 **An IMF team meets a senior tax official and his staff in Afghanistan. The fund provides for technical and other needed assistance.**
....

INTERNATIONAL FASHION FOCUS 2.1:
Luxury Week Aims Appeal to Hong Kong Consumers

How does a certain spot on the map gain attention as a global fashion center? What kind of attraction would polish Hong Kong's image as Asia's top luxury shopping venue? Let's try an invitation-only for deep-pocket customers to Luxury Week, a private 10-day fashion event with runway shows featuring designs from Calvin Klein, Diane von Furstenberg, Oscar de la Renta, Vera Wang, Zac Posen, and others. Combine all that with celebrity speakers, fashion seminars, chats with designers, parties, and, to top it off, make sure these very styles are in local stores immediately.

The major activity of visitors to Hong Kong is shopping. In fact, in 2006, tourists spent nearly $49 billion shopping, and affluent local residents spent nearly $10 billion. No wonder Hong Kong was an obvious choice for the event. Sponsored by MasterCard, Luxury Week was produced by IMG, a worldwide sports, entertainment, and media company known, in part, for its fashion showings such as Mercedes-Benz fashion weeks in New York and in other cities. More than 2,000 consumers were invited to participate in the event reinforcing Hong Kong's position as a global fashion innovator.

Source: Rosemary Feitelberg, "Luxury Week Hong Kong a Feast for Consumers," New York, *Women's Wear Daily*, August 30, 2007, p. 11. Retrieved from www.imgworld.com.

The World Trade Organization (WTO)

Established in 1995, the **World Trade Organization (WTO)** is the only global organization providing a forum for governments to negotiate trade agreements and a place for them to settle trade disputes. Headquartered in Geneva, Switzerland, it produces and enforces many rules governing trade among its 153 members. Unlike GATT, the WTO issues binding decisions.

Helping developing countries participate more fully in the global trading system is one of the WTO's most important activities. The developing countries which trade successfully tend to be those which have made the most progress in alleviating poverty and raising living standards. But there are countries, including a large number of **less-developed countries (LDCs)**, economically impoverished, poorest countries in the world, where trade is failing to make the contribution that it should for economic growth and to reduce poverty.[6]

Figure 2.4 An official of the IMF meets with a group of orphaned boys from the Kaisi Children's Home in Lusaka, Zambia. Founded in 1926, the orphanage has benefitted from IMF assistance and has become the largest and best known in the country.

....

In its efforts to lower trade barriers, the WTO conducts a series of meeting sessions, called "rounds," among members, for the purpose of negotiating favorable and equitable trade agreements. The main thrust of recent rounds, as cited in the **Doha Development Agenda (DDA)**, the Fourth Ministerial Conference of the WTO, held in Doha, Qatar, provided mandates for negotiations on a wide range of subjects, including agriculture and services. The Doha round began in early 2000. The talks provided guidelines for the implementation of agreements from the previous **Uruguay Round** of GATT negotiations, held from September 1986 to April 1994, where, among its negotiations, the General Agreement on Tariffs and Trade (GATT) was transformed into the World Trade Organization (WTO). As recently as October 2009, the Doha Agenda was still to be implemented, as the necessary will and flexibility to close the gaps are yet to be realized.[7]

The Office of the United States Trade Representative announced in August 2007 that the United States has requested the World Trade Organization (WTO) to establish a dispute settlement panel, as the next step in its WTO case challenging deficiencies in China's legal regime for protecting and enforcing copyrights and trademarks on a wide range of products. This action is consistent with the WTO's objective "to help trade flow smoothly, freely, fairly and predictably." It does this by:

> Administering trade agreements
> Acting as a forum for trade negotiations
> Settling trade disputes
> Reviewing national trade policies
> Assisting developing countries in trade policy issues, through technical assistance and training programs
> Cooperating with other international organizations

The WTO is not just about liberalizing trade. In some circumstances its rules support maintaining trade barriers, for example protecting **intellectual property rights**, patents, trademarks, and copyrights, but it is difficult to protect them from unscrupulous businesses (or governments) from other countries. Violations of intellectual property rights deprive legitimate businesses of millions of dollars, undercut innovation, and often pose serious threats to human safety and health. Imports of counterfeit apparel and toxic merchandise are discussed in Chapter 7, "Import Procedures."

Although the WTO is still young, the multilateral trading system that was originally set up under GATT is well over 60 years old. These years have seen an exceptional growth in world trade. Merchandise exports grew on average by six percent annually. GATT and the WTO have helped to create a stronger and more prosperous world trading system contributing to sustained growth.[8]

Figure 2.5 **Officials from the World Bank arrive in Africa to assess needs there.**
....

Figure 2.6 A recent WTO Ministerial Conference was held in Hong Kong, China. These conferences, meeting once every two years to provide direction for the organization, are the WTO's highest decision-making body.

·········

G8 Ministers Conferences

The **Group of Eight**, known as the **G8**, is an international forum promoting trade and economic cooperation that includes the governments of Canada, France, Germany, Italy, Japan, the United Kingdom, the United States, and Russia. Together, these countries represent about 65 percent of the world economy.[9] The group's activities include year-round conferences and policy research to promote democratic, economic, and educational reforms throughout the world. The annual summit meeting is attended by the heads of government of the member states. The European Commission, the executive branch of the European Union, which is made up of 27 "commissioners," one for each country of the EU, led by a Commission President, is also represented at the G8 meetings.

Each year, member states of the G8 take turns assuming the presidency of the group. The holder of the presidency sets the group's annual agenda and hosts the summit for that year.

Figure 2.7 At a conference of G8 ministers of the Justice and Interior held in Munich, Germany, the issue of international intellectual property rights violations was a major discussion topic.

....

Recognizing emerging nations such as China, India, and Brazil, the G8 grew to be part of the **Group of 20 (G20)**. The member nations account for 80 percent of global trade and two-thirds of the world's population.

REGIONAL ALLIANCES

Global organizations such as the WTO and structures like the World Bank were put in place by sovereign states to ensure a stable world trade and economic environment. These formats led to regional affiliations such as **bilateral alliances**, agreements between two sovereign nations, or **multinational agreements** among two or more independent countries. Examples are regional trading blocks, such as the European Union (EU) and the North American Free Trade Agreement (NAFTA) and, more recently, **free trade agreements (FTAs)**, which eliminate almost all trade restrictions and subsidies with various countries.

The European Union (EU)

One of the earliest—and historically most significant—examples of the new international order is the **European Union (EU)**, consisting of most of the nations of western Europe. It was established in 1993, to manage the economic and political integration of the member states. The idea actually began in 1950, in the aftermath of decades of wars and loss of life and property in Europe. A number of visionary European leaders were convinced that the only way to secure a lasting peace among their countries was to unite them economically and politically. Six original member countries, Belgium, West Germany, Luxembourg, France, Italy, and the Netherlands, agreed to give the power to make decisions about the coal and steel industry in their respective countries to an independent, supranational body called the High Authority.[10]

Current (2009) membership in the EU includes 27 countries: Austria, Belgium, Bulgaria, Cyprus, Czech Republic, Denmark, Estonia, Finland, France, Germany, Greece, Hungary, Ireland, Italy, Latvia, Lithuania, Luxembourg, Malta, the Netherlands, Poland, Portugal, Romania, Slovakia, Slovenia, Spain, Sweden, and the United Kingdom. Note: Canary Islands (Spain), Azores and Madeira (Portugal), French Guiana, Guadeloupe, Martinique, and Réunion (France) are sometimes listed separately even though they are legally a part of Spain, Portugal, and France. Candidate countries are Croatia, Macedonia, and Turkey.

The EU's original focus was on a common commercial policy for coal and steel and a common agricultural policy. Other policies were added as time went by, and as the need arose. Some key policy aims have changed in the light of changing circumstances. For example, the aim of its agricultural policy is no longer to produce as much food as cheaply as possible but to support farming methods that produce healthy, high-quality food and protect the environment. The need for environmental protection is now taken into account across the whole range of EU policies.

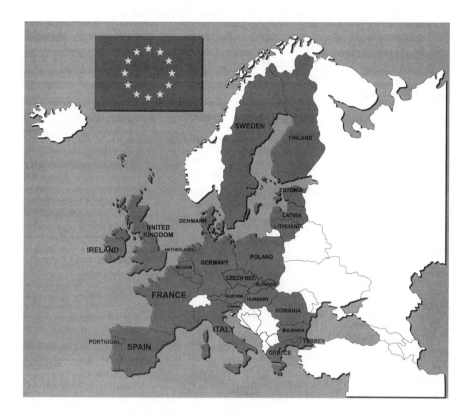

Figure 2.8 Map of the current and candidate members of the European Union.

....

The EU was created first and foremost as an economic union. The first, oldest, and largest pillar, the European Community, was founded as the European Economic Community. Creating and maintaining the EU's single market has been a prominent goal of the Community, ensuring free movement of people, goods, services, and capital.

Considered as a single economy, the EU is the largest in the world with a nominal Gross Domestic Product of $15.2 trillion in 2008.[11] The EU is also the largest exporter in the world and the second largest importer. It is the biggest trading partner to many countries, such as China and India.

It has taken years for the member states to remove all the barriers to trade between them and to turn their "common market" into a genuine single market. The single market was formally completed at the end of 1992, but there is still work to be done in some areas, for example, to create a genuinely single market in financial services, which includes a single currency, known as the **euro** (see below, Spotlight on Global Trade 2.1: History of the Euro).

CE Mark of Approval

An example of the EU's exclusionary practices is the requirement that product standards and certifications must meet certain EU health, safety, and environmental protection legislation in order to receive the CE Marking. The **CE Mark** is an abbreviation for *Conformité Européenne*, a mandatory conformity mark on many products placed on the single market in the EU. The term initially used was "EC Mark" and it was officially replaced by "CE Marking" in 1993. "EC mark" is still in use, but it is not the official term.

SPOTLIGHT ON GLOBAL TRADE 2.1:
History of the Euro

The euro (€), is the official currency of the Eurozone, which consists of most of the states of Western Europe plus some neighboring countries. The euro is the currency of the 320 million people who live in the 15 euro-area countries. Also known as the **Eurozone**, it includes the European states of Austria, Belgium, Finland, France, Germany, Greece, Ireland, Italy, Luxembourg, the Netherlands, Portugal, Slovenia, and Spain, plus the islands of Cyprus and Malta.

The euro was launched in January 1999, as an electronic currency and became legal tender three years later when 12 of the then 15 EU countries (Germany, France, Italy, Spain, Portugal, Belgium, Luxembourg, the Netherlands, Austria, Finland, Greece, and Ireland) became members of the Eurozone. The new currency, the euro, replaced the old national currencies of members in January 2002. In January 2007, the Republic of Slovenia became the first recently acceded EU Member State to introduce the euro, and the thirteenth country to join the Eurozone.

All European Union (EU) member states are eligible to join the Eurozone, if they meet certain monetary requirements. Although all countries that have joined the EU since 1993 have pledged to eventually adopt the euro, not all members have chosen to do so. The United Kingdom and Denmark negotiated exemptions, and Sweden turned down the euro in a 2003 referendum. Sweden has avoided the requirement to join the Eurozone by not meeting the membership criteria. Several small European states—The Vatican, Monaco, and San Marino—although not EU members, have adopted the euro due to currency unions with member states. Andorra, Montenegro, and Kosovo have adopted the euro unilaterally.

As of 2008, nine new EU member states have a currency other than the euro, however, all of these countries are required by their Accession Treaties to join the euro. The tentative schedule is Slovakia in 2009; Lithuania in 2010; Estonia in 2011; and Bulgaria, Hungary, Latvia, the Czech Republic, Poland, and Romania in 2012 or later. The entry of Lithuania and Estonia, as planned for January 2007, was postponed due to unacceptably high inflation rates in those countries.[12]

Figure 2.9 The euro: common currency for over 310 million people in the European Union.

The euro currency is printed in its member countries. On each coin is engraved its country of origin.

For U.S. exporters and importers, the EU and the euro have been mixed blessings. On the positive side, trade negotiations and procedures can now be undertaken with one entity, the EU, which speaks for all members, rather than dealing with individual governments. But some companies and individuals complain that the EU has become "fortress Europe," keeping out imports from non-EU nations and only promoting inter-EU imports and exports.

Figure 2.10 Ljubljana's market traders swapped the Slovenian tolar for the euro in January 2007.

....

By affixing the CE Marking, the manufacturer, its authorized representative, or person placing the product on the market or putting it into service asserts that the item meets all the essential requirements of all applicable EU directives, and that conformity assessment procedures have been applied. Note that the CE Marking is not a quality mark.[13]

On the positive side, during the past 10 years it became increasingly easy for business people, as well as tourists, to move around in Europe as passport and customs checks were abolished for EU citizens at most of the EU's internal borders allowing greater mobility for EU citizens. Since 1987, for example, more than a million young Europeans have studied abroad with support from the EU. The European Union's relations with the rest of the world have also become important. For example, the EU negotiates major trade and aid agreements with other countries and is developing a common foreign and security policy.

The North American Free Trade Agreement (NAFTA)

In January 1994, perhaps in response to the establishment of the European Union, the United States, in cooperation with Canada and Mexico, formed the **North American Free Trade Agreement (NAFTA)**, creating, at that time, the world's largest **free trade area** or region without trade borders. From the date of the signing until 2004, export-import trade between the United States and its NAFTA partners increased 129 percent, exceeding the 123 percent growth in trade between the United States and non-NAFTA partners during the same period.

Trade Diversion

One of the strongest criticisms of NAFTA is that it causes **trade diversion**, in which member states would import and export more from each other, shifting sources from one country to another, at the expense of other countries worldwide. For example, Jockey Industries of Kenosha, Wisconsin, decided to build a twin factory (known as a *maquiladora*) in Mexico to create underwear and sleepwear for its Mexican and Central American markets. Trade diversion takes place should Jockey buy its packaging materials, boxes, tape, and string, from a Mexican supplier rather than from its traditional vendor in the United States. While trade diversion has occurred in a few industries, such as textiles and apparel, where rules of origin negotiated in the agreement were specifically designed to make U.S. firms prefer Mexican manufacturers over other textile-producing nations, apparently NAFTA itself has not caused extensive across-the-board trade diversion. U.S. and World Bank studies have shown that the aggregate NAFTA imports' percentage growth was accompanied by an almost similar increase of non-NAFTA imports, suggesting that the increase in trade was not diversionary. Some economists argue that NAFTA has increased concentration of wealth in both Mexico and the United States.[14]

NAFTA MYTHS

NAFTA Myths

After nearly a decade and a half, the Office of the U.S. Trade Representative, in March 2008, dispelled the following NAFTA myths:

MYTH #1: After 14 years, we know NAFTA has not achieved its core goals of expanding trade and investment between the United States, Canada, and Mexico.

FACT: From 1993 to 2007, trade among the NAFTA nations more than tripled, from $297 billion to $930 billion. Business investment in the United States has risen by 117 percent since 1993, compared to a 45 percent increase between 1979 and 1993.

MYTH #2: NAFTA has cost the U.S. jobs.

FACT: U.S. employment rose from 110.8 million people in 1993 to 137.6 million in 2007, an increase of 24 percent. The average unemployment rate was 5.1 percent in the period 1994–2007, compared to 7.1 percent during the period 1980–1993.

MYTH #3: NAFTA has hurt America's manufacturing base.

FACT: U.S. manufacturing output rose by 58 percent between 1993 and 2006, as compared to 42 percent between 1980 and 1993. Manufacturing exports in 2007 reached an all time high with a value of $982 billion.

MYTH #4: NAFTA has suppressed U.S. wages.

FACT: U.S. business sector real hourly compensation rose by 1.5 percent each year between 1993 and 2007, for a total of 23.6 percent over the full period. During 1979–1993, the annual rate of real hourly compensation rose by 0.7 percent each year, or 11 percent over the full 14-year period.

MYTH #5: NAFTA has not delivered benefits to U.S. agriculture.

FACT: Canada and Mexico accounted for 37 percent of the total growth of U.S. agricultural exports. Moreover, the share of total U.S. agricultural exports destined for Canada or Mexico has grown in recent years from 22 percent to 30 percent. NAFTA access is most crucial for agriculture, where Mexico has its highest MFN tariffs. Mexico is the top export destination for beef, rice, soybean meal, corn sweeteners, apples, and dry edible bean exports. It is the second export market for U.S. corn, soybeans and oils, and third largest for pork, poultry, eggs, and cotton.

MYTH #6: NAFTA has reduced wages in Mexico.
FACT: Mexican wages grew steadily after the 1994 peso crisis reached pre-crisis levels in 1997, and have increased almost every year since then. Several studies note that Mexican industries that export or that are in regions with a higher concentration of foreign investment and trade also have higher wages.

MYTH #7: NAFTA investment provisions have put legitimate U.S. laws and regulations at risk.
FACT: Nothing in NAFTA's investment provisions prevents a country from adopting or maintaining non-discriminatory laws or regulations that protect the environment, worker rights, health and safety, or other public interest. The United States has never lost a challenge in the cases decided to date under NAFTA, nor paid a penny in damages to resolve any investment dispute. Even if the United States were to lose a case, it could be directed to pay compensation but it could not be required to change the laws or regulations at issue.

MYTH #8: NAFTA has done nothing to improve the environment.
FACT: NAFTA created two bi-national institutions unique to the agreement which certify and finance environmental infrastructure projects to provide a clean and healthy environment for residents along the U.S.-Mexico border. To date, they have provided nearly $1 billion for 135 environmental infrastructure projects with a total estimated cost of $2.89 billion and allocated $33.5 million in assistance and $21.6 million in grants for over 450 other border environmental projects. The Mexican government has also made substantial new investments in environmental protection, increasing the federal budget for the environmental sector by 81 percent between 2003 and 2008.[15]

The World Bank also showed that the aggregate NAFTA imports' percentage growth was accompanied by an almost similar increase of non-NAFTA imports, thus again suggesting that increase in trade was not diversionary. According to Anil Kumar, writing for the Dallas Federal Reserve Bank, in the March/April 2006 issue of *Southwest Economy*:

Preferential trade agreements impose lower tariffs on trade in goods and services among their member countries. Even with expansion of the multinational World Trade Organization in recent years, nations have found these regional deals increasingly attractive, concluding more than 180 pacts since 1990. Two types of preferential deals that are common: free-trade areas, such as NAFTA, that reduce tariffs on goods from member countries but allow each nation to set its own duties for nonmembers, and **customs unions**, such as the European Union, that agree to impose a common tariff wall on imports from nonmember countries.

In economic terms, they're similar, so the following discussion applies to both. These preferential agreements would normally violate the WTO's most-favored-nation rules, which require each member to extend to other members the lowest tariff applicable on all goods and services.[16]

While most business executives and proponents of free trade concur that NAFTA has brought economic growth and rising standards of living for people in all three countries, many economists contend it has been difficult to analyze its effects due to the large number of other factors in the global economy.

TRADE LIBERALIZATION

The United States has a genuine interest in trade liberalization as international trade is an integral part of the U.S. economy. It accounts for more than one-quarter of U.S. Gross Domestic Product (GDP) and supports more than 12 million U.S. jobs, including one-in-five manufacturing positions.

The United States has pursued the objective of trade liberalization primarily through agreements among large numbers of countries, first in successive rounds of multilateral negotiations under the General Agreement on Tariffs and Trade (GATT) and later the World Trade Organization (WTO). In recent years, however, the United States—and other countries—have also established free trade agreements (FTAs). A number of additional agreements are on the policy agendas of the U.S. Administration and the Congress.

As a result of these alliances, since the end of World War II a significant lowering of barriers to free trade has occurred. The move toward freer trade has, more than any other factor, facilitated the trend toward globalization of production and markets. From this perspective, many companies have started to view the world as a single market.

The stage is set, opportunities abound, but it's up to the individual marketer, whether a corporate manager or entrepreneur, to capitalize on export-import marketing activities.

SUMMARY

Nations are more and more interdependent through global interactions including increased trade throughout the world. With the development of liberalized trade initiatives, export and import business has grown extensively.

Starting with the Bretton Woods Conference in 1944, where both the International Monetary Fund and the World Bank were established, these organizations continue today to assist developing nations through short-term aid from the IMF (such as help with balance-of-payments deficits) and longer term assistance from the World Bank (as for building infrastructure such as communications systems, bridges, and highways).

Also stemming from Bretton Woods, the General Agreement on Tariffs and Trade (GATT) lowered tariffs among countries; its work is now absorbed by the World Trade Organization (WTO). Headquartered in Geneva, Switzerland, the WTO is responsible for creating and enforcing trade regulations among its members. Through various negotiating rounds, specific trade topics are reviewed, such as agriculture and services at the most recent Doha round.

Another international forum promoting international trade and economic cooperation is the Group of Eight (G8) consisting of the major economies of the world whose leaders meet periodically to confer on various current issues including trade.

Regional alliances also encourage international trade. One of the most significant is the European Union (EU) that currently has 27 member states consisting of most of western and eastern Europe's nations, including most of the former Eastern European, Soviet satellites. The EU is working toward economic integration by adopting the euro as a single currency, and is aiming for political integration by developing its own constitution.

The second is the North Atlantic Free Trade Agreement (NAFTA), an alliance of the United States, Canada, and Mexico whose goal is the elimination of all trade barriers among these nations. The major myths of NAFTA were addressed by the Office of the United States Trade Representative. However, some critics still contend it has been difficult to analyze NAFTA's effects due to the large number of other factors in the global economy.

The United States is among the nations that continue to work toward the liberalization and elimination of trade barriers by establishing free trade agreements to increase economic growth and prosperity throughout the world.

Key Terms

- > Bilateral alliances
- > Bretton Woods Conference
- > CE Mark
- > Customs unions
- > Doha Development Agenda (DDA)
- > Euro
- > Eurozone
- > European Union (EU)
- > Free trade agreements (FTAs)
- > Free trade area
- > General Agreement on Tariffs and Trade (GATT)
- > Group of Eight (G8)
- > Group of Twenty (G20)
- > Intellectual property rights
- > International Monetary Fund (IMF)
- > Less-developed countries (LDCs)
- > Multinational agreements
- > North American Free Trade Agreement (NAFTA)
- > Trade diversion
- > Uruguay Round
- > World Bank
- > World Trade Organization (WTO)

Review Questions

1. Explain the purpose and importance of the Bretton Woods Conference.

2. What were the three major international institutions that were established as a result of Bretton Woods? Which, if any, exist today?

3. Describe the five major activities the WTO conducts to meet its stated objective, "to help trade flow smoothly, freely, fairly, and predictably."

4. Provide three examples of regional trade alliances.

5. Explain the advantages of the individual European countries forming the EU, or European Union.

Discussion Questions and Activities

1. Using the Internet, research the history of the anti-globalization movement and list three major arguments of these protestors. Why are they often willing to subject themselves to arrest or injury in order to focus attention on their anti-globalization philosophy? Explain your own position, either pro or con.

2. WTO conferences are forums for the give-and-take among most trading countries of the world as they work toward global trade liberalization. Discuss your position vis-à-vis further liberalization of U.S. export-import trade. Discuss how the United States can champion free trade while, at the same time, protect its domestic economy, including factory jobs, from unfair foreign trade practices.

3. For many years, China's entry into the WTO was blocked by most European and Western nations, including the United States. Go to the Internet and research articles explaining why China was denied access and record the promises China made to convince the voting members to finally be admitted, which took place on December 11, 2001.

References

1. "M. Butterfly," and Miles Socha, "Giorgio Armani's New Formula." Both from *Women's Wear Daily*, January 23, 2007, pp 1, 3, 6, and 7.

2. *Encyclopedia Britannica Online*, s.v. "Bretton-Woods Conference." Retrieved on September 15, 2009, from http://www.britannica.com/EBchecked/topic/78994/Bretton-Woods-Conference.

3. International Monetary Fund, "About the IMF." Retrieved on May 23, 2008, from http://www.imf.org/external/about.htm.

4. The World Bank, "About Us." Retrieved on May 23, 2008, from http://go.worldbank.org/D6IEM83I0.

5. Duke Law Library and Technology, "GATT/WTO." Retrieved on May 23, 2008, from http://www.law.duke.edu/lib/researchguides/gatt.html.

6. The World Trade Organization, "What is the WTO?" Retrieved on May 23, 2008, from http://www.wto.org/english/thewto_e/whatis_e/whatis_e.htm.

7. World Trade Organization, "Understanding the WTO: The Doha Agenda." Retrieved on May 23, 2008, from http://www.wto.org/english/thewto_e/whatis_e/tif_e/doha1_e.htm.

8. "GATT/WTO," http://www.law.duke.edu/lib/researchguides/gatt.html.

9. World Vision, "G8 Action on World Health," http://www.g8action.org/us/issues.

10. EUROPA, "Treaty Establishing the European Coal and Steel Community, ECSC Treaty," http://europa.eu/legislation_summaries/institutional_affairs/treaties/treaties_ecsc_en.htm.

11. International Monetary Fund, "World Economic Outlook Database." Retrieved on September 16, 2009, from http://www.imf.org/external/pubs/ft/weo/2009/01/weodata/index.aspx.

12. European Commission, Economic and Financial Affairs, "The euro." Retrieved on September 16, 2009, from http://ec.europa.eu/economy_finance/the_euro/index_en.htm?cs_mid=2946.

13. CEMarking.net, "What Is CE Marking," http://www.cemarking.net/ce-marking/faqs/ce_marking?_html.

14. Kyoji Fukao, Toshihiro Okubo, and Robert M. Stern, "An Econometric Analysis of Trade Diversion under NAFTA," in *North American Journal of Economics and Finance*, Discussion Paper 491 (The University of Michigan, School of Public Policy, October 30, 2002).

15. Office of the United States Trade Representative, "NAFTA—Myth vs. Facts." Retrieved on May 24, 2008, from http://www.ustr.gov.

16. Anil Kumar. "Did NAFTA Spur Texas Exports," in *Southwest Economy* (March/April, 2006), no. 2.

Chapter 3

The U.S. Role
in Global Trade

3

in this case the retailer's name only—weekend wear for men and women. The Gap grew, offering children's wear and later intimate apparel. The company purchased Banana Republic, transforming its safari look into a more luxurious yet affordable brand of casual and dressy apparel for men and women. Turning to another price level—budget—Gap opened the Old Navy division, offering trendy looks for children, women, and men at reasonable prices. More recently, management started Piperlime, presenting online more than 100 brands of shoes and accessories for men, women, and children.

The company's expansion was not limited to the 50 states. Today Gap, Inc. is an international specialty retailer with revenues of $15.8 billion from its four divisions. Its revenue sources consist of some 3,177 stores with 150,000 employees throughout the United States, Canada, the United Kingdom, France, Ireland, and Japan, plus Internet accessibility for all of these locations. Consumers of the American sportswear look can access the Gap's various stores and Web sites from throughout the world.[1]

Source: www.gapinc.com. Accessed June 23, 2008.

TROUBLE IN WORLD TRADE?

The global financial crisis and U.S. economic downturn that began in the second half of 2008 and continued into 2009 is still unfolding as of this writing. According to the International Monetary Fund (IMF), in their World Economic Outlook Update, published in July 2009, the global economy is beginning to pull out of a recession unprecedented in the post–World War II era, but stabilization is uneven and the recovery is expected to be sluggish. Economic growth is now projected to be about 2.5 percent in 2010. Financial conditions have improved more than expected, owing mainly to public intervention, and recent data suggest that the rate of decline in economic activity is moderating, although to varying degrees among regions and individual countries.[2]

Despite these positive signs, the global recession is not yet over, and the recovery is still expected to be slow, as financial systems remain weak, support from public policies will gradually diminish, and households in countries that suffered asset price busts will try to rebuild savings. The main policy priority remains restoring a healthy world financial sector. Macroeconomic policies need to stay supportive, while preparing the ground for an orderly unwinding of unprecedented government (public) intervention in most nation's economic systems. At the same time, given weak internal demand prospects in a number of current account deficit countries, including the United States, policies need to sustain stronger demand in key surplus countries, such as China, India, and Brazil.

Considering the dynamics of global trade and the uncertain predictions for the near future of trade, it is unavoidable for some of the facts and opinions presented in this text to soon be out-of-date. What will not change, however, is the fact that the United States has had, and will continue to have, a genuine stake in globalization and in free—and fair—export-import trade.

Figure 3.2 Imported cargo will be removed from an incoming ship at the Port of Los Angeles/Long Beach, the largest and busiest port in the United States.

. . . .

The United States is the world's largest trading nation, with total trade in 2008 valued at over $4.3 trillion dollars. U.S. exports of goods and services increased $197.2 billion in 2008 to a total of $1.8 trillion, while imports grew by $174.1 billion to a total of $2.52 trillion.[3]

The slower growth rate for imports reflected the sharp drop in American consumer purchases for the last half of 2008, due to the recession, fueled by the housing and financial crisis. Most of the growth in exports occurred in the June–July period, when the dollar gained strength on the news of the recession spreading to Europe and Asia. The deepening global recession during the fourth quarter 2008 was reflected in the sharp drop in both export and import activity for the United States as even a then weaker dollar could not generate export sales in foreign markets suddenly experiencing a recession.

For only the second time in 30 years, the size of the U.S. trade deficit was reduced in 2008, as Americans continued to slash spending on imports and U.S. exports dwindled amid weakening global demand. The economic crisis had driven down U.S. imports of foreign goods even faster than the rest of the world was cutting back on buying U.S. exports.

Historically, whenever the United States experienced a major slowdown in annual domestic growth, it was followed by a reduction in the U.S. trade deficit. (See Table 3.1.) From a record high imbalance, or trade deficit of $753.2 billion in 2006, the totals fell to $700.2 billion in 2007 and even further, to $677 billion, in 2008. The unusual back-to-back annual declines last occurred during the recession years of 1990–1991, possibly indicating a long period of international trade contraction.

U.S. International Trade in Goods and Services

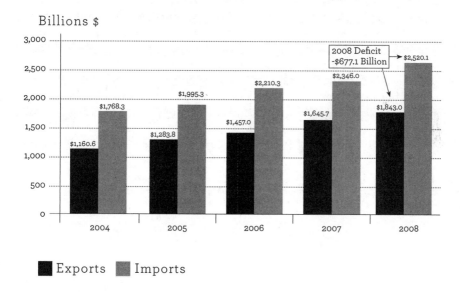

Figure 3.3 U.S. International Trade (Export-Import) in Goods and Services for 2008.

········

Source: Foreign Trade Statistics, U.S. Census Bureau, February 11, 2009.
Retrieved from http//www.census.gov/indicator/www/ustrade.html.

TABLE 3.1 U.S. TRADE IN GOODS AND SERVICES–
BALANCE OF PAYMENTS (BOP)BASIS
VALUE IN MILLIONS OF DOLLARS 1990 THROUGH 2008

Period	BALANCE			EXPORTS			IMPORT		
	Total	Goods BOP	Services	Total	Goods BOP	Services	Total	Good BOP	Services
1990	-80,864	-111,037	30,173	535,233	387,401	147,832	616,097	498,438	117,659
1991	-31,135	-76,937	45,802	578,344	414,083	164,261	609,479	491,020	118,459
1992	-39,212	-96,897	57,685	616,882	439,631	177,251	656,094	536,528	119,566
1993	-70,311	-132,451	62,141	642,863	456,943	185,920	713,174	589,394	123,780
1994	-98,493	-165,831	67,338	703,254	502,859	200,395	801,747	668,690	133,057
1995	-96,384	-174,170	77,786	794,387	575,204	219,183	890,771	749,374	141,397
1996	-104,065	-191,000	86,935	851,602	612,113	239,489	955,667	803,113	152,554
1997	-108,273	-198,428	90,155	934,453	678,366	256,087	1,042,726	876,794	165,932
1998	-166,140	-248,221	82,081	933,174	670,416	262,758	1,099,314	918,637	180,677
1999	-265,090	-347,819	82,729	965,884	683,965	281,919	1,230,974	1,031,784	199,190
2000	-379,835	-454,690	74,855	1,070,587	771,994	298,603	1,450,432	1,226,684	223,748
2001	-365,126	-429,519	64,393	1,004,896	718,712	286,184	1,370,022	1,148,231	221,791
2002	-423,725	-484,955	61,230	974,721	682,422	292,299	1,398,446	1,167,377	231,069
2003	-496,915	-550,892	53,977	1,017,757	713,415	304,342	1,514,672	1,264,307	250,365
2004	-607,730	-669,578	61,848	1,160,588	807,516	353,072	1,768,318	1,477,094	291,244
2005	-711,567	-787,149	75,582	1,283,753	894,631	389,122	1,995,320	1,681,780	313,540
2006	-753,283	-838,270	84,987	1,457,014	1,023,109	433,905	2,210,298	1,861,380	348,918
2007	-700,258	-819,373	119,115	1,645,726	1,148,481	497,245	2,345,983	1,967,853	378,130
2008	-681,130	-820,825	139,695	1,835,785	1,291,371	544,414	2,516,915	2,112,196	404,719

Source: U.S. Census Bureau, "U.S. International Trade in Goods and Services: Annual Goods (BOP basis), Services, and Total Balance, Exports and Imports, 1960–Present," Foreign Trade Historical Series, http://www.census.gov/foreign-trade/statistics/historicalgands.pdf. Retrieved September 17, 2009.

Although a narrowing of the U.S. trade deficit could be seen as a positive sign for reaching an economic balance between exports and imports, economists point out the drop reflected the slumping trade volume in a global economy that experienced a deeper recession during the first half of 2009.

Annual world trade totals for 2008 and the first half of 2009 are sharply lower, as the international credit crisis had a severe impact on all exports. Recession is not good for international trade. Traders are dependent not only upon strong consumer demand for goods and services, but also liquid credit to fund documentary letters of credit (see Chapter 10) to pay for imported goods and services, or to get paid for exports.

No one could have predicted that such financial icons as Bear Stearns and Lehman Brothers would disappear in one year (2008). Some economists try to explain this phenomenon by citing the downside of globalization, suggesting that the global scope of our financial system and its rapid growth have made it more difficult to regulate by private or government entities. But students of "what went wrong?" will also have to consider the contributions made by greed and speculation by investment bankers and traders, poor management practices by some of the world's largest banks, and government policies that encouraged subprime market lending for unqualified home mortgages.

When financial markets fail, as they did in 2008, capitalism loses liquidity, exchanges of goods and services fall—both domestically and internationally—output is reduced, and employment is cut. Asset owners lose the wealth they thought would sustain them not only for daily expenses, but also for their retirement years.

Free-trade proponents are quick to point out, however, that export-import trade has become an integral part of the U.S. economy and is anticipated to be a vital contributor to any recovery from the current economic crisis. The U.S. balance of trade—the difference between the dollar value of exports (goods and services sold abroad) and the dollar value of imports (goods and services purchased abroad)—is one indicator that reveals the impact of the current crisis on the U.S. economy. Since 1975, the United States has recorded a trade deficit, as imports exceeded exports over a one-year period. One reason for the continuing trade deficit is the size and purchasing power of the U.S. domestic market. Also, continued dependency of American industry and consumers on foreign fossil fuels has made it unlikely the nation will, in the foreseeable future, experience a trade surplus, where exports would exceed imports.[4]

The balance of trade is usually divided into a goods and a services component, to comply with international reporting standards. The U.S. balance of *services* trade has been in a surplus since 1971. The export of services, such as financial, legal, accounting, and banking activities, continues to help reduce the overall trade deficit. U.S. services exports totaled $551.6 billion in 2008, up $54.4 billion (10.9 percent) from 2007. This rise in exports helped the United States to have a record trade surplus in services at $144.1 billion, up $24.9 billion (20.9 percent) from 2007. The top services export categories include items such as business, professional and technical services, insurance services, and financial services

($241.0 billion), travel ($111.5 billion), royalties and license fees ($91.1 billion), transportation ($60.2 billion), passenger fares ($31.4 billion), and government services ($16.3 billion).[5]

Historically, the value of U.S. trade—exports plus imports—as a percentage of GDP, has averaged approximately 20 percent. The comparable figure for Canada, our most important trade partner, is 60 percent of its GDP allocated to trade.

KEY U.S. TRADE RELATIONSHIPS

U.S. bilateral trade relationships have been the cornerstone of its free enterprise system, providing open access to foreign imports while encouraging **free trade**—international trade with no or few limitations—that ensure American goods and services can be exported to global markets. Key trade partners of the United States—those who have a surplus or deficit in trade with this country—have not been spared from the global economic crisis. Their individual trade account figures are down and GDP growth has come to an alarming halt as of the first half 2009.

TABLE 3.2 U.S. EXPORTS, IMPORTS, AND TOTAL TRADE 2008 (BY COUNTRY) FOR TOP TEN TRADE PARTNERS

(by goods only; in billions of U.S. dollars)

Rank	Country	Exports	Imports	Total Trade	Percent of Total Trade
	Total, All Countries	1,300.5	2,100.4	3,400.9	100%
1	Canada	261.4	335.6	596.9	17.6%
2	China	71.5	337.8	409.2	12%
3	Mexico	151.5	215.9	367.5	10.8%
4	Japan	66.6	139.2	205.8	6.1%
5	Germany	54.7	97.6	152.3	4.5%
6	United Kingdom	53.8	58.6	112.4	3.3%
7	South Korea	34.8	48.1	82.9	2.4%
8	France	29.2	44.0	73.2	2.2%
9	Saudi Arabia	12.5	54.8	67.3	2%
10	Venezuela	12.6	51.4	64.0	1.9%

In terms of total goods trade—exports and imports—Canada remains the number one trade partner of the United States.

Source: FTDWebMaster, Foreign Trade Division, U.S. Census Bureau, Washington, DC 20233. Retrieved on August 1, 2009.

TABLE 3.3 TOP TEN COUNTRIES WITH WHICH THE U.S. HAS A TRADE SURPLUS YEAR-TO-DATE, JULY 2009

(by goods only; in millions of U.S. dollars)

Country name	Year-to-date surplus in millions of U.S. dollars
Netherlands	9,993.65
Hong Kong	9,300.14
Australia	6,021.67
Singapore	3,675.21
Belgium	5,053.30
United Arab Emirates	6,149.54
Chile	1,341.30
Brazil	2,718.04
Panama	2,096.67
Argentina	771.91

With imports greater than exports for the past 40 years, the United States has a favorable, or surplus, balance of trade with a few countries, at dollar amounts much less than our top export markets.

Source: www.census.gov/foreign-trade/top/dst/2009/07/surplus.html. Retrieved on September 20, 2009.

TABLE 3.4 TOP TEN COUNTRIES WITH WHICH THE U.S. HAS A TRADE DEFICIT YEAR-TO-DATE, JULY 2009

(by goods only; in millions of U.S. dollars)

Country name	Year-to-date deficit in millions of U.S. dollars
China	-123,468.18
Japan	-21,836.82
Germany	-14,761.45
Mexico	-24,107.83
Venezuela	-9,451.58
Canada	-10,743.93
Ireland	-12,640.24
Nigeria	-6,236.90
Russia	-7,745.68
Italy	-7,989.71

The U.S. goods trade deficit with most of its trade partners is due not only to the American consumer's strong interest in foreign goods, including a deficit of over $123 billion with China for just the first seven months of 2009, but also to a weakness in exporting.

Source: www.census.gov/foreign-trade/top/dst/2009/07/deficit.html. Retrieved on September 20, 2009.

U.S.–Canada Trade

The U.S. and Canadian economies are closely intertwined; they are each other's largest trading partner. The United States is the largest foreign investor in Canada and the U.S. is the most popular destination for Canadian investment. The two countries share the world's longest open border, with 90 percent of Canada's 33 million people living within 100 miles of the U.S. border.

As a result, Canada was the United States's largest bilateral trading partner in 2008, with more than $1.6 billion in goods crossing the border each day. Combined export and import trade totaled $597 billion in 2008. U.S. exports to Canada were $261 billion and imports were $335 billion, resulting in a U.S. goods deficit of $74.2 billion in 2008.

Approximately 80 percent of Canadian exports go to the United States while the U.S. share of Canada's total imports is about 55 percent. U.S. exports to Canada exceed U.S. exports to the entire European Union, even though the EU has 15 times Canada's population. The two-way trade that crosses the Ambassador Bridge between Michigan and Ontario equals all U.S. exports to Japan.[6]

Figure 3.4 The Ambassador Bridge, spanning Michigan and Ontario, connects not just the countries of the United States and Canada, but also the largest export-import trade partnership in the world.

·········

TABLE 3.5 U.S. TRADE WITH CANADA: 2008

NOTE: All figures are in millions of U.S. dollars, and not seasonally adjusted unless otherwise specified.

Month	Exports	Imports	Balance
January 2008	20,485.6	27,359.1	-6,873.5
February 2008	21,255.8	27,499.0	-6,243.2
March 2008	22,978.2	29,968.0	-6,989.8
April 2008	23,463.8	31,232.6	-7,768.8
May 2008	24,386.5	30,270.8	-5,884.3
June 2008	23,741.4	31,285.3	-7,544.0
July 2008	22,325.4	32,208.4	-9,883.0
August 2008	22,075.6	29,994.4	-7,918.8
September 2008	22,294.2	29,653.6	-7,359.3
October 2008	22,058.7	27,707.3	-5,648.5
November 2008	19,172.4	22,692.9	-3,430.5
December 2008	16,912.2	19,710.0	-2,797.8
TOTAL	261,149.8	339,491.4	-78,341.6

*TOTAL may not add due to rounding.
*Table reflects only those months for which there was trade.
*CONTACT: Data Dissemination Branch, U.S. Census Bureau, 301-763-2311.
*SOURCE: U.S. Census Bureau, Foreign Trade Division, Data Dissemination Branch, Washington, DC, 20233.

Trade with Canada is facilitated by proximity, common culture, language, similar lifestyle pursuits, and the ease of travel among citizens for business or pleasure. American products have gained an increased competitive edge over goods from other countries as the North American Free Trade Agreement (NAFTA) and geographical proximity gives U.S. exporters an advantage. In 2008, the U.S. goods trade deficit with Canada was $78 billion, largely due to high commodity prices.

U.S.–China Trade

China is the United States's second largest trading partner with $409 billion in two-way goods trade in 2008—a six percent increase over 2007. In 2008, China became the third-largest market for U.S. exports, with a total of $69 billion, an increase of 7.5 billion over the previous year. Exports included electrical machinery, soybeans, aircraft, iron and steel products, and industrial engines. In 2008, imports from China increased by five percent over the previous year, to total a record $337 billion. TVs and DVDs, drilling and oil field equipment, telecommunications equipment and computers, toys and textiles and apparel were among the leading exports to the United States.[7]

TABLE 3.6 U.S. TRADE WITH CHINA: 2008

NOTE: All figures are in millions of U.S. dollars, and not seasonally adjusted unless otherwise specified.

Month	Exports	Imports	Balance
January 2008	5,556.7	26,193.0	-20,636.3
February 2008	5,698.1	24,095.9	-18,397.8
March 2008	6,294.4	22,440.2	-16,145.9
April 2008	5,651.2	25,951.7	-20,300.4
May 2008	6,275.7	27,634.5	-21,358.9
June 2008	6,188.2	27,930.6	-21,742.5
July 2008	6,234.6	31,247.3	-25,012.6
August 2008	6,201.3	31,823.7	-25,622.4
September 2008	5,257.6	33,078.7	-27,821.1
October 2008	6,083.4	34,032.4	-27,949.0
November 2008	5,181.0	28,265.0	-23,084.1
December 2008	5,110.7	25,079.5	-19,968.8
TOTAL	69,732.8	337,772.6	-268,039.8

*TOTAL may not add due to rounding.
*Table reflects only those months for which there was trade.
*CONTACT: Data Dissemination Branch, U.S. Census Bureau, 301-763-2311.
*SOURCE: U.S. Census Bureau, Foreign Trade Division, Data Dissemination Branch, Washington, DC 20233.

Figure 3.5 China is the third-largest market for U.S. exports. Many U.S. exports are sold in department stores and high-end shops on the seven-hundred-year-old Wangfujing Street, in Beijing, China.

....

SPOTLIGHT ON GLOBAL TRADE 3.1:
U.S. Free Trade Agreements

The United States has pursued the objective of trade liberalization primarily through trade negotiations among many countries, first in successive rounds of multilateral negotiations under the General Agreement on Tariffs and Trade (GATT) and later the World Trade Organization (WTO). In recent years, however, the United States—as well as most countries world-wide—has established bilateral or multilateral free-trade agreements (FTAs) between two or more countries to eliminate tariff and **non-tariff barriers (NTB)** affecting trade among themselves.

Prior to the year 2000, the United States had only three comprehensive FTAs on the books: Canada, Israel, and Mexico. Since then, the United States has concluded FTAs with Australia, Bahrain, Chile, Jordan, Oman, Morocco, Singapore, Peru, and the six Central American parties to CAFTA (Costa Rica, Dominican Republic, El Salvador, Guatemala, Honduras, and Nicaragua). The United States is presently negotiating FTAs with another dozen or so countries, including:

> South Korea
> Panama
> Thailand
> United Arab Emirates
> Colombia and Ecuador (as part of the Andean process)
> The five parties to the US-SACU talks (Botswana, Lesotho, Namibia, South Africa, and Swaziland).

Countries reportedly being considered for upcoming U.S. FTA consideration include Malaysia, Algeria, Egypt, Tunisia, Saudi Arabia, and Qatar. Congressional action on any of the FTAs was put on hold at the start of the new administration in early 2009, as the deepening global financial crisis led to more talk of protectionism than free trade agreements.

Concerns over rising protectionism have become a global issue. The World Trade Organization's Director-General Pascal Lamy, in presenting his report on recent trade developments associated with the financial crisis to an informal meeting of the Trade Policy Review Body on February 9, 2009, warned that with trade growth already stalled "the fragile economic prospects of every WTO Member [country] have become especially vulnerable to the introduction of any new measure that closes off market access or distorts competition." "This is particularly the case for developing countries," he said. A few days earlier, in a speech before the International Chamber of Commerce, on February 3, 2009, Lamy warned members against "sliding down a slippery slope of tit-for-tat (protectionist) measures," quoting Mahatma Gandhi who said, "An eye for an eye makes the whole world blind." He urged the business community to support the Doha Round [trade talks], which he said "can be part of the solution to the economic downturn."

For U.S. exporters trying to combat rising protectionism in trade partner countries, FTAs have proven to be a very effective way to open up these markets. Each participating country applies its own independent schedule of tariffs to imports from countries that are not members.

These comprehensive free trade agreements are intended to expand export and import opportunities for American manufacturers, workers, farmers and ranchers, plus a myriad of marketing and service organizations. To ensure U.S. access to specific foreign markets for selling our products and services, or to expand our foreign manufacturing options, the U.S. has signed and ratified a number of Free Trade Agreements (FTAs) which provide for immediate or staged elimination of duties on imports and qualifying exports to partner countries.

The U.S. international trade balance, previously presented in negative numbers as a major problem for the recovery of the economic recession, has actually flipped from a deficit to a surplus with our Free Trade Agreement partners. In the first five months of 2008, the trade balance in manufactured goods rose to a $2.7 billion *surplus* with our FTA partners. That was a major recovery, as the U.S. recorded a $12.3 billion deficit during the same period the year before. The FTAs are in addition to the North American Free Trade Agreement (NAFTA), the agreement between the United States, Canada, and Mexico. The final provisions of NAFTA were fully implemented on January 1, 2008. Launched on January 1, 1994, NAFTA is one of the most successful trade agreements in history and has contributed to significant increases in export-import trade and investment among the United States, Canada, and Mexico.

The duty preference systems, the primary benefit of FTAs, increases the price competitiveness of U.S. products compared with those provided by local suppliers and third-country suppliers that do not receive such duty benefits. FTAs also afford benefits in a broad range of service sectors, for example when retailers can export franchises and establish distribution companies; enhance the protection of intellectual property; open up government procurement opportunities; and facilitate U.S. trade and investment through more open and transparent rule-making procedures and nondiscriminatory laws and regulations.

Comprehensive summaries of these FTAs can be found on the Office of the U.S. Trade Representative website: www.ustr.gov/Trade_Agreements. A few specific agreements will be examined further.

The United States engages in free trade agreements to expand export and import opportunities for American manufacturers, workers, farmers and ranchers, plus a variety of marketing and service organizations. To ensure U.S. access to specific foreign markets for selling its products and services, or to expand its foreign manufacturing options, the U.S. has signed and ratified a number of FTAs, as listed above.

Duty preferences do increase the price competitiveness of U.S. products compared with those provided by local suppliers and third-country suppliers that do not receive the same benefits. Historically, FTAs have allowed U.S. textile and apparel manufacturers easier access to a growing number of global markets.

U.S.–AUSTRALIA FREE TRADE AGREEMENT

The U.S.–Australia Free Trade Agreement went into effect on January 1, 2005, and up to this point has achieved the most significant immediate reduction of industrial tariffs in a U.S. free trade agreement. It provides for immediate benefits for America's manufacturing workers and companies. On the day this FTA entered into effect, tariffs that had averaged 4.3 percent were eliminated on more than 99 percent of the tariff lines for U.S. manufactured goods exported to Australia.

Exports of these goods account for 93 percent of total U.S. goods sold in Australia's market, and reduced tariffs create new export opportunities for America's manufacturers. With virtually all U.S. manufactured exports becoming duty-free immediately, the National Association of Manufacturers (NAM) estimates that the manufacturing sector could sell $2 billion more per year to Australia and that U.S. national income could grow by nearly that much.

Textile and apparel tariffs will phase out over a maximum of 15 years for goods that meet the agreement's yarn-forward rule of origin. The FTA promotes new opportunities for U.S. fiber, yarn, fabric and apparel manufacturing.

CAFTA-DR FREE TRADE AGREEMENT

The **Central America-Dominican Republic-United States Free Trade Agreement (CAFTA-DR)** includes seven signatories: the United States, Costa Rica, Dominican Republic, El Salvador, Guatemala, Honduras, and Nicaragua. The United States is implementing the CAFTA-DR on a rolling basis as countries make sufficient progress to complete their commitments under the agreement.

Small and medium-sized enterprises (SME) benefit from the tariff-eliminating provisions of free trade agreements, and should benefit from the significant tariff cuts required under the CAFTA-DR. The transparency obligations, particularly those contained in the customs chapters, are also very important to SMEs, which may not have the resources to navigate customs and regulatory red tape.

The CAFTA-DR export zone created the United States' second largest free trade zone in Latin America, after Mexico. In addition to tariff reduction, CAFTA-DR provides new market access for U.S. consumer and industrial products and agricultural products. Small businesses have taken advantage of previous trade agreements designed to eliminate trade barriers.

CAFTA-DR liberalizes the services sectors, protects U.S. investments in the region, and strengthens protections for U.S. patents, trademarks, and trade secrets. The agreement covers customs facilitation and provides benefits to small and medium-sized exporters. Provisions are also included that address government transparency and corruption, worker rights, protection of the environment, trade capacity building, and dispute settlement.

At the signing of the CAFTA trade bill, on August 2, 2005, the President stated that "it is more than a trade bill; it is a commitment among freedom-loving nations to advance peace and prosperity throughout the region. As the oldest democracy in the Western Hemisphere, the United States has a moral obligation and a vital national security interest in helping democracies in our neighborhood succeed, and CAFTA advances this goal."

THE UNITED STATES-ISRAEL FREE TRADE AREA (FTA)

Effective September 1, 1985, the U.S.–Israel Free Trade Area Agreement (FTA) was the first free trade agreement the United States signed with another country. The FTA eliminated duties on manufactured goods as of January 1, 1995. Although it was designed to stimulate trade between the United States and Israel, it also allowed both countries to protect sensitive agricultural subsectors with non-tariff barriers, including import bans, quotas, and fees. In 2008, Israel was America's 19th leading trade partner.

With the exception of agriculture products, the United States-Israel FTA has eliminated nearly all tariffs on trade and administrative import licensing requirements between the two countries. To fully take advantage of the benefits offered under the FTA, U.S. exporters should carefully review the information regarding the Certificate of Origin for U.S. exports to Israel.

Because of the FTA, U.S. companies have gained greater Israeli market access, reduced transaction costs, increased sales, and enhanced export revenues. Over the years, the FTA has supported strong U.S. export growth in the Israeli market by making U.S. products and services more attractive to Israeli consumers. Thanks in large part to the FTA, U.S. companies exported more than $20 billion worth of goods and services to Israel in 2007, making Israel the largest U.S. export market in the Middle East. U.S. companies are encouraged to take advantage of this historic agreement to expand their export opportunities in the Middle East's most dynamic market.

The FTA has no expiration date and provides for the elimination of duties for merchandise from Israel entering the United States. The United States is Israel's largest trading partner, and there are opportunities there for U.S. exporters. A recognized leader in high-tech industries, Israel's investment in research and development is higher than that of any other single member of the **Organization for Economic Cooperation and Development (OECD)**, an international establishment, created after World War II under the Marshall Plan, to help rebuild and promote social and economic growth among countries. In fact, after the United States and Canada, Israel has the most companies listed on the **National Association of Securities Dealers Automated Quotations (NASDAQ)**, the automated over-the-counter securities exchange, generally consisting of medium-sized firms.

Israel's population of 6.7 million lives in an area roughly the size of New Jersey. Their business environment and style will seem familiar to American businesses, but personal relationships can play a relatively larger role within Israel's tight-knit population than in the United States. Israel's per capita income is 75% of the average in OECD nations, and remained strong through the recent economic slowdowns.

Free trade negotiations between the United Arab Emirates (UAE) and the United States began in 2005, but as of January, 2007, no agreement had been signed. U.S. oil and gas exploration and development companies stand to lose billions if the administration cannot work out the FTA. This agreement was expected to build on existing FTAs in the region and would promote the Middle East Free Trade Area (MEFTA) initiative to advance economic reforms and openness in the Middle East and the Persian Gulf, thus establishing a regional free trade area by 2013.

A successful conclusion of a comprehensive MEFTA would generate export opportunities for U.S. goods and service providers, solidify the UAE's trade and investment liberalization, and strengthen intellectual property rights protections and enforcement. It also would be in the best interest of national security.

THE U.S. BILATERAL INVESTMENT TREATY (BIT)

The **U.S. Bilateral Investment Treaty (BIT)** program helps protect private investment, develops market-oriented policies in partner countries, and promotes U.S. exports. A BIT is an agreement establishing the terms and conditions for private investment by nationals and companies of one state in the state of the other. This type of investment is also referred to as Foreign Direct Investment (FDI).

The BIT program's basic aims are to:

> Protect investment abroad in countries where investor rights are not already protected through existing agreements (such as modern treaties of friendship, commerce, and navigation, or free trade agreements);

> Encourage the adoption of market-oriented domestic policies that treat private investment in an open, transparent, and non-discriminatory way; and

> Support the development of international law standards consistent with these objectives.

Examples of other global economic and trade alliances include: the **Association of Southeast Asian Nations (ASEAN)** group made up of Bangladesh, India, Pakistan, Vietnam, Cambodia, Indonesia, Laos, and Sri Lanka) the **Caribbean Basin Countries**, including Costa Rica, Dominican Republic, El Salvador, Guatemala, Haiti, Honduras, Jamaica, and Nicaragua; and the **Andean Countries**, which include the textile and apparel-producing nations of Bolivia, Colombia, Ecuador, and Peru.

There are critics of Free Trade Agreements, however, citing political and social arguments against them. They claim that U.S. FTAs are, along with the EUs, the most far reaching in terms of achieving substantial change—or legal grounds for it—in other countries' social and economic policies by setting U.S. friendly standards for investor privileges, environmental protection, workers' rights, intellectual property rights, deregulation of service industries and privatization in general, wherever they are signed. Critics point out that world trade is increasingly being dominated by **preferential trade agreements (PTAs)**, agreements between two countries to lower or eliminate trade barriers that have taken precedence over multilateral trade negotiations. Within Asia and the Pacific an explosion of bilateral deals is taking place that seems likely to produce a tangle of trade blocs centered on major Asian or Pacific countries.

While many of the emerging free trade agreements appear to be consistent with WTO guidelines, the complex **rules of origin**—the rules that determine the country of origin of an imported product—threaten to complicate international commerce and divert trade rather than creating it. Rules of origin play an important role in international trade, since the application of duties and other restrictions on entry often depends on the source of the imports. The FTA agreements provide for harmonization in the practices of WTO members in determining the country of origin of products on both the practices and patterns of textile and apparel trade between signatory countries in trade agreements and between those countries and non-signatories. In the North American Free Trade Agreement (NAFTA), a product is said to originate in the free trade area when it is grown, harvested, wholly produced, or substantially transformed in the free trade area. Substantial transformation occurs when processing causes a product to shift from one tariff classification to another.

NAFTA rules of origin are designed to ensure that the benefits of free trade accrue to the NAFTA Parties by requiring that the products traded with NAFTA preference be of North American origin, and by preventing non-NAFTA products from receiving NAFTA treatment.

The rules of origin trade barriers seem to have a greater effect on the import and export of apparel and textiles than on any other classification of goods traded. Perhaps the recent changes, noted below, scheduled to be implemented in 2008 by NAFTA, on new rules of origin, will help address the needs of the apparel and textile industries.

NAFTA New Rules of Origin Changes for 2008

Trade ministers from Canada and Mexico and the U.S. Trade Representative, the three NAFTA countries, met August 14, 2007 in Vancouver, Canada, and announced new rules of origin liberalization that would be implemented in 2008.

Proposed changes would give producers more flexibility in sourcing inputs, which makes it easier for them to qualify for preferential tariff treatment under the NAFTA Agreement.

In a joint statement the trade officials announced, "The rules of origin revisions, affecting an estimated $100 billion in trilateral trade, follow changes implemented in 2005 and in 2006. These efforts confirm NAFTA's ability to adapt to ever-changing competitive conditions including new sourcing patterns and production methods. In this context, the Working Group on Rules of Origin will continue its work to pursue further liberalization opportunities." New rules of origin for U.S.-Canada trade became effective July 1, 2009.

U.S.–Mexico Trade

Mexico is the United States's third largest single-country trading partner (Canada is first) and has been among the fastest growing major export markets for the United States, since the signing of the North American Free Trade Agreement (NAFTA), between the United States, Canada and Mexico, in 1994. NAFTA has built both a strong trade relationship and a more equitable set of trade rules as Mexico's barriers have been reduced or eliminated.

TABLE 3.7 U.S. TRADE WITH MEXICO: 2008

NOTE: All figures are in millions of U.S. dollars, and not seasonally adjusted unless otherwise specified.

Month	Exports	Imports	Balance
January 2008	11,990.6	17,054.5	-5,063.9
February 2008	11,961.9	17,674.5	-5,712.7
March 2008	11,793.1	17,707.1	-5,914.0
April 2008	12,492.9	19,364.9	-6,871.9
May 2008	12,297.9	18,837.2	-6,539.3
June 2008	13,383.3	19,179.9	-5,796.6
July 2008	13,800.8	19,238.0	-5,437.2
August 2008	13,749.7	19,522.8	-5,773.1
September 2008	12,789.2	17,926.2	-5,137.0
October 2008	14,875.5	19,695.7	-4,820.2
November 2008	11,944.7	15,471.6	-3,526.9
December 2008	10,140.5	14,269.1	-4,128.6
TOTAL	**151,220.1**	**215,941.6**	**-64,721.6**

*TOTAL may not add due to rounding.
*Table reflects only those months for which there was trade.
*CONTACT: Data Dissemination Branch, U.S. Census Bureau, 301-763-2311.
*SOURCE: U.S. Census Bureau, Foreign Trade Division, Data Dissemination Branch, Washington, DC 20233.

U.S. imports from Mexico include: manufactured goods, oil and oil products, silver, fruits, vegetables, coffee and cotton. U.S. exports to Mexico totaled $151.5 billion in 2008, while we imported $215.9 billion worth of Mexican products, for a trade deficit of $64.4 billion.[8]

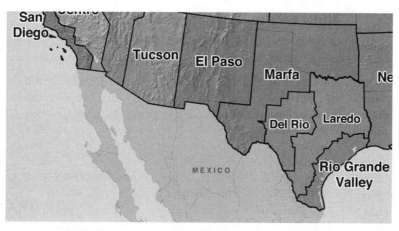

Figure 3.6 The long border between the United States and Mexico may breed illegal immigration, but it also represents over $350 billion in two-way trade between the two countries.
....

Figure 3.7 Traffic waiting to enter the United States from Tijuana, Mexico, to San Ysidro, California. It is the most frequently crossed international border in the world, with about 250 million legal crossings every year.
....

TABLE 3.8 U.S. TRADE WITH JAPAN: 2008

NOTE: All figures are in millions of U.S. dollars, and not seasonally adjusted unless otherwise specified.

Month	Exports	Imports	Balance
January 2008	4,950.6	11,709.0	-6,758.4
February 2008	5,523.9	12,542.0	-7,018.1
March 2008	5,626.6	13,015.6	-7,388.9
April 2008	5,431.2	13,045.3	-7,614.1
May 2008	6,024.6	11,244.4	-5,219.8
June 2008	5,752.4	12,144.3	-6,391.8
July 2008	5,600.9	12,029.0	-6,428.0
August 2008	5,908.0	11,136.9	-5,228.8
September 2008	5,434.4	11,008.0	-5,573.7
October 2008	5,338.6	11,475.7	-6,137.1
November 2008	5,058.0	10,108.2	-5,050.2
December 2008	4,492.5	9,804.0	-5,311.5
TOTAL	65,141.8	139,262.2	-74,120.4

*TOTAL may not add due to rounding.
*Table reflects only those months for which there was trade.
*CONTACT: Data Dissemination Branch, U.S. Census Bureau, 301-763-2311.
*SOURCE: U.S. Census Bureau, Foreign Trade Division, Data Dissemination Branch, Washington, DC 20233.

U.S.–Japan Trade

Japan, the world's second-largest economy, is the fourth-largest export market for the United States, after Canada, China, and Mexico. The country is the second-largest foreign investor in the U.S., behind only the U. K., with more than $200 billion invested.

The U.S.–Japan alliance is not only important in terms of two-way trade, but it also is the cornerstone of U.S. security interests in Asia and is fundamental to regional security and prosperity. In 2008, the U.S. exported $65 billion in goods and services, but imported nearly $140 billion from the island nation. The resulting U.S. trade deficit with Japan, totaling over $74 billion in 2008, was second only to China's $266 billion.[9] (See Table 3.8.)

Figure 3.8 The Ginza in Tokyo, Japan, is a famous shopping district by day and entertainment center by night. In addition to $10 cups of coffee, you can find almost every leading brand of global fashion and apparel.

....

Figure 3.9 Native Berliners and tourists alike flock to the world-famous Kurfürstendamm, known to many as "Ku'damm," Germany's most popular shopping street and promenade. Its department stores, elegant boutiques, and cafes offer shopping, entertainment, or just a meeting place.

. . . .

U.S.–Germany Trade

Germany, the largest economy in the European Union and the third-largest in the world, had a trade surplus with the United States of $42.8 billion in 2008. U.S. exports to Germany totaled $54.7 billion, while imports of German goods and services into the U.S. amounted to $97.5 billion. (See Table 3.9.)

According to the World Trade Organization (WTO), Germany is the world's top exporter, when measured as a percentage of Gross Domestic Product. Germany is also the world leader in mechanical engineering, holding about 20 percent of this global market. Core German exports include such engineering products as vehicles, machinery, chemical goods, electronics, ship building, and optics. The "land of ideas" is also among the world's largest and most technologically advanced producers of iron, steel, coal, cement, food and beverages, and textiles. In recent years, traditional German industries like steel-making and textiles have shrunk considerably.[10]

Germany remains the United States' most important trade partner within the EU and receives the largest amount of U.S. overseas investment that results in over 800,000 direct jobs. About 2,700 U.S. companies, including branches, have relocated in Germany, again the highest in a list of U.S. foreign investments.

TABLE 3.9 U.S. TRADE WITH GERMANY: 2008

NOTE: All figures are in millions of U.S. dollars, and not seasonally adjusted unless otherwise specified.

Month	Exports	Imports	Balance
January 2008	4,064.5	7,078.5	-3,014.1
February 2008	4,631.0	7,978.7	-3,347.7
March 2008	4,630.2	9,157.4	-4,527.2
April 2008	4,760.7	9,217.1	-4,456.4
May 2008	4,804.5	8,403.0	-3,598.5
June 2008	4,960.0	8,959.1	-3,999.1
July 2008	4,747.1	9,229.9	-4,482.9
August 2008	4,676.9	7,968.9	-3,292.0
September 2008	4,281.0	7,131.9	-2,850.9
October 2008	4,763.1	8,084.8	-3,321.8
November 2008	4,366.2	7,158.1	-2,791.9
December 2008	3,820.3	7,129.2	-3,308.9
TOTAL	54,505.3	97,496.6	-42,991.3

SOURCE: U.S. Census Bureau, Foreign Trade Division, Data Dissemination Branch, Washington, D.C. 20233.

U.S.–U.K. Trade

Two-way trade between the United States and the United Kingdom amounts to over $111 billion a year. More than 5,000 U.S. companies are based in the United Kingdom, with almost 10,000 across the whole of the EU. The United States is Britain's largest single export market, importing $58 billion of U.K. goods in 2007. The United Kingdom is the sixth biggest exporter to the United States, after Canada, Mexico, Japan, China, and Germany. The United States is also the leading overseas destination for British investment. U.S. exports to the United Kingdom totaled $53.7 billion in 2008.[11] (See Table 3.10.)

TABLE 3.10 U.S. TRADE WITH THE UNITED KINGDOM (GREAT BRITAIN) 2008

NOTE: All figures are in millions of U.S. dollars, and not seasonally adjusted unless otherwise specified.

Month	Exports	Imports	Balance
January 2008	4,708.1	4,581.4	-126.7
February 2008	4,765.9	4,838.4	-72.5
March 2008	4,642.9	4,664.0	-21.1
April 2008	4,959.6	5,102.4	-142.8
May 2008	4,822.9	5,588.7	-765.8
June 2008	5,101.3	5,271.5	-170.2
July 2008	4,803.3	5,650.1	-846.9
August 2008	4,447.5	5,016.7	-569.2
September 2008	3,887.4	4,696.8	-809.4
October 2008	4,330.8	5,154.6	-823.9
November 2008	3,546.1	4,105.0	-558.8
December 2008	3,583.4	3,917.8	-334.4
TOTAL	53,599.1	58,587.4	-4,988.3

TOTAL may not add due to rounding.
Table reflects only those months for which there was trade.
CONTACT: Data Dissemination Branch, U.S. Census Bureau, 301-763-2311.
SOURCE: U.S. Census Bureau, Foreign Trade Division, Data Dissemination Branch, Washington, DC 20233.

Figure 3.10 London's pedestrian-only Carnaby Street is famous for the shops and cafes that line its wide walkways.

. . . .

U.S.–EU Trade

Both Germany and the United Kingdom are part of the **European Union (EU)**, an organization of 27 countries across the European continent that goes far beyond its origins as a regional economic agreement among just neighboring European states, in 1951. The EU today has many of the attributes associated with independent nations: its own flag, anthem, founding date and currency, as well as a defined common foreign and security policies in dealing with other nations.[12]

TABLE 3.11 U.S. TRADE WITH EUROPEAN UNION: 2008

NOTE: All figures are in millions of U.S. dollars, and not seasonally adjusted unless otherwise specified.

Month	Exports	Imports	Balance
January 2008	21,151.4	27,757.8	-6.606.4
February 2008	23,431.0	30,473.0	-7,042.0
March 2008	23,594.6	31,692.1	-8,097.5
April 2008	23,664.4	32,752.3	-9,087.9
May 2008	23,797.3	32,658.1	-8,860.8
June 2008	24,834.1	33,387.5	-8,553.4
July 2008	23,664.2	34,822.8	-11,158.6
August 2008	23,597.6	29,706.6	-6,109.0
September 2008	20,826.3	29,150.3	-8,324.0
October 2008	22,861.5	32,068.2	-9,206.7
November 2008	20,658.9	26,550.0	-5,891.1
December 2008	19,728.8	26,598.8	-6,869.9
TOTAL	**271,810.1**	**367,617.4**	**-95,807.4**

SOURCE: U.S. Census Bureau, Foreign Trade Division, Data Dissemination Branch, Washington, D.C. 20233.

The European Union and the United States are the two largest economies in the world. Together they account for about half of the entire world economy. The EU and the United States also have the biggest bilateral trading and investment relationship. Transatlantic flows of trade and investment amount to around $1 billion a day, and, jointly, U.S.-EU global trade accounts for almost 40 percent of world trade. More than $642.4 billion in total two-way trade was recorded for 2008. The U.S. deficit with the EU stood at $93 billion at the end of 2008, as the U.S. exported to member countries $272 billion worth of American goods, but imported from them $367.6 billion in goods and services.[13] (See Table 3.11.)

The descriptions of U.S. trade relationships, cited above, illustrate the links between trade and economic prosperity. The contribution of U.S. exports and imports to an anticipated economic recovery can be explained in statistics that show U.S. goods and services exports totaled over 12 percent of its GDP in 2008.

U.S. PERSPECTIVES ON GLOBAL TRADE

The July 2008 failure of the Doha Round of WTO trade talks, originally aimed at break-ing down world trade barriers designed to help not only the developing nations, but also U.S. exporters, was notable as, "the first failure of a major international trade negotiation since the 1930s and the implications could be particularly serious for the United States," according to economist C. Fred Bergsten at the Economic Policy Institute (EPI), an in-dependent, non-profit, non-partisan research institute—or "think tank"—based in Wash-ington, D.C.[14] He blamed the collapse of trade talks, which had been under way for seven years, on both the United States and the European Union, because they offered too little too late. But Bergsten also pointed to India and China as the biggest villains, because they were unwilling to give up trade barriers that protect their agricultural products, services, and manufactured goods. These nations had demanded a safeguard clause that would al-low them to raise tariffs on key crops, such as cotton, sugar and rice, if there were a sud-den surge in imports.

A *Wall Street Journal* editorial titled, "The End of Free Trade?" stated that the demise of the Doha trade round was "another blow to the struggling world economy," and ques-tioned whether the setback is temporary or if it marks the end of the post-World War II free-trade era, "that has done so much to spread prosperity." The editorial continued, "Freer trade and more open markets have opened vast new opportunities for global busi-ness, spreading competition and innovation that have helped to raise living standards across the globe."[15]

While free trade proponents were extremely disappointed at the failure of the Doha talks, many critics of globalization and free trade were actually happy with the results. For example, the perspective of the Fair Trade Federation is that free trade is not neces-sarily "fair" trade. They are not necessarily protectionist, but rather favor a system of exchange that creates greater equity and partnership in international trade by:

> Creating Opportunities for Economically and Socially Marginalized Producers
> Developing Transparent and Accountable Relationships
> Building Capacity
> Promoting Fair Trade
> Paying Promptly and Fairly
> Supporting Safe and Empowering Working Conditions
> Ensuring the Rights of Children
> Cultivating Environmental Stewardship
> Respecting Cultural Identity[16]

By approaching development as a whole process, rather than just a fair price, fair trade organizations cultivate partnerships with their suppliers and contribute to the development of communities. Their concept of fair trade is not about charity; it uses a fairer system of exchange to empower producers and to create sustainable, positive change. The Fair Trade

Federation offers these guidelines, especially for students or those new to global trade[17]:

> Fair trade is about offering appropriate products to the public. Consumers can choose fairly-traded clothing, coffee, food, furniture, home décor, house wares, jewelry, tea, toys, personal accessories, and many other products.

> Fair trade is also about keeping prices affordable for consumers. This relationship can be made possible, because fair trade advocates typically work directly with artisans and farmers, assuming the function of the middle men who usually increase the price at each level of distribution. In theory, retail prices should be more competitive—and producers more fairly compensated—when compared to conventional wholesale distribution, but either the producer or the consumer must be willing to do more of the selling and buying functions.

> Finally, fair trade makes a tremendous impact on communities. Children's school fees are paid; nutritional needs met; health care costs are covered; the poor, especially women, are empowered; the environmental impact of production, sourcing, and transport is mitigated to the fullest extent possible. Such an impact is created, because fair trade approaches development as a complete process.[18]

In the wake of the failed talks, economists and politicians continue to debate the costs—or the benefits—of free trade. Robert E. Scott, an international economist at EPI, released a 2008 study stating that the U.S. workforce has lost 2.3 million jobs due to competition with China since that country joined the WTO in 2001. Many workers found new jobs—but at lower wages than they would have earned in their old jobs. Scott's report concludes that the growing U.S. trade deficit with China has displaced huge numbers of jobs in the United States and has been a prime contributor to the crisis in manufacturing employment over the past six years. Moreover, the United States is piling up foreign debt, losing export capacity, and facing a more fragile macroeconomic environment.[19]

Is America's loss China's gain? The EPI says no. China has become dependent on the U.S. consumer market for employment generation, has suppressed the purchasing power of its own middle class with a weak currency, and, most importantly, has held hundreds of billions of hard currency reserves in low-yielding, risky assets instead of investing them in public goods that could benefit Chinese households. Its vast purchases of foreign exchange reserves have stimulated the overheating of its domestic economy, and inflation in China has accelerated rapidly in the past year. In the opinion of the EPI, its repression of labor rights has suppressed wages, thereby artificially subsidizing exports.[20]

The Financial Services Forum, a financial and economic policy organization comprised of the chief executive officers of 20 of the largest and most diversified financial institutions doing business in the United States, in a June 2007 study, "Succeeding in the Global Economy: A Policy Agenda for the American Worker," claimed that only three percent of lost U.S. jobs are tied directly to competition with imports or outsourcing overseas, according to their research.[21]

The Forum study points to survey data from the U.S. Bureau of Labor Statistics that reveal: "in layoffs of 50 or more people between 1996 and 2004, less than 3 percent were attributable to import competition or overseas relocation." This study comes amid a growing backlash against global trade that has threatened to curtail U.S. trade agreements. The banking, investment and other CEOs who belong to the group have consistently cited protectionism as the leading threat to continued U.S. and global economic growth. The paper, written by a bipartisan group of economists, calls for providing additional help to more workers as a way to defuse tensions over trade. Its authors argue that current protectionist sentiment in the U.S. can be moderated only by providing more assistance to workers on the losing end of globalization.[22]

The biggest challenge, therefore, is to create a $22 billion [Trade] Adjustment Assistance Program that would provide health insurance, supplement unemployment benefits, and buttress income while displaced workers develop the skills they need to find new jobs. "From a public-policy standpoint, it's the labor market dislocations that are behind the waning support for open trade in the U.S.," said Matthew Slaughter, an economist at Dartmouth University and one of the authors of the Forum study. Better assistance to displaced workers would help alleviate concerns, he added.[23]

The current U.S. recession began in December 2007, according to the National Bureau of Economic Research (NBER). The recession has since affected other countries, and many forecasters predict that world output would contract during 2009. Even with determined steps to return the global financial sector to health and continued use of macroeconomic policy levers to stimulate consumer demand, economic activity is projected to contract by 1.3 percent in 2009. This represents the deepest post–World War II recession by far.

Global output per capita is projected to decline in countries representing three-quarters of the global economy. Growth is projected to reemerge in 2010, but at 2.5 percent it would be sluggish relative to past recoveries. These projections are based on an assessment that financial market stabilization will take longer than previously predicted, even with strong efforts by global policymakers. Thus, financial conditions in the mature markets are projected to improve only slowly, as insolvency concerns are diminished by greater clarity over losses on bad assets and injections of public capital, and risks and market volatility are reduced.[24]

According to the Federal Reserve Bank of St. Louis's May, 2009 report, "International Economic Trends," "the world's economies are tied together by global financial markets and international trade. Shocks that affect the U.S. economy—the world's largest—will surely affect the rest of the world. Many analysts blame the current recession on the financial crisis that resulted from large losses on securities backed by U.S. residential mortgage loans. Some analysts also attribute the economic slowdown to a spike in energy prices. If the current recession engulfs more countries and world GDP contracts in 2009 as predicted by the IMF, then this recession will prove to be the broadest, and certainly the deepest, of the past 40 years."[25]

TABLE 3.12 HARD TIMES

The IMF's March 2009 projections show a contraction in world growth this year, followed by a small recovery (percent change, unless otherwise noted)

| | 2008 | Proj. | |
		2009	2010
WORLD OUTPUT	3.2	-1.0 to -0.5	1.5 to 2.5
Advanced economies	0.8	-3.5 to -3.0	0.0 to 0.5
United States	1.1	-2.6	0.2
Euro area	0.9	-3.2	0.1
Japan	-0.7	-5.8	-0.2
Emerging and developing economies	6.1	1.5 to 2.5	3.5 to 4.5

Source: www.imf.org/external/pubs/ft/survey/so/2009.new031909a.htm. Retrieved on May 5, 2009.

In the United States, the contraction in economic activity in 2009, as shown in Table 3.12, is expected to push up the output gap to levels not seen since the early 1980s. Assuming that financial market conditions improve relatively rapidly in the second half of 2009, based on the implementation of a detailed and convincing plan for rehabilitating the financial sector, as well as continued policy support to bolster domestic demand, growth is expected to turn positive in the course of the third quarter of 2010.

International trade is still stimulating economic growth in the United States, in spite of its continuing trade balance deficit—the U.S. imports much more than the U.S. exports. The deficit is very high relative to the GDP—about five percent—which begs the question: How likely is it that this growth will persist?

Note that a country's GDP is the total market value of its outputs—goods and services—over a period of time, usually one year. GDP is the total of four main components:

> consumption expenditures,
> private business and residential investment,
> government consumption expenditures and investment, and net exports.

Forecasts of lower world GDP growth as a result of recent financial turmoil and U.S. dollar appreciation in 2009, will further curb U.S. net exports growth. Although large contributions of net exports to U.S. GDP are unusual, if the demand for U.S. goods and services from abroad weathers the current financial crisis, international trade, exports in particular, might be a catalyst to the nation's eventual economic recovery.

Figure 3.11 U.S. president Barack Obama and his wife, Michelle, meeting with British prime minister Gordon Brown and his wife, Sarah, during the G-20 meeting hosted by Great Britain, in London, April 1, 2009.

....

For goods and services producers engaged in global trade, it is increasingly difficult to obtain trade finance from foreign and U.S. banks, as continued bank failures made all banks suspect that international trade exchanges may also fail, if the issuing banks do not have sufficient funds to guarantee letter of credit payments. (See Chapter 10 for a complete explanation of letters of credit and other international trade finance methods.) In spite of this, most economists and government leaders insist that capitalism will survive.

Figure 3.12 The G7 began in 1975 as an informal forum of coordination among the key world industrialized countries (Canada, France, Germany, Italy, Japan, United Kingdom, and United States). Russia joined the G7 in 1998, so the organization is now known as the G8 and hosts Finance Ministers and Central Bank Governors to discuss economic and financial developments and policy priorities.

....

G20 SUMMITS—WASHINGTON, D. C. (NOVEMBER 2008) AND LONDON, ENGLAND (APRIL 2009)

Participants in the G20 Summits, held in Washington, D.C., in November 2008, and in London, in April 2009, represented a grouping of major industrialized and developing countries.[26a,26b] They pledged their cooperation to subject all financial markets, products and participants to strict future supervision, tougher accounting rules, a review of compensation practices and enhanced cooperation between national regulators. The London Summit called for quicker progress on the steps agreed to in Washington.

G20 members are drawn from all continents and represent two-thirds of global population and about 90 percent of world GNP. The G20's broad representation of countries at different stages of development gives its consensus outcomes greater impact than those of the original G7 and subsequent G8. One step in the right direction was a renewed commitment from the summits to reach an agreement in the stalled WTO Doha Round of world trade talks.

Members of the G20 Summits also have pledged to reject protectionism as a response to the financial crisis—a move reminiscent of the Smoot-Hawley Tariff Act of June 1930, that raised import tariffs by up to 50 percent on a wide range of goods from abroad and led to the globalization of the U.S. Great Depression, as foreign trade partners retaliated to protect their own markets. Recently, some government leaders and many world traders were concerned that President Obama has moved in a protectionist direction, as shown by his September 14, 2009 duties levied on imports of tires from China.

Figure 3.13 **Indian spinning mill.**

....

GROUP OF SEVEN MEETING—ROME

The **Group of Seven (G7)** finance ministers met in Rome in February 2009 to affirm their pledges to avoid resorting to protectionism as they try to stimulate their own economies in the face of the world's worst economic crisis since the depression era of the 1930s. The G7 will next meet in January 2010 in Italy.[27]

RECENT U.S. TRADE TRENDS

As the world's largest economy, the eyes of all trade partners are on the United States to lead the way out of the global economic crisis of 2008. Japan and Germany were especially concerned with moves toward global protectionism as they are both net exporters. Germany, with 40 percent of is output export-driven was one of the countries most affected by the worldwide recession. The United States and Europe are the focus of most of the headlines, but even the emerging markets have been hit hard, as they lack the resources to restore confidence in their financial systems. The weaker countries have little control over their exchange rates and need to issue debt in foreign currencies.

Even China and India, relatively insulated from free market supply and demand forces prior to 2008, have experienced manufacturing contraction and import credit problems with their foreign customers that were thought to be impossible in previous history. The withdrawal of credit after a boom can lead to deep recessions and major internal political and economic disruptions. After years of economic expansion and double digit growth rates, 2008 saw the shrinking of demand for China's exports, caused by the global recession, which led to a slowdown in China's economy.

Countries that became rich during the massive real estate and commodities expansion period of the 2001–2008, became very vulnerable when faced with the global recession of 2008. Reductions in foreign aid from the wealthy countries caused hardship among the extremely poor ones.

The global recession reduced the ability to trade, which limits one potential source of growth for nations or companies. The flight to quality drives up the value of the dollar, making it even harder for U.S. companies to export goods and services. Economic distress overseas creates political instability in important countries, such as Pakistan, that agreed, in 2008, to terms of an International Monetary Fund (IMF) bailout, but the international agency lacked the capacity to protect the global economy as a whole.

As a result, the global economic winds have been shifting. Countries most responsible for global growth over the latter half of the twentieth century—the U.S., Japan, and the EU—are no longer the key drivers. The developing countries, led by China, India, Brazil, and Russia, often referred to as the "BRIC" group of emerging markets, once observers from the sidelines, are assuming a greater role—and responsibility—for global economic growth and prosperity.

Trade is critical to America's economic recovery and return to prosperity—fueling economic growth, supporting good jobs at home, raising living standards and helping Americans provide for their families with affordable goods and services.

In just the last 15 years, freer trade has helped raise the Gross Domestic Product (GDP) by almost 50 percent. Over the same period the United States has added over 23 million jobs, according to the Office of the United States Trade Representative's (USTR) February, 2008 report.[28]

The United States is one of the most open economies in the world, and as a result is one of the strongest, most dynamic and competitive. Although the global economy has recently suffered its worst slowdown in modern history, the U.S. continues to make major contributions to global Gross National Product (GNP). In spite of recent declines, U.S. exports are still providing support for the economy in difficult times. American farmers, factory workers and entrepreneurs are among the most innovative in the world and know that when the economy is threatened, that's when their ability to deliver safe, quality products and services is needed most. Free trade provides a competitive edge around the world that is certain to speed up economic recovery for the U.S. and its trade partners and the world at large. Through the combined efforts of nations, it is hoped that good will ultimately come from this crisis and that the global financial system will make the necessary adjustments to insure growth and continued globalization.

Of course, there are many challenges ahead, along with a fear that markets abroad may become closed to U.S. goods, farm products, and services, if countries erect trade barriers as they are unable to deal with lost manufacturing jobs at home. Negotiators will continue efforts to reduce trade barriers so that farmers, ranchers, manufacturers and service providers gain better access to the 95 percent of the world's customers living elsewhere.

Every day American families benefit from globalization and unrestricted access to the world's markets, as trade delivers a greater choice of goods, and services—everything from food and furniture to cars and computers—at lower prices. The USTR report links U.S. economic growth with U.S. exports, noting these contributions:

> manufactured exports increased 128 percent in the last ten years and support more than one of every six manufacturing jobs, according to the U.S. Dept. of Commerce;

> one of every three acres of U.S. land is planted for exported goods and agriculture exports supports an estimated 806 thousand jobs, according to the U.S. Dept. of Agriculture;

> the U.S. had a record $104 billion surplus in the services trade in 2007 on exports totaling $473 billion and these exports have more than doubled—up 136 percent— since 1994 and account for 8 out of 10 jobs in the United States;

> jobs supported by goods exports pay an estimated 13–18 percent more than the U.S. national average.

> further reduction of trade barriers will stimulate more exports that will create more higher paying U.S. jobs.[29]

TABLE 3.13 U.S. FREE TRADE AGREEMENTS

The United States has free trade agreements with 17 countries. These are:

1. Australia	7. El Salvador	13. Morocco
2. Bahrain	8. Guatemala	14. Nicaragua
3. Canada	9. Honduras	15. Oman
4. Chile	10. Israel	16. Peru
5. Costa Rica	11. Jordan	17. Singapore
6. Dominican Republic	12. Mexico	

The United States has signed free trade agreements with Colombia, Korea, and Panama, but as of September 2009, Congress has not enacted legislation to approve and implement each individual agreement in order for them to go into effect.
Source: Office of the U.S. Trade Representative, retrieved September 18, 2009 from http://www.ustr.gov.

Figure 3.14
A Middle Eastern
shopping bazaar.

....

Prosperity Flows from Trade

American families benefit from trade and open markets every day. International trade liberalization, often through bilateral and international Free Trade Agreements, provide American consumers a greater choice of goods—everything from apparel to appliances, computers to cars—at lower prices:

> U.S. annual incomes are $1 trillion higher, or $9,000 per household, due to increased trade liberalization since 1945, according to the Institute for International Economics (IIE), a private, nonprofit, nonpartisan research institution devoted to the study of international economic policy.

> Two major trade agreements of the 1990s—the North American Free Trade Agreement and the Uruguay Round—have generated annual benefits of $1,300–$2,000 for the average American family of four.

> If remaining global trade barriers are eliminated, IIE estimates U.S. annual incomes could increase by an additional $500 billion, adding about $4,500 per household.[30]

Trade not only creates jobs in the United States and among its trade partners, it also builds international partnerships for security, when transparency counters corruption, strengthens the rule of law and encourages economic integration. Critics of U.S. Free Trade Agreements, however, suggest they are attempts at achieving substantial change—or legal grounds for it— in other countries' social and economic policies by setting U.S.-friendly standards for investor privileges, environmental protection, workers' rights, intellectual property, deregulation of service industries and privatization in general, wherever they are signed.[31]

Recent trade actions seen to offer evidence of more positive results of FTAs, as follows:

CAFTA-DR FTA

The **Central America-Dominican Republic Free Trade Agreement**, of August 2, 2005, supports freedom, democracy and economic reform in the western hemisphere. In the 1980s,

Figure 3.15 More than half of all U.S. apparel imports come from China.

....

Central America was characterized by civil war, chaos, dictators, and Communist insurgencies. Today, elected leaders in the region, through CAFTA-DR and other efforts, are embracing transparency and economic reform, fighting corruption, and strengthening the rule of law.

The CAFTA-DR Free Trade Agreement is in the best interest of United States commerce. The comprehensive agreement not only slashed tariffs, but also reduced barriers for services, provided for leading-edge protection and enforcement of intellectual property, kept pace with new technologies, ensured regulatory transparency, and required enforcement of domestic labor and environmental laws. With the agreement in place, doing business in Central America and the Dominican Republic has become easier, faster, and more transparent.[32]

The CAFTA-DR region is an important market for U.S. yarn and fabric manufacturers and therefore it is in the U.S. interest to do as much as possible to support the growth of Central American and Dominican Republic apparel manufacturers. In 2004, the United States sold $4.15 billion worth of yarns and fabrics to CAFTA-DR countries and 61 percent of apparel shipped from Central America and the Dominican Republic qualified under the **Caribbean Basin Trade Partnership Act (CBTPA)** provision requiring the use of U.S. yarns and fabrics. In contrast, Asian apparel producers use very little U.S. yarn or fabric. The CAFTA-DR will help retain and promote textiles trade with Central America and the Dominican Republic, a benefit to U.S. exporters.[33]

MEFTA Free Trade Area

To re-ignite economic growth and expand opportunity in the Middle East, the U.S. proposed, on May 9, 2003, the establishment of a **U.S.-Middle East Free Trade Area (MEFTA)** within a decade. According to the United Nations, the Middle East attracted just 0.7 percent of global foreign direct investment throughout the 1990s. Exports from the region—over 70 percent of which are accounted for by oil and oil-related products—grew at 1.5 percent per year over the same period, far below a global average growth rate of 6 percent. On a per capita basis, exports are significantly lower today than 20 years ago. The MEFTA was billed as part of a plan to fight terrorism—in this case, by supporting the growth of Middle East prosperity and democracy—through trade. Although the United States initially set the deadline for MEFTA at 2013, officials now refer to a target of 2014.

The countries targeted to join MEFTA are: Algeria, Bahrain, Egypt, Iran, Israel (and through Israel, the Palestinian Authority), Jordan, Kuwait, Lebanon, Libya, Morocco, Oman, Qatar, Saudi Arabia, Tunisia, and Yemen.[34]

According to the World Bank, about 25 percent of people in the region live on less than $2 per day. The UN reports that Arab countries have the world's lowest percentage of people who use the Internet or have access to a computer. The United States is committed to expanding trade in the region and providing economic hope for millions in the Middle East. The 9/11 Commission unanimously recommended that the United States expand trade with the Middle East as way to "encourage development, more open societies, and opportunities for people to improve the lives of their families."[35]

Non-ratified FTAs

Of concern to the U.S. international trade community is the failure, for over two years, of Congress to ratify key market-opening free trade agreements with Colombia, Panama and South Korea. All three have been approved by each country's negotiating team, but need U.S. congressional approval before they become law. The trade agreements will allow U.S. exports to these countries to be completed without expensive import taxes that act as disincentives to trade. Foreign access to U.S. markets not only benefits U.S. industry with more price-competitive imports, but also gives foreign countries the revenues that could be used to purchase more U.S. exports—a win-win situation.

Global economic balance had created a favorable opportunity for U.S. exports until the economic meltdown of 2008. Developing countries had been growing twice as fast as developed countries and accounted for about 50 percent of global domestic product and world trade. Events of 2008–2009 and beyond are expected to diminish the ability of developing countries to keep up with previous growth rates.[36]

For example, in the emerging markets, where growth rates have been the highest in the world for the past five years, inflation has been rising at a faster rate than in developed countries. In China, strong foreign demand for its consumer and industrial goods, as well as double-digit domestic growth, pushed prices up for energy, apparel, and food items. Prospects for inflation in 2009 and 2010 were not very encouraging at the time of this writing, as China has seen both a drop in demand for its exports; more protectionist sentiment on the part of its foreign customers, as it tries to keep jobs at home; and more inflationary pressures of the cost of raw materials and other goods it must import.

TABLE 3.14 LEADING TEXTILES AND APPAREL SHIPPERS TO THE UNITED STATES

Ranked by Value

2007	Year-to-date, November 2008
1. China	1. China
2. Mexico	2. Vietnam
3. India	3. India
4. Vietnam	4. Mexico
5. Indonesia	5. Indonesia
6. Bangladesh	6. Bangladesh
7. Pakistan	7. Pakistan
8. Honduras	8. Honduras
9. Cambodia	9. Cambodia
10. Italy	10. Italy

Source: Office of Textiles and Apparel, International Trade Administration, U.S. Department of Commerce.

[U.S. IMPORTS OF TEXTILES AND APPAREL]

$96.4 billion in imports of textiles and apparel to the U.S. in 2007;
$86.7 billion in January-November 2008

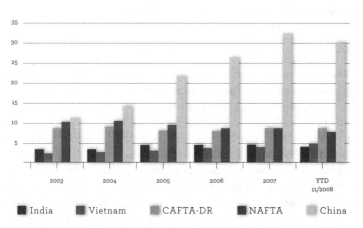

Figure 3.16 India, Vietnam, CAFTA-DR, NAFTA, and China together account for over 60 percent of U.S. imports of textiles and apparel.

Source: U.S. Department of Commerce, International Trade Administration.

From an international trade perspective, developing countries may be providing a new source of global demand for American exports—everything from agricultural commodities and raw materials to finished consumer goods and services. With the domestic economy in a recession, U.S.-based multinationals, including Coca-Cola, General Electric, Proctor & Gamble, as well as Levis and McDonald's among many others, are now focusing on satisfying consumer demand in developing countries.

U.S. industry continues to rank at the top of most measures of global competitiveness. The United States also remains the world's leading exporter of services, such as insurance, banking, legal, accounting and advertising/marketing industries.

THE END OF TEXTILE AND APPAREL QUOTAS

From 1974, until the end of the GATT Uruguay Round in 1994, apparel and textile trade was governed by the **Multifiber Arrangement (MFA)**, a general legal framework for determining the conditions under which textile and apparel trade could be controlled. Quotas, or limits on the volume or quantities of specific textiles or apparel items from a certain country, were designed to help those countries whose domestic industries were facing serious damage from rapidly increasing imports. However, the quotas conflicted with GATT's general preference for customs tariffs instead of restricting quantities. Quotas also were inconsistent with the GATT principle of treating all trading partners equally, because they specified how much the importing country was going to accept from individual exporting countries.[37]

In 1994, as a result of the Uruguay Round of negotiations, GATT was absorbed into the World Trade Organization (WTO). The WTO also absorbed the MFA, which was replaced by the **Agreement on Textiles and Clothing (ATC)**. The purpose of the ATC was to phase out the MFA and its quota system over ten years. The ATC and all quota restrictions terminated on January 1, 2005. The end of the ten-year transition period means that trade in textile and clothing products is no longer subject to quotas under a special program outside normal WTO/GATT rules but is now governed by the general rules and disciplines embodied in the multilateral trading system.[38]

Although the United States has entered into a number of Free Trade Agreements through the World Trade Organization, regional groups such as ASEAN, and with many individual countries in both hemispheres, complex **rules of origin**, the rules that determine the country of origin of an imported product, threaten to complicate international commerce and divert trade rather than creating it. However, except for negotiated exceptions, textile and apparel goods must be produced starting at the yarn stage in FTA countries in order to receive duty-free treatment. Legislation is pending to give producers more flexibility in sourcing inputs, which would make it easier for them to qualify for preferential tariff treatment.[39]

The growth of the U.S. trade deficit in textiles and apparel in 2007 and 2008 was attributed to an increase of imports from Asia, particularly China, which occurred when quotas on these goods were eliminated in 2005. Preliminary figures released by the U.S. Department of Commerce show that Chinese apparel for the first time accounted for more than 50 percent of U.S. imports in November, 2008.[40]

TABLE 3.15 TOP 10 MARKETS FOR U.S. TEXTILES AND APPAREL

Ranked by Value

2007	Year-to-date, November 2008
1. Canada	1. Canada
2. Mexico	2. Mexico
3. Honduras	3. Honduras
4. Dominican Republic	4. Dominican Republic
5. El Salvador	5. China
6. China	6. El Salvador
7. Japan	7. Japan
8. United Kingdom	8. United Kingdom
9. Germany	9. Germany
10. Belgium	10. Belgium

Source: Office of Textiles and Apparel, International Trade Administration, U.S. Department of Commerce.

Watching China and other sourcing countries is the U.S. Department of Commerce's **Office of Textiles and Apparel (OTEXA)**. The agency develops programs and strategies to improve the competitiveness of the U.S. textile, apparel, footwear, and travel goods industries. It is a resource for current trade data and industry news, as indicated by the following illustrations.[41]

Although it ushered in a new era for global trading in clothing and textiles, the impact of the ATC has been affected by three factors:

> First, the ATC was limited only to the removal of quotas; parties to the agreement could still impose import tariffs on clothing and textiles;
> Second, the impact of the ATC was lessened because it did not prevent countries from utilizing safeguard measures to block imports, such as anti-dumping duties, taxes on goods exported to a foreign country for a lower price than sold in the home country or for less than it cost to produce and countervailing duties–special taxes imposed on goods from countries that unfairly subsidize their exports in an effort to disrupt and eventually dominate foreign markets.
> Third, as part of its entry to the WTO in December, 2001, China agreed to special provisions that allowed other WTO members to use safeguard measures against their clothing and textile exports if the importing country believes that the imports are causing or threatening to cause domestic market disruption.[42]

In November 2005, the U.S. government, citing the WTO "safeguard" measures above, imposed quotas on 34 categories of textiles and apparel from China, including low-priced shirts and trousers, that became subject to 21 annual quota limits. The move was to control surging imports of clothes from Asia, following the end of the ATC. The U.S.–China "Bilateral Textile Agreement" was implemented on January 1, 2006, and expired on December 31, 2008. By order of the Committee for the Implementation of Textile Agreements, the Bureau of Customs and Border Protection no longer requires Electronic Visa Information System (ELVIS) filing for textiles and textile products produced or manufactured in the People's Republic of China and exported to the United States on or after January 1, 2009.[43]

Although it has been years since the ATC was implemented, there are differences in opinion on its overall impact. But most studies agree that one of the biggest beneficiaries is the People's Republic of China. That country's large labor pool of low-cost skilled workers and large industrial capacity gives it an opportunity to take advantage of the clothing and textile trade opportunities created by the removal of quotas. It is still unclear how the end of quotas has affected clothing and textile trade for other countries, including the United States, since the ability of China to expand its clothing and textile exports to this country has faced some constraints.

Future U.S. export and import trade policies regarding textiles and apparel will most likely impact the nation's overall international trade positions and administration—as they have in the past. In that sense, students and business professionals should monitor U.S. government agencies, such as the U. S Department of Commerce's Bureau of Industry and Security and Office of Textiles and Apparel, and Customs and Border Protection, as well as international media, for updates, trends and events including:

> The Vietnam import monitoring program for certain apparel products that ended on January 20, 2009.
> Continuing U.S. trade in textiles and apparel subject to normal WTO disciplines and U.S. trade remedy mechanisms.
> Activities of the U.S. International Trade Commission, which, at the request of Congress, is monitoring U.S. imports of textiles and apparel from China.
> Rulings by other U.S. government agencies, such as the Consumer Product Safety Commission, the Federal Trade Commission and the Food and Drug Administration that may impact future imports of consumer products.

Also recommended is the frequent monitoring of foreign press Web sites representing the major U.S. export-import trading partners—China, Japan, India, Mexico, Canada and the EU—for current trade issues and pending legislation that will have an effect on business with U.S. companies. Business and trade publications, such as *Women's Wear Daily*, which serving the fashion industry, are reliable information resources and also provide opportunities for novices to research an industry or specific company prior to applying for or accepting employment.

SUMMARY

For the past sixty years, the United States has been at the forefront in the effort to do away with trade barriers and encourage prosperity worldwide. A leader in global competitiveness, the U.S. has increased both exports and imports over the years, resulting in a growing overall trade deficit, especially in the textiles and apparel sectors.

Although large corporations are leaders in global exports and imports, small and medium-sized businesses (SMEs) have begun to enter global markets. Advances in electronic technologies, new sources of information, communications breakthrough speeding data transmissions, and supply-chain management improvements have aided small and large corporations in their global marketing efforts. Today, more than one-quarter of all U.S. exports are from SMEs.

The 2008 failure of the Doha Round of international trade negotiations has created a negative environment vis-à-vis trade agreements. Fair-trade advocates are actively promoting those principles, since they believe free trade is not focusing on human and environmental challenges created by globalization.

Competitive pressures have touched just about every industry, as consumer and industrial goods and services can now be purchased via the Internet (e.g., eBay, virtual shopping malls) from sources all over the globe. Whether it's Tide or a pair of pants produced in China or Bangladesh, globalization has made it possible for customers to get what they want, when they want it—the key to successful global distribution.

The stage is set, opportunities abound, but it's up to individual marketers, be they corporate managers or entrepreneurs, to capitalize on global export-import activities. Future U.S. export growth potential will depend on the extent to which Doha's failure will impact domestic businesses, particularly when small and medium-sized enterprises become aware of these trends and respond to them.

Another factor will be the continued recovery of the global economy in general and specifically export-import trade. This country's continued commitment to international trade organizations and bilateral or multilateral trade agreements and alliances will accelerate U. S. economic recovery and future prosperity. Students and business professionals should monitor both U. S. and foreign trade media and public press reports for shifts in trade policies and procedures.

Key Terms

- Agreement on Textiles and Clothing (ATC)
- Andean Countries
- Association of Southeast Asian Nations (ASEAN)
- Caribbean Basin Trade Partnership Act (CBTPA)
- Caribbean Basin countries
- Central America-Dominican Republic-Free Trade Agreement (CAFTA-DR)
- Doha Trade Talks
- Fair trade
- Free trade
- Free Trade Agreements (FTAs)
- Group of Seven (G7)
- Multifiber Arrangement (MFA)
- National Association of Securities Dealers Automated Quotations (NASDAQ)
- Non-tariff barriers to trade (NTBs)
- Office of Textiles and Apparel (OTEXA)
- Organization for Economic Cooperation and Development (OECD)
- Preferential trade agreements (PTAs)
- Private label
- Rules of origin
- Small and medium-sized businesses (SMEs)
- Supply-chain management
- Trade balance
- U.S. Bilateral Investment Treaty (BIT)
- U.S.-Middle East Free Trade Area (MEFTA)

Review Questions

1. Describe the status of the United States today in terms of exports, imports, and trade deficit. What is the relationship of the U.S. textile, apparel, and footwear industries to overall trade trends?

2. To what extent do U.S. small and medium-sized businesses participate in world trade?

3. In what ways can export and import businesses make use of the U.S. Department of Commerce's Office of Textiles and Apparel (OTEXA)?

4. State the purpose of free trade agreements (FTAs). Why is the United States interested in lowering trade barriers?

5. Explain the history and purpose of the Doha trade negotiations. How do you think their failure will impact trade liberalization for the foreseeable future?

Discussion Questions and Activities

1. Access Everything International at http://faculty.philau.edu/russowl/russow.html. Everything International provides links to a wide variety of international business, education, and research Internet sites. In the past ten years, over two million viewers have accessed this site. More than 200 libraries, colleges, universities, schools, businesses, and government agencies use Everything International as a resource and recommend it to their members and customers. Read the opening introduction to "Village of 1,000," then click on the title to access the site's "If the World Were a Village of 1,000 in the Year 2005." Discuss in class how life would be in the "Village." What lessons do think would apply to global business success or failures?

2. Go to the CIA's World Fact Book Web site at: www.cia.gov/library/publications/the-world-factbook/ and read the Guide to Country Profiles for an idea of what kind of country-specific information you can extract from this research resource. Then return to the main menu and click on History of The World Factbook for an excellent introduction to The Intelligence Cycle, the process by which information is acquired, converted into intelligence, and made available to policymakers. Read the Brief History of Basic Intelligence and The World Factbook for insight into why the U.S. has collected foreign intelligence since the days of George Washington and how that information may be used in conducting global trade activities.

3. Divide the class into two groups: one to debate the pros of "free trade," and the other to present the case for "fair trade." Research Web sites on Free Trade vs. Fair Trade to prepare for the debate.

References

1. "About Gap Inc." Retrieved on June 6, 2008, from www.Gapinc.com/public/About/about.shtml.

2. "World Economic Outlook Update," July 8, 2009, The International Monetary Fund. Retrieved on July 10, 2009, from http://www.imf.org/external/pubs/ft/weo/2009/update.htm.

3. U.S. Census Bureau, Foreign Trade Division, "U.S. 2008 Trade Highlights." Retrieved on May2, 2009, from http://www.census.gov/foreign-trade/www/press.html.

4. U. S. Census Bureau, Foreign Trade Division, "U. S. Trade in Goods and Services—Balance of Payments (BOP) Basis." Retrieved on May 3, 2009, from http://www.census.gov/foreign-trade/www/press.html.

5. Bureau of Economic Analysis, U.S. Department of Commerce, "U. S. Balance of Services Trade 2008." Retrieved on May 1, 2009 from http://www.bea.gov/newsreleases/international/trade/tradnewsrelease.htm.

6. "Trade with Canada," USTR NEWS, Office of the United States Trade Representative, April 27, 2009. Retrieved May 1, 2009, from http://www.ustr.gov/assets/document_library/press_releases2009/april/asset_upload_file624__1559.

7. "Trade with China," Export.gov, U.S. Government Export Portal. Retrieved on May 7, 2009 from http://www.export.gov/china/archivepress.asp.

8. "Trade with Mexico: 2008." Retrieved on May 7, 2009, from http://www.ustr.gov/assets/document_library/reports_publications/2008/2008_nte_reports.

9. "U.S. Census Bureau, Foreign Trade Division, FT-900 SUPPLEMENT February 2009, Exhibit 14: Exports, Imports, and Balance of Goods By Selected Countries and Areas—2009 (Trade With Japan: 2008)." Retrieved on May 7, 2009, from http://www.census.gov/foreign-trade/www/press.html.

10. "U.S. Census Bureau, Foreign Trade Division, FT-900 SUPPLEMENT February 2009, Exhibit 14: Exports, Imports, and Balance of Goods By Selected Countries and Areas—2009 (Trade With Germany: 2008)," http://www.census.gov/foreign-trade/www/press.html.

11. "U.S. Census Bureau, Foreign Trade Division, FT-900 SUPPLEMENT February 2009, Exhibit 14: Exports, Imports, and Balance of Goods by Selected Countries and Areas—2009 (Trade With the U.K.: 2008)." http://www.census.gov/foreign-trade/www/press.html.

12. Ibid. "U.S. Census Bureau, Foreign Trade Division, FT-900 Supplement February 2009, Exhibit 14: Exports, Imports, and Balance of Goods By Selected Countries and Areas—2009 (Trade With the EU: 2008)." Retrieved on May 7, 2009 from http://www.census.gov/foreign-trade/www/press.html.

13. "Trade with the European Union." Retrieved on May 7, 2008, from http://www.census.gov/foreign-trade/balance/c0003.html.#2008.

14. C. Fred Bergsten, "Rescuing the Doha Round," Foreign Affairs, May/June 2009, Vol. 3, No 88. Retrieved on May 8, 2009,

from www.foreignaffairs.com/articles/61212/c-fred-bergsten/rescuing-the-doha-round.

15. "The End of Free Trade?" The Wall Street Journal, Editorial Section, July 31, 2008, sec. A, p. 14.

16. "Welcome to the Fair Trade Federation," the Fair Trade Federation, p.4. Retrieved on August 26, 2008, from http://www.fairtradefederation.org/ht/display/Faqs/faqcat_id/1737.

17. Ibid.

18. Ibid.

19. Robert Scott, "The China Toll: Widespread Wage Suppression, 2 Million Jobs Lost in the U. S.," EPI Briefing Paper #219; News From EPI, July 30, 2008. Retrieved on August 15, 2008, Economic Policy Institute, from http://www.epi.org/content.cfm/bp219.

20. Ibid.

21. Grant D. Aldonas, Robert Z. Lawrence, and Matthew J. Slaughter, "Succeeding in the Global Economy: A New Policy Agenda for the American Worker," The Financial Services Forum, June 26, 2007. Retrieved on May 2, 2009, from http://www.financialservicesforum.org/site/apps/nlnet/content2.

22. Ibid.

23. Ibid., Slaughter.

24. Alan J. Auerbach, "Implementing the New Fiscal Policy Activism," National Bureau of Economic Research, working paper No. 14725, February, 2009. Retrieved on May 8, 2009, from http://www.nber,irg/papers/w14725.

25. Craig P. Aubuchon and David C. Wheelock, "International Economic Trends," *Federal Reserve Bank of St. Louis*, May, 2009. Retrieved on May 8, 2009, http://www.imf.org/external/pubs/ft/weo/2009/01/index.htm.

26-a. G20 Summit-Washington, D. C. (November, 2008), www.g20.org/about_faq.aspx.

26-b.G-20 Summit-London, England (April, 2009), www.g20.org/Documents/final-communique.pdf.

27. February, 2009, G-7 Summit of Rome, www.economywatch.com/international-organizations/g7-group-of-seven.html.

28. Office of the United States Trade Representative's (USTR) February, 2008 report. Retrieved on May 4, 2009, from (http://www.ustr.gov/assets/document_library/fact_sheets/2008/ass).

29. Ibid.

30. The Institute for International Economics, report retrieved on March 2, 2009, from http://www.iee.com/publications/papers/print.cfm?doc=pub&ResearchID=1056.

31. "US FTAs," *bilaterals.org*. Retrieved on May 7, 2009, from http://www.bilaterals.org/rubrique-print.php3?id_rubrique=55.

32. "Free Trade with Central America and the Dominican Republic," 2007 CAFTA-DR Fact Sheets, Office of the United States Trade Representative. Retrieved on May 2, 2009, from www.export.gov/fta/cafta/index.asp.

33. "Caribbean Basin Trade Partnership Act (CBTPA) to be Extended," *Trade Watch*, February, 2008, The Official E-letter of the Caribbean Export Development Agency. Retrieved on May 4, 2009, from http://tradewatch.carib-export.com/News/TRADEPOLICYDEVELOPMENTS/Stories/.

34. "The U. S. Middle East Initiative." Retrieved on May 6, 2009, from www.calchamber.com/BusinessResources/InternationalResources/TradeIssues/Pages/USMiddleEastFreeTradeInitiative.

35. "MEFTA," *bilaterals.org, April, 2009*. Retrieved on May 8, 2009, from http://www.bilaterals.org/rubrique.php3?id_rubrique=174.

36. Op. cit. "The World Economic Outlook: Crisis and Recovery," April 2009 Edition.

37. Multifibre Arrangement (MFA) 1974–1994, *WTO Trade Topics–Textiles Monitoring Body (TMB)*, p.1. Retrieved on May 5, 2008, from http://www.wto.org/english/tratop_e/texintro_e.htm.

38. The Agreement on Textiles and Clothing (ATC). Retrieved on May 7, 2009, from www.wto.org/english/docs_e/legal_e/16-tex_e.htm

39. "Rules of Origin," retrieved on May 7, 2009, from http://www.wto.org/english/tratop_e/roi_htm.

40. "U. S.: More than half of apparel imports now come from China," *Just-style*, December 15, 2008. Retrieved on May 8, 2009, from http://www.just-style.com/articleprint.aspx?ud=102846.

41. OTEXA, retrieved on May 7, 2009, from http://otexa.ita.doc.gov/.

42. Op. cit., ATC

43. OTEXA, Committee for the Implementation of Textile Agreements, Dec. 5, 2008. Retrieved on May 8, 2009, from http://otexa.ita.doc.gov/fr2006/china2elv(11-08).htm.

U.S. Exporting Policies and Procedures

Part II

Figure 4.1 An interest among Chinese consumers of sportswear and recreational gear led L.L. Bean to open its first store in China.

4

BASICS OF EXPORTING

What do people in the country of China and the state of Maine have in common? For one thing, it seems that consumers in both places have similar tastes in sportswear and sporting goods. These like interests are leading Freeport, Maine's L.L. Bean to open five stores in China, starting in the city of Beijing, the first venture for L.L. Bean in that country.

"Throughout China there is a growing interest in participating in outdoor and recreational activities," noted Chris McCormick, President and CEO of the Maine retailer. "L.L. Bean is a natural fit within this market. This is an area we have been studying for some time as we've considered ways to expand our international presence and diversify our business. China provides many opportunities with its growing marketplace."

L ocated in an open air mall, the 3,000-square-foot store's layout resembles that of the flagship, headquartered in Freeport, Maine. The interior offers a weathered woodsy New England atmosphere, with company photos and displays illustrating outdoor recreation activities. Product lines include outerwear and sportswear for men, women, and children, footwear, luggage, and hiking and camping equipment.

L.L. Bean stores in China are facilitated through a partnership with Youngone Corporation of Korea.[1] The company's own research findings plus the partnering agreement help pave the way to expanding its customer base, increasing sales, and gaining profits in Asia.

WHAT IS EXPORTING?

Exporting is distributing a product, service, technology, or idea, which originates in one country and is sent beyond its borders to distributors or end-users in another country. Every day people and businesses around the globe use **products**, or *goods and services*, that were produced in the United States and exported to their country. American-made goods can be found in Japanese kitchens (Kellogg's Corn Flakes), French offices (Parker Pens), and Mexican construction projects (U.S-made steel and cement components), or camping gear in China (L.L. Bean). Harley-Davidson motorcycles, Hanes hosiery and underwear, Holiday Inns, and McDonald's and Kentucky Fried Chicken franchises are influencing lifestyles in nations worldwide.

Why have these and many other U.S. firms ventured into foreign markets when they may still have untapped opportunities in the United States? With 95 percent of the world's population living outside the United States, even small-to-medium-sized firms now acknowledge that exporting must be an important consideration when planning their future business strategies. With domestic competition intense and foreign imports growing rapidly in most industry sectors, a global marketing strategy may be necessary not only for increased sales and profits but also for business survival.

REASONS FOR EXPORTING

Exporting is beneficial to the country as well as to the company. Creating more jobs, stimulating economic growth from higher employment, and adding tax revenues are some of the reasons U.S. federal and state governments vigorously promote exporting. Exports also help reduce the U.S. deficit in the International Trade Account (the difference between a nation's exports and imports). Record annual U.S. trade deficits in excess of $600 billion were recorded in 2007 and 2008, as imports continued to grow much faster than exports.

Successful exporters wonder why only about 65,000 firms—10 percent of all businesses—are active in foreign trade, according to the U.S. Department of Commerce estimates. Success stories emphasize that increased sales and expanded profits can result from exporting, but many corporate managers still regard international marketing as mysterious, time consuming and too expensive for them. Global trade consultants believe that fear of the un-known and ignorance of export policies and procedures are the real reasons keeping firms from trying to export.

On the other hand, successful participants in exporting extol its benefits, as follows:

> Increased Revenues and Profits: Expanded markets can lead to more sales and profits—usually over a reasonable period of time. Foreign accounts may take more time and money to sign up, but they usually are more reliable and loyal for the long-term. For example, U.S. specialty department stores today such as Lord & Taylor, realizing they are operating domestically in mature markets, look increasingly to overseas expansion for this very reason (see Chapter 9).

> Counter-cyclical Marketing: Combating external market influences such as the economy and weather. The various phases of the business cycle (stability, growth, decline, and recovery) describe the state of the economy at a given time. Should the economy in the United States see a downturn, some of the other world markets may lag behind for several months to a year. Putting more emphasis on exports could level out the peaks and valleys of the nation's economic health. In the case of the changing seasons and the effect of weather, companies producing seasonal products (bathing suits, skis, and boats) look south of the Equator for markets during the U.S. winter months.

> Extended product life cycles: If domestically-marketed products become technologically obsolete, or fall out of fashion with their target market, chances are good that a developing market (over half of the world's economies) would welcome imports of less expensive, older models of electronics such as cell phones and computers.

> Diversification: Even though the United States is the world's largest market, **consumer demand**, the amount consumers are willing to buy, still fluctuates according to the economic climate. Selling to foreign markets enables firms to balance market changes. This applies for product diversification as well. For example, the Juicy Couture (division of Liz Claiborne) contemporary apparel marketing organization, has opened 50 stores in Asia, along with its partner there, in addition to maintaining some 60 stores stateside.[2]

> Enhanced company image: Export marketing tells customers that a company understands how important it is to be truly global in today's competitive climate. This creates a new perception for a company. It also provides the appearance of a well-established firm with 21st century management. The Judith Ripka fine jewelry company is one example of an organization whose owners count on international distribution to enhance its image in the global luxury goods market. As Ripka's president Charles Jayson puts it, "In terms of global expansion, there's a global shift taking place and we have to follow the money."[3]

> Reduced Unit Costs: New exporters often find foreign-based orders will lower cost-per-unit for their entire output. By utilizing excess manufacturing capacity or reducing existing inventories, exporters can take advantage of these economies-of-scale.

SPOTLIGHT ON GLOBAL TRADE 4.1:
Exploding Exporting Myths

In order to take the mystery and confusion out of global marketing, some of the many myths surrounding exporting need to be exposed. Before you begin, please know that each one is false.

> **Myth #1:** Exporting is only for large-staffed, well-known and well-financed companies that can hire experienced staffs, conduct marketing research, modify products, and increase production to satisfy demand.
> **Myth #2:** Export success depends on a large export department.
> **Myth #3:** Exporting is too risky, especially for smaller or medium-sized companies unable to absorb losses from non-payment.
> **Myth #4:** Exporting regulations are too complex, with punishments for violations too common and severe.
> **Myth #5:** Violations of patents, copyrights, and trademarks are so common that new exporters risk losing their property rights.
> **Myth #6:** Only experts know how to navigate today's myriad of international trade laws, policies, and procedures. How-to-export tutorials and procedural guides are not readily available.

Taken as a group, the above myths, if true, would be strong disincentives for entering the export business. To repeat, however: *all of the myths cited are false.* According to U.S. Department of Commerce studies, companies of all sizes are engaging in export; in fact 60 percent of all successful exporting companies have 100 or fewer employees. What matters is the effective planning, research, pricing, and delivery of a product wherever the demand may be profitably served.

Source: Harvey R. Shoemack, *Introduction to the Export-Import Business*, (Northbrook, Illinois); The International Marketing Center Ltd., Unpublished text, n/d, pp. 2–10, 2008.

Figure 4.2 The Milan store is the first one in Europe for Juicy Couture.
. . . .

In spite of these significant advantages to exporting, many U.S. firms still do not export, for the following reasons:

> no need; the U.S. market is still large enough for anticipated growth;
> perception that the mysteries of foreign marketing—different language, etiquette, new business customs—are too difficult or time-consuming to deal with;
> requires a greater use of resources (people, money, and time) than does domestic marketing, and
> more complex, sometimes more costly, particularly in coping with payment and financing procedures.[4]

Figure 4.3 Fine jewelry is popular all over the world. Gold bracelets and similar jewelry by Judith Ripka are found in the company's stores and boutiques in the United States, Canada, the Caribbean, and Russia, among other locations.
....

CHALLENGES TO EXPORTING

Of course, challenges do accompany the benefits of exporting but, with careful planning and preparation, they are often surmountable. Some of these challenges include the fact that exporting frequently requires a substantial investment in travel and research, possibly hiring new staff, and perhaps modifying product or packaging. Moreover, the commitment of top management is crucial, not just early on, but for the long haul. It takes not willingness alone, but sustained effort, resources, and time to establish and maintain relationships in foreign markets. This means learning cultural differences, as an automobile manufacturer failed to do when, deciding to market its small automobile in Spanish-speaking countries, named the car Nova—easily translated into "doesn't go." In addition to knowing the language, learning cultural differences also means being available to overseas customers, dealing with extensive paper work, and being aware of and alert to local existing and potential competition.

DECIDING TO EXPORT

The decision to export should be based on practical reasons, supported by current and accurate statistical market research. Emotional rationalizations—such as the company owner, or CEO, suggesting exporting as a means for traveling the world with a business write-off—are usually poorly planned and unrealistically funded, thus quite often destined to fail. Such actions may actually discourage firms from continuing efforts to sell in foreign markets, when good planning and research could have built a substantial profit center for the company.

Is Our Product Exportable?

The company's key question—do we have an exportable product?—is followed swiftly by others, such as do we have adequate resources of personnel, time, and money, and are we backed by management's long-term commitment to succeed in international marketing? In attempting to export T-shirts to China, the sportswear company American Apparel knew that although its product is exportable, the company could not register the name "American Apparel" there because Chinese copyright laws forbid including the name of a country in a brand name.[5]

To be exportable, a product must meet the following criteria:
> legally exportable from the United States, according to the **Export Administration Regulations (EARs)**, rules of the U.S. Department of Commerce, for specific product and country classifications (see Chapter 5 for export controls and procedures);
> easily imported into the targeted foreign market country, without unreasonable taxes (duties) or administrative expense;
> exempted from any market-related restrictions, such as size of unit, nature of the product (ice cream melts if not kept frozen), or modification costs;
> possesses unique qualities that provide a competitive edge over foreign or international products (design, quality, or technology, since a low price is no longer a guarantee of success in international business);

> satisfies an existing and growing demand for the product's category and specific characteristics, and
> enjoys no existing prejudice against imports from the United States.[6]

Exporting Goods versus Exporting Services

Exporting goods (such as Michael Kors apparel) differs from exporting services (management

---

SPOTLIGHT ON GLOBAL TRADE 4.2:
Making the Export Decision

The product a company intends to export must meet certain marketability requirements. Answers to the questions below call for research of current data concerning each potential market. Assessing a product's export potential should yield useful answers.

1. What need does the product fulfill?
2. Does the need exist abroad?
3. Is a profitable market share attainable, or is the need already being met?
4. Is the proposed export competitive in features, benefits, and pricing?
5. Can the product stand alone or does it require basic or supplemental products to operate? (Example: what use are computers without software to run them?)
6. Does the product require modifications? (Example: Since the Japanese drive on the left side of the street, their factories mount the steering wheel on the right; to market their automobiles in the U.S., the steering wheel needed to be mounted on the left.)
7. If so, will the cost of modification make the product too expensive for the targeted export market?
8. Is the product easily packaged and shipped?
9. Are there legal/governmental export restrictions or non-tariff barriers to trade and/or investment?
10. Are there industry-specific controversies that might create barriers for export? (Example: Could certain chemicals be converted for use as chemical or biological weapons?)

What matters is the effective planning, research, pricing, and delivery of a product wherever the demand may be profitably served.

Source: Harvey R. Shoemack, *Introduction to the Export-Import Business*, (Northbrook, Illinois); The International Marketing Center Ltd., Unpublished text, n/d, pp. 2–10, 2008.

---

consulting on textile technologies) because each operates in a unique environment. Marketing tangible goods requires packaging, customs, and physical delivery. Exporting services requires empowering staff, that is, enabling export project managers to create marketing plans, travel between headquarters and overseas assignments, obtain work permits, and maintain cross-cultural communications in the language of the designated market.

Do We Have Sufficient Resources?

After a company determines that its products or services are exportable, it must ask if the export activity is compatible with corporate objectives and operations management. Management needs to address the following questions:

> What are our firm's export marketing goals? Are they realistic?
> Are the exporting goals consistent with overall corporate strategic planning?
> Can current company resources of personnel, production capacity, and finances support increased demands?
> Does the corporate Business Plan include an Export Marketing Strategy that also provides a road-map to foreign marketing success?
> Adequate personnel resources are essential for successful exporting. Since market development involves frequent and lengthy foreign travel on the part of key marketing or sales executives, can these managers be spared without compromising domestic productivity?
> Will top managers be able to spend the time necessary for domestic meetings to plan export marketing strategies, as well as travel overseas to meet with prospective distributors, agents or joint venture partners? Many foreign company executives will judge a company's level of commitment by the caliber and experience of managers sent to their country.
> The bottom line is always about money. Overseas travel, meals, and lodging are usually much more expensive (and more so with a weak dollar), as is participation at foreign trade shows (highly recommended—but go as a visitor first, then possibly become an exhibitor.) If top management is not fully committed, and proper funding not allocated, chances for success are diminished.

ARE WE PREPARED TO EXPORT?

What makes a business export-ready? Simply put, the business has an exportable product (from a legal and marketing point of view), as well as the capacity, resources, and management commitment to compete on an international scale. The trick is to figure out whether or not this is true of your company—and if it isn't yet, how to make it happen.

The first step is to think about the knowledge and resources your business already has. To begin, consider:

Your expectations—do you have:

> clear and achievable export objectives;
> a realistic idea of what exporting entails;

> an openness to new ways of doing business, and
> an understanding of what is required to succeed in the international marketplace?

Human resources—do you have:
> the capacity to handle the extra demand associated with exporting;
> top management committed to exporting;
> efficient ways of responding quickly to customer inquiries;
> personnel with culturally-sensitive marketing skills, and
> ways of dealing with language barriers?

Financial and legal resources—can you:
> obtain enough capital or lines of credit to produce the product or service;
> find ways to reduce the financial risks of international trade;
> find people to advise you on the legal and tax implications of exporting;
> deal effectively with different monetary systems, and
> ensure protection of your intellectual property?

Competitiveness—do you have:
> the resources to do market research on the exportability of your product or service;
> proven, sophisticated market-entry methods, and
> a product or service that is potentially viable in your target market?

GETTING STARTED IN EXPORTING

Although many government agencies have questionnaires to help determine export-readiness status, there is no clear-cut definition of being export ready. However, export service providers have determined some aspects that firms need to be aware of when becoming export ready; such guidelines help prepare for global market entry. In most cases, they are extensions and adaptations of existing marketing-related programs companies are already implementing to serve their domestic markets.

Key factors to consider for becoming export-ready include:

Export-Readiness Evaluation

To check for export readiness, start with a company SWOT assessment (strengths, weaknesses, opportunities, threats (see Chapter 6). Add the company's level of management commitment. If sufficient commitment is not present, don't go any further. Most firms can experience some success in establishing international sales and distribution during the first year, but becoming established often can be a much longer process, requiring more dedication and perseverance than that needed to market domestically.

TABLE 4.1 COMPARISON OF FOREIGN MARKET ENTRY MODES

Mode	Conditions Favoring This Mode	Advantages	Disadvantages
Exporting	• Limited sales potential in target country; little product adaptation required • Distribution channels close to plants • High target country production costs • Liberal import policies • High political risk	• Minimizes risk and investment • Speed of entry • Maximizes scale; uses existing facilities	• Trade barriers and tariffs add to costs • Transport costs • Limits access to local information • Company viewed as an outsider
Licensing	• Import and investment barriers • Legal protection possible in target environment • Low sales potential in target country • Large cultural distance • Licensee lacks ability to become a competitor	• Minimizes risk and investment • Speed of entry • Able to circumvent trade barriers • High ROI	• Lack of control over use of assets • Licensee may become competitor • Knowledge spillovers • License period is limited
Joint Ventures	• Import barriers • Large cultural distance • Assets cannot be fairly priced • High sales potential • Some political risk • Government restrictions on foreign ownership • Local company can provide skills, resources, distribution network, brand name, etc.	• Overcomes ownership restrictions and cultural distance • Combines resources of two companies • Potential for learning • Viewed as insider • Less investment required	• Difficult to manage • Dilution of control • Greater risk than exporting and licensing • Knowledge spillovers • Partner may become a competitor
Direct Investment	• Import barriers • Small cultural distance • Assets cannot be fairly priced • High sales potential • Low political risk	• Greater knowledge of local market • Can better apply specialized skills • Minimizes knowledge • Spillover • Can be viewed as an insider	• Higher risk than other modes • Requires more resources and commitment • May be difficult to manage the local resources

Source: "A Comparison of Market Entry Strategies," reprinted with permission from *The Global Entrepreneur*, by James Foley, Dearborn Financial Publishing Inc., 1999.

Market Entry Options

Investigate the characteristics and size of the markets you are thinking of entering. Methods and approaches to market research are covered later in this chapter. Initially, exporters may be able to serve up to a dozen foreign markets with existing sales and marketing staff. Many firms considered to be successful exporters serve fewer than 30 overseas markets. Europe, the Pacific Rim countries, Latin America, and a few other select countries easily represent more than 30 potential markets for most products.

Market Entry Strategies

There are numerous entry strategies available to consider, but three are basic to most successful exporting companies:

Stocking Distributors

The majority of export sales are done through distributors. They are generally responsible for all aspects of marketing and distribution of imported product in their country. **Stocking distributors** purchase products in stocking quantities, have a sales and support staff similar to the U.S. operation, and warehouse and ship products to customers.

Piggybacking

For new-to-export companies, successful international marketing may come through **piggybacking**, in this instance meaning seeking out and tying in with other non-competitive, complimentary product line exporters in their industry. Thus, through practice, the new exporter can learn the industry specifics of overseas distribution. Start by introducing the proposed export idea to your existing distributors. They may be interested in helping you establish relationships with their own distributors, so they become a stronger factor in their own markets.

Export Management Companies

Private firms can serve as the export department for several producers of goods or services, either by taking title or by soliciting and transacting export business on behalf of its clients in return for a commission. **Export management companies (EMCs)** work on a salary or retainer plus commission basis. Others, known as *export trading companies (ETC)*, can be very helpful to the firm that either doesn't want to do the actual exporting itself, or wants to serve countries not considered to be primary markets. ETCs usually take title to the goods they export.

INTERNATIONAL FASHION FOCUS 4.1:
Global Shopping Preferences

How do people prefer to shop in various parts of the world? According to Cotton Incorporated's *Lifestyle Monitor*, Europeans shop most frequently while window displays attract the attention of Japanese shoppers, and Germans are drawn to clothes made of denim. And obviously, young people everywhere are the most dedicated shoppers. Also, today's consumers are seeking out quality when buying fashion goods.

A recent lifestyle survey, part of a series sponsored by the Cotton Trade Association, studied trends and fashion consumers' shopping habits in ten South American, European, and Asian countries. Through face-to-face and telephone interviews, the survey obtained the following facts:

More than half of the Europeans surveyed shopped for apparel once a month or more. They also spent the most in terms of the U.S. dollar, up to $440, while Americans spent $220 in the study's three-month time period.

The findings also pointed out that consumers are able to feed their desire for new looks in fashion by thinking globally and acting locally. If fashion goods are being produced in a given country, they naturally get to the stores faster than imports. This may be one of the reasons Asian customers—living where much fashion merchandise is manufactured—are influenced by television and fashion-forward store displays; they can see the latest fashions and know these are the newest looks.

Another finding the study reinforced is the worldwide popularity of denim. Demanded by young consumers everywhere, denim appears to be growing in versatility as it is combined into stretch fabrics for sportswear, T-shirts, and (of course) jeans.

Source: "On the World Stage," Lifestyle Monitor, Cotton Incorporated, *Women's Wear Daily*, September 18, 2008. p. 2.

There is no single, correct way for a firm to market internationally. A combination of the above, plus a company's unique strategies, can lead to a successful formula for most firms. In many instances, teaming up with another organization, in particular one possessing local market knowledge and resources, can ease entry into a foreign market. As the chapter's opening vignette shows, partnering with a Korean company proved useful to L. L. Bean in its first venture into China.

DETERMINING YOUR EXPORT POTENTIAL

Is your company too small to export? Probably not, particularly if you have a Web site which may bring in customers from other countries without additional promotion on your part. To succeed in international markets, you don't have to be a big-name firm with lavish resources and an entire department devoted to exporting. In the United States alone, more than 60,000 small and medium-sized companies are currently engaged in exporting. Each of these accounts for anywhere from occasional sales to $5 million in exported goods and services each year.

Can your product find a worthwhile market outside of the United States? Getting this right is crucial—if there's no demand for what you are offering, obviously you'd be unwise to proceed. But how do you come up with the answer that best suits your situation? Here are some factors to consider:

Customer Profile
> Who already uses your product or service?
> Is your product in broad general use or limited to a particular group?
> Are there other significant demographic patterns to its use?
> Will climactic or geographic factors affect the use of your product?

Product Modification
> To make your product appeal to customers, are modifications required?
> What is its shelf life? Will this be reduced by time in transit?
> Is the packaging costly? Can it be modified easily to satisfy the demands of foreign customers?
> Is special documentation required? Does it need to meet any technical or regulatory requirements?

Transportation
> How easily can it be shipped?
> Would transportation and shipping costs make competitive pricing a problem?

Local Representation
> Does the product require professional assembly or other technical skills?
> Is after-sales service needed? If so, is it available locally or do you have to provide it? Do you have the resources to do this?

Exporting Services

> If you're exporting services, what is unique or special about them?
> Are your services considered to be world-class?
> Do you need to modify your services to allow for differences in language, culture, and business environment?
> How do you plan to deliver your services: in person, with a local partner, or electronically?

Capacity

> Will you be able to serve both your existing domestic customers and your new foreign clients?
> If your domestic demand increases, will you still be able to look after your export customers or vice versa?[7]

DEVELOPING AN EXPORT MARKETING PLAN

Before deciding to allocate personnel and resources to exporting, invest your energies in preparing an Export Marketing Plan. Think of the plan not only as a roadmap to profits, but also as a test for deciding whether or not you should venture into international trade. Many individual entrepreneurs and businesses have discovered reasons (competitive, financial, or marketing) for postponing or canceling a proposed expansion into global marketing. After analyzing the firm's export potential, they are unable to justify the action.

As you will discover, foreign markets can differ greatly from those at home. Some of these differences include: climate and other environmental factors such as local infrastructure (transportation, highways, and bridges; communications); social and cultural traditions and practices; local availability of raw materials or product alternatives; lower wage costs; varying amounts of purchasing power; the availability of foreign exchange, and government import controls.

Once you have decided that your company is able to overcome those potential barriers and is committed to exporting, the next step is to develop a marketing plan. A clearly written marketing strategy offers six immediate benefits:

> Written plans display strengths and weaknesses more readily, they are a great help in formulating and polishing an export strategy.
> Written plans are not easily forgotten, overlooked, or ignored by those charged with executing them. If deviation from the original plan occurs, it is likely due to a deliberate choice.
> Written plans are easier to communicate to others and are less likely to be ignored by those charged with executing them.
> Written plans allocate responsibilities and provide for an evaluation of results.

> Written plans are essential when seeking financial assistance. They indicate to potential lenders that you are serious about your export venture.
> Written plans give management a clear understanding of what will be required and thus help ensure the commitment to exporting. Actually, a written plan signals that the decision to export has already been made.

This last advantage is particularly important. Building an international business takes time—months, if not years, before an exporter begins to see a return on its investment of time and money. Budgeting for these commitments is an essential element of export marketing planning. By committing to the specifics of a written plan, top management can make sure that the firm sets out to finish what it begins, and that the hopes that prompted its export efforts will be realized.

As you can tell from Table 4.2, in developing a Business Plan the first step is to create a company profile, a description of the company and its products, plus its mission and goals. This type of plan serves to guide any marketing business, domestic or global. In planning to enter international trade, the next step is to create an Export Marketing Plan, indicating export commitment, resources, and strategies (see Table 4.3). To provide adequate data on export potential, the next action is to conduct relevant market research.[8]

TABLE 4.2 BASIC BUSINESS PLAN

Preparing a Basic Business Plan is an absolute prerequisite for export business success. The major sections of the plan should include:

> individual or company profile;
> market research data;
> sales/marketing objectives;
> marketing strategy/timetable (what, when ,who, and how), and
> resources inventory (people, money, and time).

Source: Harvey R. Shoemack, *Introduction to the Export-Import Business*, (Northbrook, Illinois); The International Marketing Center Ltd., Unpublished text, 2008.

TABLE 4.3 SAMPLE OUTLINE FOR AN EXPORT MARKETING PLAN

Table of Contents
Introduction: Why This Company Should Export
(Executive Summary—one or two pages maximum)

Part I—Export Policy Commitment Statement

Part II—Situation/Background Analysis
> Product
> Operations
> Personnel and Export Organization
> Resources of the Firm
> Industry Structure, Competition, and Demand

Part III—Marketing Components
> Identifying, Evaluating, and Selecting Target Markets
> Product Selection
> Pricing
> Distribution and Delivery
> Promotion
> Terms and Conditions
> Internal Organization and Procedures
> Sales Goals: Profit and Loss Forecasts

Part IV—Tactics: Action Steps
> Primary Target Countries
> Secondary Target Countries
> Indirect Marketing Efforts

Part V—Export Budget: Pro Forma Financial Statements

Part VI—Implementation Schedule
> Follow-up
> Periodic Operational and Management Review
  (Measuring Results Against Plan)

Addenda: Background Data on Target Countries and Markets
> Basic Market Statistics: Historical and Projected
> Background Facts
> Competitive Environment

Source: Harvey R. Shoemack, *Introduction to the Export-Import Business*, *(Northbrook, Illinois)*;
The International Marketing Center Ltd., Unpublished text, n/d, pp. 4-13, 2008.

INITIATING MARKET RESEARCH

The purpose of overseas **market research**, data concerning consumers, is to collect information about the marketplace abroad that results in planned marketing activities with the goal of generating new revenues. Results of such research can reveal useful information such as the largest market for a company's product, its fastest growing markets, market trends and outlook, market conditions and practices, and competitive firms and products.

Research data that is already compiled by other sources such as the government, trade associations, or the Internet, (such as the per capita income of a given country) is known as **secondary data**. Original data that is collected first-hand via surveys, personal interviews, or focus groups (such as consumers' ideas on a new product concept) is called **primary data**. Most companies find they need to use both sources to achieve the results they are seeking.

Gathering data from secondary sources is less expensive than collecting primary data, and a company may decide to begin its research here, consulting various sources such as trade statistics for a country or product. However, secondary sources have their limitations: available figures may be old, out-of-date, distorted, or not otherwise relevant. Nevertheless, some secondary data may be quite useful, and here is an easy place to begin research. In fact, utilizing secondary data may be the only step the company needs to take, provided its distributors have more advance research capabilities.

In conducting primary research, a company collects data directly from the foreign marketplace through interviews, observation, and surveys with representatives and potential buyers. Although primary market research is time consuming and expensive, it has the advantage of being tailored to the company's needs and provides answers to specific questions.

Where to Begin

Because of the cost of primary market research, most forms rely heavily on secondary data sources. Three sources exporters find useful are:

The Library and the Internet

Start exploring your global market potential with library and Internet research. To stay alert to current world events that influence the international marketplace, monitor the Internet. Watch for announcements of specific projects, or visit likely markets. For example, a thawing of political hostilities often leads to the opening of economic channels among countries.

Analyze Web-based and economic statistics sites. General country-specific information—critical to any export plan—may be found on the *CIA World Factboook* Web site at: www.cia.gov/library/publications/the-world-factbook/index.html. Demographic and general economic statistics, such as population size and composition, per capita income, and production levels by industry can be important indicators of the market potential for a company's products. Trade statistics are generally compiled by product category and by country. These statistics provide U.S. firms with information concerning product

SPOTLIGHT ON GLOBAL TRADE 4.3:
Export Questionnaire

This questionnaire highlights the characteristics common to successful exporters. They should help you to assess your export readiness, as well as identify areas where your business needs to strengthen and improve its export activities.

1. Does your company have a product or service that has been successfully sold in the domestic market?   Yes   No

2. Does your company have or is it preparing an international marketing plan with defined goals and strategies?   Yes   No

3. Does your company have sufficient production capacity that can be committed to the export market?   Yes   No

4. Does your company have the financial resources to actively support the marketing of your products in the targeted overseas markets?   Yes   No

5. Is your company's management committed to developing export markets and willing and able to dedicate staff, time, and resources to the process?   Yes   No

6. Is your company committed to providing the same level of service given to your domestic customers?   Yes   No

7. Does your company have adequate knowledge in modifying product packaging and ingredients to meet foreign import regulations and cultural preferences?   Yes   No

8. Does your company have adequate knowledge in shipping its product overseas, such as identifying and selecting international freight forwarders and freight costing?   Yes   No

9. Does your company have adequate knowledge of export payment procedures, such as developing and negotiating letters of credit?   Yes   No

Scoring: Add up the number of "yes" answers

> 1 or 2 yes   You may be on the right track, but you have a long way to go
> 3 or 4 yes   A good beginning, but you still have work to do
> 5 or 6 yes   You are well on the way to being a successful exporter
> 7 or 8 yes   You are almost there; you just need to fine-tune your plans
> 9 yes   You are ready to export

shipments during certain time periods. Review international market reports, locate potential overseas trade contacts, and prepare a list of services that can help you. You may even be able to form your own export team—those private and government sources that can assist you in each step of your export development process.

International Marketing Experts

There are several ways of obtaining advice from the experts in a given field. These include:

> contact experts at the U.S. Department of Commerce, the Small Business Administration, and other government agencies;
> attend seminars, workshops, and international trade shows;
> hire an international trade and marketing consultant;
> talk with successful exporters of similar products;
> contact trade and industry association staff, and
> enroll in a college-level course in exporting and importing and/or international trade.

Gathering and evaluating secondary market research data can be complex and sometimes tedious; however, many Web sites, publications, and people can add information to the knowledge you seek.

Figure 4.4 Essential country-specific information may be found in the CIA World Factbook.

....

TABLE 4.4 NINE FACTORS IN TARGET MARKET SELECTION

1. Location
2. Culture
3. Government Regulations

4. Political Climate
5. Socio-economic Factors
6. Infrastructure

7. Distribution Channels
8. Market Size
9. Competition

TABLE 4.5 MARKET SCREENING: HOW TO SELECT FOREIGN MARKETS

> Initial Screening:
Basic Needs Potential
Foreign Trade and Investment

> Second Screening: Economic and Financial Forces/Environments

> Third Screening:
Political Forces/Environments
Legal Forces/Environments

> Fourth Screening: Socio-cultural Forces/Environments

> Fifth Screening: Competitive Forces/Environments

> Final Selection:
Personal Visits to Foreign Market Country
Attendance at Trade Shows in the Country
Locally Conducted Market Research (if necessary)

A Step-by-Step Approach

As you can tell from Tables 4.4 and 4.5, screening and selecting target markets calls for locating relevant data. The following approach to research may be useful; it involves screening potential markets, assessing the targeted markets, and drawing conclusions:

Screen Potential Markets

> **STEP 1:** Obtain statistics indicating product exports to various countries. Published statistics provide a reliable indicator of where U.S. exports are currently being shipped. The U.S. Census Bureau Web site provides these statistics every month. They are also available using the National Trade Data Bank. (Note: A small fee is involved for personal service or available to use free at local federal depository libraries. See reference in Step 5.)

> **STEP 2:** Identify five or more large and fast-growing markets for the firm's product. Look at the growth over the past three years. Has it been consistent? Did the market grow even during a recession, or did it resume with economic recovery?

> **STEP 3:** Identify some smaller but rapidly emerging markets that may provide ground-floor opportunities. If the market is just beginning to open up, there may be fewer competitors than in established markets. Given a lower starting point here, growth rates should be substantially higher to qualify as potential markets.

> **STEP 4:** Target three to five of the most statistically promising markets for further assessment. Consult with the Department of Commerce's U.S. Export Assistance Center (USEAC; www.doc.gov), business associates, freight forwarders, and others knowledgeable concerning export to further evaluate these targeted markets.

Assess Targeted Markets

> **STEP 5:** Examine trends for company products as well as related items that could influence demand. Calculate the overall product consumption and the amount accounted for by imports. U.S. government sources include the official U.S. Department of Commerce export Web site (www.export.gov); the National Trade Data Bank (NTDB) (www.stat-usa.gov/tradetest.nsf) and the National Technical Information Service (NTIS) (www.ntis.gov/); Industry Sector Analysis (ISAs); and the Country Commercial Guides (CCGs) (www.bis.doc.gov). These are among the sites that give economic backgrounds and market trends for each country. Demographic information (such as population size, composition, and age) can be obtained from *World Population (Census) and Statistical Yearbook*, United Nations, as well as the *CIA World Factbook*.

> **STEP 6:** Discover sources of competition, including the extent of domestic industry production and the major foreign competitors in each target market by using ISAs and competitive assessments. This information is available from the NTDB and the NTIS.

> **STEP 7:** Analyze factors affecting the marketing and use of the product in each market, such as end-use sectors, channels of distribution, cultural idiosyncrasies, and business

practices. Again, the ISAs and the Customized Market Analyses (CMAs) offered by the Department of Commerce are useful.

> **STEP 8:** Identify any foreign barriers (tariff or non-tariff) for the product to be exported, plus any U.S. barriers such as export controls (see Chapter 5).

> **STEP 9:** Take advantage of any U.S. or foreign government incentives that promote exporting your particular product. Attending a foreign trade show can result in comprehensive market data to affirm or cancel plans to enter that market.

Draw Conclusions

The data gathered from taking the preceding steps should provide enough information to determine your next move. However, further data sources are available in the Appendix at the end of this chapter.

FORMULATING PRO-ACTIVE STRATEGIES: COMMUNICATION AND TRADE SHOWS

Once you have determined your plan, you will need to consider how you are going to present your company and product information to interested parties overseas; and in turn, how you can obtain information from them. Many firms today use a Web site as one way to accomplish this. For instance, your Web site can be a virtual catalogue of your products or services, but should also include an international sales program that provides the standard terms and conditions for selling your products overseas.

Figure 4.5 **Première Vision textile trade show in Paris brings buyers from all over the world.**
....

You will probably want to develop international distributor support programs for promotions, including advertising, selling, and after-sales services. These include items such as translation, price quotations, discount structures, warranties, services, parts, and training.

When you have made your commitment, assessed your ability to serve international markets, developed an international marketing plan, and created your communication tools, you are considered to be export ready. Now you can use the numerous federal and state agency programs for exporters. As mentioned earlier, a great place to start is with **trade shows**, periodic wholesale markets for buyers and sellers in related industries. Trade shows are a key method for exposing your company and its products to pre-qualified trade prospects and buyers. International trade shows are the single best method for contacting distributor prospects and are widely attended. For example, Germany hosts more than 200 trade shows each year (an average of two per week). While many companies new to export cannot afford to attend trade shows overseas, most domestic trade shows have a foreign component. In fact, one of the more popular programs offered by the U.S. Department of Commerce is its Foreign Buyers Program which promotes and brings international visitors to many domestic trade shows. By this time, you are off and running. Now what happens?

FOLLOWING THROUGH WITH AN EXPORT ORDER

Suppose, as a novice exporter exhibiting your products at the appropriate industry trade show, you have collected attendees' business cards, and a while later one of these prospects sends you an order inquiry and request for a quotation. You respond with a **pro forma invoice**, a form describing the merchandise including its specifications, packaging, per unit price, and payment terms. Your prospect responds with a purchase order, including payment confirmation. Based on the terms of the sale, the prospective importer arranges for financing with its bank. Simultaneously, you plan for production. The importer's bank, after verifying that company's credit-worthiness, prepares the necessary documents and informs your bank that the financial requirements have been satisfied. When your bank notifies you, your company prepares the goods for export and contacts a freight forwarder (or the shipper if you are not using a freight forwarder) to pick up the shipment.

When the shipper receives the goods, you are given a **bill of lading (B/L)**, (or **air waybill**), containing a full description of the shipment contents. You then prepare the required documents which may include an insurance policy, consular invoice, and other permits or certificates specified in the terms of sale. These documents go to your bank (or to your freight forwarder who also coordinates all documentation). Your bank informs the importer's bank that the documents have been received. The importer's bank then sends payment to your bank on your behalf. Meanwhile, the goods are en route. When your bank receives the payment, all of the transaction documents go to the importer's bank and are forwarded to the importer who then can claim the goods on their entry into the country. Your first export transaction is complete. May it lead to many more! (See Chapter 10 for payment procedures.)

SUMMARY

Today, in order for many businesses to grow their markets and remain competitive, exporting is a necessity. (For some profiles of selected fashion businesses participating in exporting, see Chapter 9.) Exporting is beneficial to a country as well as to its businesses, as it helps lower unemployment and trade deficits.

To be successful, an exporting organization contemplating establishing overseas channels needs a commitment from top management, including a long-term willingness to invest resources to the venture. In order for a product to be exportable, it must meet certain criteria, particularly those of creating a competitive edge and satisfying existing demand.

Some of the challenges potential exporters need to face include determining the company's readiness to export and its export potential. Once a decision is reached, several overseas market entry options are available. Developing a basic Business/Marketing Plan and an Export Marketing Plan geared to the particular foreign market are the next essential steps. To make the plans effective, the findings gained from conducting market research serve as the foundation for developing overseas marketing strategies.

Two useful places to begin research are the local library and the Internet. Other sources include consulting the U.S. Department of Commerce, relevant trade associations, and enrolling in college courses in international trade. A step-by-step approach culminates in attending trade shows, and ultimately participating as an exhibitor.

Key Terms

> Air waybill
> Bill of lading (B/L)
> Consumer demand
> Export Administration Regulations (EARs)
> Export management companies (EMCs)
> Exporting

> Market research
> Piggybacking
> Primary data
> Products
> Pro forma invoice
> Secondary data
> Stocking distributors
> Trade shows

Review Questions

1. Why is exporting important to U.S. businesses both large and small?

2. Explain four reasons for businesses to export.

3. Name three or four of the concerns top management must resolve in ascertaining that a business is export-ready.

4. Cite five factors to consider in determining a company's export potential.

5. Explain several reasons why a written Export Marketing Plan is important.

Discussion Questions and Activities

1. Why is it necessary to consider a venture into export as requiring a long-term commitment from top management?

2. If a major company executive likes to travel, what would be the advantages of that person's assuming the responsibility for managing the export venture? What could be the disadvantages of such an arrangement?

3. Why is it important for a company to do market research when creating an Export Marketing Plan? What would be the advantages and disadvantages of engaging an independent firm to conduct the research?

4. What are some of the benefits of attending relevant trade shows before attempting to participate in one?

References

1. Chantal Todé, "L. L. Bean to open first store in China this month," *DM News*, September 17, 2008. Retrieved September 22, 2008 from http://dmnews.com/LL-Bean-to-open-first-store-in-China-this-month.

2. "The WWD List," *Women's Wear Daily*, August 28, 2008, p.12.

3. Caroline Tell, "Judith Ripka Seeks to Expand Worldwide Presence," *Women's Wear Daily*, August 25, 2008, p. 9.

4. Harvey R. Shoemack, *Introduction to the Export-Import Business*, Northbrook, Illinois: The International Marketing Center, Ltd. Unpublished work. N/D, pp. 2 and 3.

5. Lisa Movius, "Role Reversal: American Apparel Heads to China," *Women's Wear Daily*, August 21, 2008, p.14.

6. Op. Cit., Shoemack, pp. 2-5.

7. Ibid. pp. 2-12 and 2-13.

8. Ibid, Shoemack.

Additional References

Rob Walker, *Buying In: The Secret Dialog between What We Buy and Who We Are*. New York: Random House, 2008.

Fareed Zakaria, *The Post-American World*. New York: W. W. Norton & Company, Inc., 2008.

Appendix: Basic Resource Links Data

Further information may be secured from additional government and private resources available to help companies new-to-export:

PRIVATE SERVICES. The number of private resources is too great to list here, but a few of the essentials every exporter needs include:

> AN INTERNATIONAL BANKER to receive payment from export sales;

> A FOREIGN FREIGHT forwarder for shipping and documenting your exports;

> AN ATTORNEY for reviewing intellectual property rights, and

> PREPARING agent-distributor contracts.

Also, companies will find the services of an accountant, insurance agent and export packer to be useful. These, and other resources, can be accessed through the *Yellow Pages*, or by other firms already exporting and using these services, or by most export assistance service providers.

GOVERNMENT SERVICES. Two key agencies are generally available to provide export promotion services to companies across the nation:

> State Trade Office. Almost all states have an international group within their Department of Economic Development (some states refer to this agency as their Department of Commerce). They will provide numerous trade promotion services for firms ready to develop their global market potential. They do this by helping with global marketing and making overseas contacts.

> FEDERAL GOVERNMENT AGENCIES. Commercial Service is a Commerce Department agency that helps U.S. companies, particularly small and medium-sized businesses, conduct sales in international markets. The agency's network includes 107 U.S. Export Assistance Centers throughout the country, and more than 150 offices overseas. In 2005, the U.S. Commercial Service facilitated over $23 billion in U.S. exports, and conducted nearly 150,000 counseling sessions with American companies.

State and federal export promotion agencies can be contacted via their Internet Web site.

> Other agencies. As companies begin their search for resources, they may find other agencies that provide special services that help with export development. These include the SBA, the Service Core of Retired Executives (SCORE), Small Business Development Centers (SBDC), state or city chambers of commerce, local or regional economic development agencies, university and community college extension and outreach offices, and special organizations that focus on specific areas of international activities.

There is a Catch-22 to be aware of when using these services. They are promoted as services to assist firms that are pre-qualified as export ready. They can identify and contact international intermediary prospects (distributors, agents, and representatives) in a given foreign country, but it is important firms are prepared to respond quickly and effectively to inquiries they generate. Companies must be ready to support those willing to represent them in the foreign market.

Links

Automated Export System
www.aesdirect.gov

Bureau of Industry and Security
www.bis.doc.gov

Bureau of the Census
www.census.gov

Defense Trade Reduction
Agencywww.dtra.mil

Foreign Corrupt Practices Act
www.usdoj.gov/criminal/
fraud/fcpa/

International Trade Data
System
www.itds.gov

Market Access and Compliance
http://trade.gov/mac/

Office of Defense Trade
Controls
www.pmddtc.state.gov

Office of Foreign Assets
Control (OFAC)
www.treas.gov/ofac

Schedule B Export Codes
www.census.gov/
foreign-trade/schedules/b/

The Chemical Weapons
Convention
www.cwc.gov

Trade Advocacy Center
www.export.gov/advocacy

Trade Compliance Center
http://tcc.export.gov/

Trade Information Center
www.export.gov

U.S. Commercial Service
www.trade.gov/cs/

U.S. Customs and Border
Protection
www.cbp.gov

U.S. Department of Commerce
www.doc.gov

U.S. International Trade
Administration
www.ita.doc.gov

U.S. International Trade
Commission
www.usitc.gov

U.S. Trade Representative
www.ustr.gov

ATA Carnet
www.atacarnet.com

Incoterms
www.iccwbo.org/incoterms/
id3045/index.html

National Association of
Foreign Trade Zones
www.naftz.org

Overseas Private
Investment Corporation
www.opic.gov

China's Export Controls
www.nti.org/db/china/
excon.htm

Chapter 5

U.S. Export Controls
and Procedures

Don't Let This HAPPEN TO YOU!

Actual Investigations *of* Export Control *and* Antiboycott Violations

July 2008 Edition

U.S. DEPARTMENT OF COMMERCE
Bureau of Industry and Security
Export Enforcement

Figure 5.1 The Bureau of Industry and Security publishes a report of export violations.

• • • • • •

5

U.S. EXPORT CONTROLS AND PROCEDURES

A Texas doctor and college professor illegally exported vials of a deadly bacterium to Tanzania, but claimed to the FBI that the shipment of his plague had been stolen. As a result of the government's investigation and his subsequent export control violation trial, the doctor was convicted on 47 counts of a 69-count indictment, was fired from his college, and sentenced to two years in prison.[1]

In another criminal case, Worldwide Sports & Recreation, Inc., while doing business as Bushnell Corporation, exported Night Ranger night vision devices to Japan and 14 other countries, without the required BIS export licenses. Bushnell sold the cameras to a Japanese company, but transferred them to a U.S. company in Florida with the knowledge that the cameras were going to be exported to Japan.

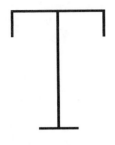he foreign company and the domestic intermediary pleaded guilty and cooperated, but the penalty to Bushnell was a $650,000 criminal fine and five years probation. Bushnell also agreed to pay an administrative penalty of $223,000 and to a one-year suspended denial of export privileges.[2]

These cases are examples of how U.S. export control laws help protect the United States and its trading partners by keeping certain goods and technologies away from unfriendly countries and terrorists who could use them to attack the U.S. or other nations. This chapter provides an overview of complex and lengthy policies and procedures of U.S. export control laws and will offer suggestions for exporters to follow in maintaining compliance with these laws.

Many of the U.S. executive branch agencies are responsible for regulating exports from the United States. The U.S. Department of Commerce is responsible for controlling goods and technology that are capable of being used for commercial purposes, but also present foreign policy or national security concerns when used for military applications.

THE EXPORT ADMINISTRATION REGULATIONS

The Commerce Department's **Bureau of Industry and Security (BIS)** is the primary government agency responsible for implementing and enforcing the **Export Administration Regulations (EARs)**, which regulate the export and re-export of most commercial items. The **Export Enforcement Arm (EEA)** of the BIS protects the U.S. national security, foreign policy, and economic interests by educating potential exporters on how to improve their compliance practices. Its job is to intercept illegal exports, investigate violations, and help prosecute violators of export control laws.[3]

The U.S. government prosecutes intentional violations of U.S. export control laws by assessing substantial fines and even prison terms for criminal violators. Even if no criminal charges are claimed, administrative (civil) penalties, such as fines and a denial of export privileges, can be assessed for other violations of the EAR. Fines for export violations can reach up to $1 million per violation in criminal cases, $50,000 per violation in administrative cases, and up to $120,000 per violation in certain cases involving national security issues.

BIS enforcement efforts continue to focus on transactions that impose the most serious threat to U.S. national security, such as proliferation networks. In 2008, BIS investigations resulted in the criminal conviction of 40 individuals and businesses for export control violations. The penalties for these convictions came to over $2.7 million in criminal fines, over $800,000 in forfeitures, and over 218 months of imprisonment. Additionally, BIS investigations resulted in the completion of 50 administrative cases against individuals and businesses, which were concluded with over $3.4 million in administrative penalties and nine denial orders.[4]

Criminal and administrative violations may result in the offending individual or organization being prohibited from receiving U.S. exports and others may receive goods only if they have been licensed. The BIS Web site, www.bis.doc.gov/, features a link to actual investigations of Export Control and Antiboycott Violations, titled, "Don't Let This Happen to You!"[5]

In most export-control cases, however, BIS negotiates settlement in administrative cases before they get to a formal administrative hearing. The settlements are the result of **voluntary self-disclosures (VSDs)**, that is, the individual or company voluntarily admitting to export law violations. These voluntary admissions of administrative errors are looked upon by the BIS as significant mitigating factors when negotiating settlements of administrative cases. To encourage VSDs, in appropriate cases, fines and other administrative penalties could be significantly reduced if the BIS became aware of the violations as a result of voluntary disclosure.[6]

The EAR place legal responsibility on anyone who has information, authority or functions relevant to carrying out export business subject to the EAR. Included are exporters, freight forwarders, carriers (ships, planes, rail, and truck), consignees (those parties receiving the exports), and any other relevant party.

The EAR applies not only to parties within the United States, but also to individuals and companies in foreign countries who are involved in transactions subject to the EAR.

REASONS FOR EXPORT CONTROLS

Export controls are necessary for three major reasons: national security, foreign policy, and short supply.

National Security (NS)

Controls are placed on exports of certain strategic commodities or technology, "which would make a significant contribution to the military potential of any other country or combination of countries which would prove detrimental to the national security of the United States," are for National Security reasons.[7]

Foreign Policy (FP)

Foreign Policy export controls are placed on some commodities "where necessary to further significantly the foreign policy of the United States or to fulfill its declared international obligations. Foreign Policy controls may be commodity oriented (crime control, and regional stability) or country specific (Iran, North Korea, Taliban-controlled Afghanistan, Cuba, and other embargoed countries).[8]

Short Supply (SS)

Controls that are used "where necessary to protect the domestic economy from the excessive drain of scarce materials and to reduce the serious inflationary impact of foreign demand," (example: petroleum products), are known as Short Supply.[9]

Other controls include: Anti-Terrorism (AT), suspected terrorist-enabling products; Missile Technologies (MT), such as specifications on missile delivery systems; Nuclear Proliferation (NP), products or technologies that further nuclear expansion; Chemical and Biological weapons (CB); Crime Control(CC); Regional Stability (RS); computers (XP), and the United Nations (UN) controls.[10]

THE EAR AND DUAL-USE ITEMS

Note that EAR does *not* control all goods, services, and technologies. Other U.S. government agencies regulate more specialized exports. For example, the U.S. Department of State has authority over defense articles and defense services. A list of other agencies involved in export controls can be found in the EAR which is available on the U.S. Government Printing Office Web site: www.bis.doc.gov/licensing/exportingbasics.htm.[11]

The exports regulated by BIS are often referred to as **dual-use items**. They may have a commercial application, but also a potential military or proliferation use, as a weapon of extreme violence, conventional arms, or end-use violations by terrorists.[12]

Nearly all U.S. exporters trade in items that are subject to the export control laws administered by the BIS. Controlled items tend to be sophisticated hardware, software or technologies. However, purely commercial items without an obvious military use, such as chemical ingredients used in ballpoint pens, may be precursors to chemical weapons, are also subject to the EAR.

So it is essential for potential exporters, before processing a transaction, to consider exactly what they are selling, to whom it will go, and how it will ultimately be used. They must be certain their exports will not adversely affect national security or U.S. foreign policy interests.

Most of the dual-use export control system is spelled out in the Export Administration Regulations Web site (www.gpo.gov/bis/). The information presents a general understanding of the U.S. regulations and how to use them. It is designed for those firms and individuals who are new to exporting and in particular, new to export controls. However, since the regulations are still complex to novices, they will likely turn to a licensed **freight forwarder**—an independent service organization that, for a fee, expedites export shipments by providing information and assistance on U.S. export regulations and documentation, shipping methods, freight costs, and major foreign import regulations.

The BIS Web site provides a link to the EAR, the Bureau's regulations governing exports of dual-use items. The site also provides discussions of certain key regulatory policy areas, including policies governing exports of high performance computers, exports of encryption products, deemed exports, U.S. anti-boycott regulations, special regional considerations, the multilateral export control regimes, and the technical advisory committees.

The EAR site also includes answers to frequently asked questions, detailed step-by-step instructions for determining if a transaction is subject to the regulations, how to request a commodity classification or advisory opinion, and how to apply for a license. Using the government Web site or the assistance of a freight forwarder cannot substitute for consulting the EAR.[13]

NEW DUAL-USE EXPORT CONTROL INITIATIVE

In March 2009, at the annual BIS Export Control Forum, Newport Beach, California, the U.S. government announced a series of new steps to ensure that dual-use export control policies and practices support the National Security Strategy while facilitating U.S. economic and technological leadership. The U.S. faces unprecedented security challenges from threats of terrorism to proliferation of nuclear, biological, and chemical weapons and advanced conventional weapons to instability in a number of regions in the world. The security issue is further impacted by an unprecedented economic challenge from the increasing worldwide diffusion of high technology and globalization of markets. Therefore, government policies must ensure that the dual-use export control system is precisely focused to meet those challenges. In response to this continuing threat, the following new steps are being taken to tighten U.S. dual-use export control system:[14]

Foreign End-Users

The dual-use export control system increasingly focuses on foreign end-users of U.S. high technology products. This program encourages growth in trade to reliable foreign customers, while denying access to sensitive technologies to proliferators, international terrorists, and other foreign parties acting contrary to U.S. national security and foreign policy interests.

Keeping track of foreign end-users involves the Validated End User (VEU) process, which is intended to facilitate legitimate exports to civilian end-users and reliable foreign companies, while also imposing additional scrutiny of exports to foreign parties with a record of activities contrary to U.S. foreign policy and national security interests. An explanation of the new VEU, which would allow the export, re-export, and transfer of eligible items to specified end-users in eligible destinations, including the PRC (China), without a license, can be viewed at: http://www.bis.doc.gov/finalchina.html.[15]

U.S. Competitiveness

To sustain U.S. global economic competitiveness and innovation—keys to the nation's domestic economic recovery long-term national security—the U.S. government's export control agencies constantly reassess domestic policies to ensure that the most sensitive items are regulated.

The current focus on U.S. competitiveness includes developing a regular process for systematic review of the list of controlled dual-use items, and has revised controls on intra-company transfers and encryption products, and provides a review of re-export controls.

Transparency

U.S. exporters need sufficient information to support both domestic security and competitiveness goals. There must be enough clear communication between the government and potential exporters to enable compliance. By publishing on the Department of Commerce's Web site, advisory opinions and lists of foreign parties warranting higher scrutiny, the government's transparency fosters public awareness.

A number of industry associations, as well as individual companies, work closely with government agencies to implement these reforms to ensure that dual-use exports are controlled and security threats are addressed, while also maintaining the economic competitiveness of this country.

TABLE 5.1 COMMERCE CONTROL LIST CATEGORIES TO DETERMINE EXPORT CONTROL CLASSIFICATION NUMBER (ECCN)

0 = Nuclear Materials, Facilities, and Equipment (and Miscellaneous Items)
1 = Materials, Chemicals, Microorganisms, and Toxins
2 = Materials Processing
3 = Electronics
4 = Computers
5 = Telecommunications and Information Security
6 = Sensors and Lasers
7 = Navigation and Avionics
8 = Marine
9 = Propulsion Systems, Space Vehicles, and Related Equipment

TABLE 5.2 FIVE PRODUCT GROUPS

A. Systems, Equipment, and Components
B. Test, Inspection, and Production Equipment
C. Material
D. Software
E. Technology

All ECCNs are listed in the Commerce Control List (CCL) (Supplement No. 1 to Part 774 of the EAR) which is available on the government printing office Web site. The CCL is divided into ten broad categories, and each category is further subdivided into five products.

Source: www.bis.doc.gov/licensing/exportingbasics.htm.

In addition to the U.S. export control policy for dual-use items, the Bureau of Industry and Security is also charged with the development, implementation, and interpretation of the anti-boycott provisions of the Export Administration Act. The anti-boycott provisions encourage, and in some cases require, U.S. businesses to refuse to participate in foreign boycotts that the United States does not sanction, such as the Arab boycott of Israel. Domestic companies are also required to report receipt of boycott-related requests.[16]

The EAR imposes responsibilities on all parties to an export transaction: manufacturers/exporters, freight forwarders, transport carriers (ship, air, rail, and truck) and consignees (those receiving the exported goods).

EXPORT LICENSING REQUIREMENTS

As stated in Chapter 4, any item sent from the United States to a foreign destination is an export. Items include commodities, software or technology, such as clothing, building materials, circuit boards, automotive parts, blue prints, design plans, retail software packages, and technical information.

How an item is transported outside of the United States does not matter in determining export license requirements. For example, an item can be sent by regular mail or hand-carried on an airplane. A set of technical diagrams can be sent via fax to a foreign destination, software can be uploaded to or downloaded from an Internet site, or technology can be transmitted via e-mail or during a telephone conversation. Regardless of the method used for the transfer, the transaction is considered an export for export control purposes.[17]

An item is also considered an export even if it is leaving the United States temporarily, if it is leaving the United State but is not for sale, such as a gift, or if it is going to a wholly-owned U.S. subsidiary in a foreign country. Even a foreign-origin item exported from the United States, transmitted or transshipped through the United States, or being returned from the United States to its foreign country of origin, is considered an export. Finally, release of technology or source code subject to the EAR to a foreign national in the United States is considered to be an export to the home country of the foreign national under the EAR. An innocent review of technical drawings, while sitting on a park bench at lunch, may result in those drawings being considered an export, if a foreign national should sit down next to you and look at those drawings. If so, the incidental action would require compliance with all EARs regarding exports to the country of the foreign national.[18]

HOW TO DETERMINE IF YOU NEED
A COMMERCE EXPORT LICENSE

A relatively small percentage of total U.S. exports and re-exports, dual-use in particular, require an **export license**, which would come from the Bureau of Industry and Security (BIS). License requirements depend on an item's technical characteristics, the destination, the end-user, and the end-use. The exporter-of-record must determine whether an export requires a license. When making that determination, consider the following questions:

> What are you exporting?   > Where are your exports going?
> Who will receive your export?   > What will be the end-use of your export?[19]

What Are You Exporting?

A key in determining whether an export license is needed from the Department of Commerce is researching whether your intended export has a specific **Export Control Classification Number (ECCN)**, the alpha-numeric code that identifies the level of export control for all export "items, including products, technology, and software that are exported from the United States." (See Figure 5.3.) All ECCNs are listed in the **Commerce Control List (CCL)**, which includes items subject to their export licensing authority. The CCL does not include those items exclusively controlled for export or re-export by another department or agency of the U.S. Government. In instances where agencies other than the Department of Commerce administer controls over related items, entries in the CCL contain a reference to these controls. The Bureau of Industry and Security maintains the Commerce Control List within the Export Administration Regulations. The CCL is available on the Government Printing Office Web site at www.gpo.gov.[20]

BIS also maintains the **Commerce Country Chart (CCC)**, which can be found in Supplement No. 1 to part 738 of the EARs. It contains licensing requirements based on destination and Reasons for [export] Controls.

Classifying Your Item

The proper classification of your item is essential to determining any licensing requirements under the Export Administration Regulations. You may classify the item on your own, ask your freight forwarder, or submit a classification request and BIS will determine the ECCN for you.

Commerce Control List Categories

When reviewing the CCL to determine if your item is specified by an ECCN, you will first need to determine in which of the following 10 broad categories of the Commerce Control List your item is included and next consider to which of the five specific product groups your exports apply. (See Table 5.1.)

For example, assume that you have lie detectors—polygraph, or psychological stress analysis equipment—that are used to help law enforcement agencies. What would be your ECCN? Start by looking in the Commerce Control List under the category of electronics (Category 3) and product group which covers equipment (Product Group A). Then read through the list to find whether your item is included in the list. In this example the item is 3A001 (see Figure 5.3).

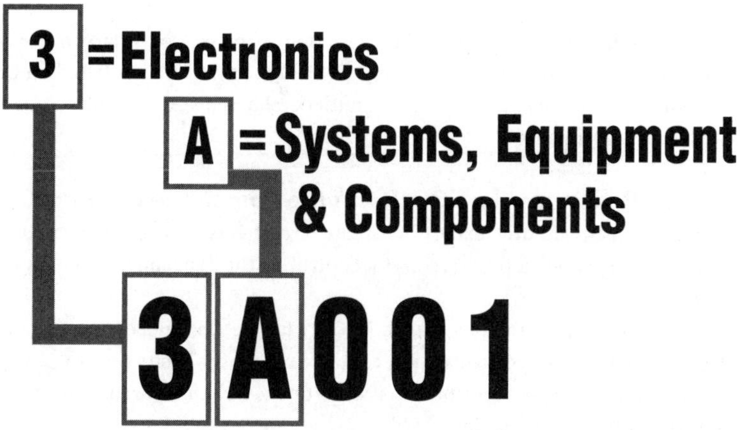

3 =Electronics
A =Systems, Equipment & Components
3A001

Figure 5.2 According to the Bureau of Industry and Security Web site, "A key for exporters to determine whether an export license is needed from the U.S. department of Commerce is to reference the CCL for a specific Export Control Classification Number (ECCN). An alpha-numeric code (see above), the ECCN describes a particular item or type of item, and shows the export controls the U.S. government has placed on that item. If an item is subject to U.S. Department of Commerce jurisdiction and is not listed on the CCL, it is designated as EAR99. Those items are usually low-technology consumer goods that do not usually require a license to be exported."

. . . .

Source: Export Control Basics at http://www.bis.doc.gov/exportingbasics.htm.

If your item falls under U.S. Department of Commerce jurisdiction and is not listed on the CCL, it is designated as **EAR99**. These items generally consist of low-technology consumer goods and do not require a license in many situations. However, if your proposed export of an EAR99 item is to an embargoed country, to an end-user of concern or in support of a prohibited end-use, a license is required and you will most likely have difficulty in obtaining one.[21]

Where Are Your Exports Going?

Restrictions vary from country to country. The most restricted destinations are the embargoed countries and those countries designated as supporting terrorist activities. As of this writing, embargoed countries include Cuba, Iran, Sudan, Taliban controlled Afghanistan, and Syria. There are U.S. export restrictions on some products, for example nuclear devices, that are worldwide.

The EAR describes embargoed destinations and refers to certain additional controls imposed by the **Office of Foreign Assets Control of the Treasury Department (OFAC)**, which administers and enforces economic and trade sanctions based on U.S. foreign policy and national security goals against targeted foreign countries, terrorists, international narcotics traffickers, and those engaged in activities related to the proliferation of nuclear, biological, and chemical weapons. The OFAC acts under presidential wartime and national emergency powers, as well as authority granted by specific legislation, to impose controls on transactions and freeze foreign assets under U.S. jurisdiction. Many of the sanctions are based on United Nations and other international mandates, are multilateral in scope, and involve close cooperation with allied governments.[22]

How to Cross-Reference the ECCN with the Commerce Country Chart

Once you have classified potential export items, the next step is to determine whether you need an export license based on the "reasons for control" of the item and the country of ultimate destination.

Begin this process by cross-referencing the ECCN with the **Commerce Country Chart (CCC)**, which identifies the reasons for export controls by country. When used together, they define the items subject to export controls based solely on the technical parameters of the item and the country of ultimate destination.

Below the main heading on the CCC, you will find the "Reason for Control" (NS for National Security, AT for Anti-Terrorism, CC for Crime Control). Below the titles, the columns on the Country Chart indicate the specific licensing requirements for exports identified by your ECCN as they apply to different countries.

If there is an "X" in the box based on the reason(s) for control of your item and the country of destination, a license is required, unless a **license exception** excluding that item from licensing is available. The EAR sets forth the license requirements and licensing policy for most reasons for control.

If there is no "X" in the control code column(s) specified under your ECCN and country of destination, you will not need an export license unless you are exporting to an end-user or end-use of concern.[23]

TABLE 5.3 COMMERCE COUNTRY CHART (REASON FOR CONTROL)

Countries	Chemical & Biological Weapons			Nuclear Nonproliferations		National Security		Missile Tech	Regional Stability		Firearms Convention	Crime Control			Anti-Terrorism	
	CB 1	CB 2	CB 3	NP 1	NP 2	NS 1	NS 2	MT 1	RS 1	RS 2	FC 1	CC 1	CC 2	CC 3	AT 1	AT 2
Guyana	X	X		X		X	X	X	X	X	X	X		X		
Haiti	X	X		X		X	X	X	X	X	X	X		X		
Honduras	X	X		X		X	X	X	X	X	X	X		X		
Hong Kong	X	X		X		X		X	X	X		X		X		
• Hungary	X					X		X	X							
• Iceland	X			X		X		X	X							

The Commerce Country Chart identifies reasons for U.S. export controls by matching the ECCN number with the export target country.

Source: http:www.bis.doc.gov/licensing/bis_exports.pdf.

Who Will Receive Your Export?

It is part of any firm's export control compliance to review several lists of individuals and entities to whom and to which no exports are permitted—no matter what the product may be. These lists should be reviewed prior to each export transaction and recommended even before going through the trouble of applying for an export license. Violators of the EAR may be placed on one of the following lists: the **Entity List; Treasury Department Specially Designated Nationals and Blocked Persons List**; the **Denied Persons List**; the **Debarred List**, and the **Unverified List**. Placement on a list can apply even to goods or services that don't normally require a license. It is a violation of the EAR to participate in an export transaction subject to the EAR, with a denied party.[24]

Certain individuals and organizations may only receive goods if they have been licensed, even items that do not normally require a license based on the ECCN and Commerce Country Chart or the "catch-all" EAR99 designation.

The Export Administration Regulations provide that the Bureau of Industry and Security may inform exporters, individually or through amendment to the EAR, that a license is required for exports or re-exports to certain prohibited parties. The EAR contains a list of such entities, including the following:

Entity List

The **Entity List**, established in February 1997, informs the public of parties whose activities imposed a risk of diverting exported and re-exported items into programs related to nuclear, biological, and chemical weapons. Since then, the grounds for listing a person, company, or even a country on the Entity List have expanded to include entities sanctioned by the State Department for which United States foreign policy goals are served by imposing additional license requirements on exports and re-exports to them.[25]

Publishing this list puts exporters on notice of export license requirements that apply to exports to these parties. While this list will assist exporters in determining whether an entity poses proliferation concerns, it is not comprehensive. It does not relieve exporters of the responsibility to determine the nature and activities of their potential customers using BIS's *Know Your Customer and Red Flags* guidance. (See Spotlight on Global Trade: Red Flag Indicators.)[26]

Denied Persons List

U.S. firms may not participate in an export or re-export transaction subject to the EAR with a person whose export privileges have been denied by the BIS. A list of those firms and individuals is available on the BIS Web site (www.bis.doc.gov/dpl/thedeniallist.asp). Note that some denied persons are located within the United States. If approached by a person whose export privileges have been denied, you must not make the sale and should report the situation to BIS's Office of Export Enforcement.[27]

The Treasury Department's Specially Designated Nationals and Blocked Persons List

The Treasury Department's Specially Designated Nationals and Blocked Persons List is maintained by the Office of Foreign Assets Control (OFAC) (of the U.S. Department of

TABLE 5.4 SUPPLEMENT NO. 4 TO PART 744—ENTITY LIST

This Supplement lists certain entities subject to license requirements for specified items under this part 744 of the EAR. License requirements for these entities includes exports and re-exports, unless otherwise stated. This list of entities is revised and updated on a periodic basis in this Supplement by adding new or amended notifications and deleting notifications no longer in effect.

Country	Entity	License Requirement	License Review Policy	Federal Register Citation
Canada	Ali Bakhshien, 909-4005 Bayview Ave., Toronto, Canada M2M 3Z9.	For all items subject to the EAR. (See 744.11 of the EAR).	Presumption of denial.	73 FR 54504, 9/22/08.
	Kitro Corporation, 909-4005 Bayview Ave., Toronto, Canada M2M 3Z9.	For all items subject to the EAR. (See 744.11 of the EAR).	Presumption of denial.	73 FR 54504, 9/22/08.
China, People's Republic of	13 Institute, China Academy of Launch Vehicle Technology, (CALT), a.k.a. 713 Institute or Beijing Institute of Control Devices.	For all items subject to the EAR.	See 744.3(d) of this part.	66 FR 24265, 5/14/01.
	33 Institute, a.k.a. Beijing Institute of Automatic Control Equipment.	For all items subject to the EAR having a classification other than EAR99 or a classification where the third through fifth digits of the ECCN are 999", e.g., XX999.	See 744.3(d) of this part.	66 FR 24266, 5/14/01.

The *Entity List* is just one of several lists a potential exporter or importer is required to check to be sure their customer or "end user" of their item is not in violation of the U.S. Export Administration Regulations, which would prohibit the transaction.

Source: www.access.gpo.gov/bis/ear/pdf/744spir.pdf.

Treasury). It is comprised of individuals and organizations that represent restricted countries or those known to be involved in terrorism and narcotics trafficking.[28]

The Unverified List

Composed of firms for which BIS was unable to complete an end-use check (www.bis.doc.gov/enforcement/unverifiedlist/unverified_parties.html). Firms on the unverified list present a "red flag" that exporters have a duty to inquire about before making an export to them.[29]

What Will Be the End-Use of Your Export?

Some end-uses are prohibited while others may require a license. For example, you may not export to certain entities involved in the proliferation of nuclear, biological, and chemical weapons and the missiles to deliver them, without specific authorization, no matter what your item is.

SPOTLIGHT ON GLOBAL TRADE 5.1:
Red Flag Indicators

Things to Look for in Export Transactions

Exporters can avoid transactions that may lead to possible violations of the Export Administration Regulations by watching out for the following irregularities. Also helpful is the BIS Web site, *Know Your Customer Guidance*, at www.bis.doc.gov/complianceandenforcement/knowyourcustomerguidance.htm.

> The customer or its address is similar to one of the parties found on the Commerce Department's [BIS's] list of denied persons.
> The customer or purchasing agent is reluctant to offer info information about the end-use of the item.
> The product's capabilities do not fit the buyer's line of business, such as an order for sophisticated computers for a small bakery.
> The item ordered is incompatible with the technical level of the country to which it is being shipped, such as semiconductor manufacturing equipment being shipped to a country that has no electronics industry.
> The customer is willing to pay cash for a very expensive item when the terms of sale would normally call for financing.
> The customer has little or no business background.
> The customer is unfamiliar with the product's performance characteristics but still wants the product.
> Routine installation, training, or maintenance services are declined by the customer.
> Delivery dates are vague, or deliveries are planned for out-of-the-way destinations.
> A freight forwarding firm is listed as the product's final destination.
> The shipping route is abnormal for the product and destination.
> Packaging is inconsistent with the stated method of shipment or destination.
> When questioned, the buyer is evasive and especially unclear about the whether the purchased product is for domestic use, for export, or for reexport.

If you have a reason to believe a violation is taking place or has occurred, you may report it to the Department of Commerce by calling it's 24-hour hotline number at 1-800-424-2980, or if you prefer, request a form to submit a confidential tip.

Source: www.bis.doc.gov/complianceandenforcement/redflagindicators.htm.

EXPORT AUTHORIZATION

There is no such thing as an "exporter's license." Authorization to export is determined by the transaction: what the item is, where it is going, who will receive it, and what it will be used for. The majority of U.S. commercial exports do not require a license. The three types of export authorization are: no license required (NLR); license, and license exception.[30]

No License Required (NLR)

Most exports from the United States do not require a license, and are therefore exported under the designation "NLR." Except in those relatively few transactions when a license requirement applies because the destination is subject to embargo or because of a proliferation end-use or end-user, no license is required when:

> the item to be shipped is not on the CCL (i.e. it's EAR99); or
> the item is on the CCL but there is no "X" in the box on the Country Chart under the appropriate reason for control column on the row for the country of destination. (See the country chart example earlier in this chapter)

In each of these situations, you would enter "NLR" on your export documents.

License

If your item requires a license to be exported, you must apply for one to the BIS. If your application is approved, you will have an export license number and expiration date to use on your export documents. A BIS-issued license is usually valid for two years.

License Exception

If a license is normally required for your transaction, a license exception may be available. License Exceptions, and the conditions on their use, are set forth in the EAR. If an export is eligible for a license exception, use the designation of that license exception (example, LVS, GBS, and TMP) on the export documents.

APPLYING FOR AN EXPORT LICENSE

If an export license is required, exporters must prepare a Form BIS-748P, "Multipurpose Application Form" and submit it for review and approval. The application form can be used for requesting authority to export or re-export, or to request BIS to classify your item for you. Requirements for submitting a license are detailed in the EAR.

The best and fastest way to submit an export application form is to use the on-line Simplified Network Application Process Redesign (SNAP-R), http://www.bis.doc.gov/snap/index.html. SNAP-R includes enhanced security, the ability to attach supporting documentation electronically, user access rights, and the ability for BIS licensing officers to view work items and supporting documents electronically. Exporters can also request a Form BIS-748P from the U.S. Department of Commerce Office of Exporter Services. Exporters must be certain to follow the instructions on the form carefully. In most cases, technical brochures and support documentation must also be included.[31]

Export License Application Processing

BIS conducts a complete analysis of the license application along with all documentation submitted in support of the application. The Bureau reviews the item, its destination, its end use, and considers the reliability of each party to the transaction. In addition to the review, applications are often sent for interagency review by the Departments of State, Energy, and/or Defense.

License Status

For the status of pending export license applications and commodity classification requests, exporters can contact the **System for Tracking Export License Applications (STELA)**. STELA is an automated voice response system that will provide up-to-the-minute status on any pending license application or commodity classification. Provide the number of your license application in order to determine licensing status.[32]

How to Avoid Delays

If submitting a hard copy application through the mail, exporters should take care to avoid common errors that often account for delays in processing. These are:

> failing to sign the application;
> failing to submit a typewritten application;
> inadequately responding to the section of the application where the specific end use of the products or technical data is to be described;
> answering vaguely or entering "unknown" is likely to delay the application process or even cause a rejection of the application, and
> inadequately responding to the section of the application, "Description of Commodity or Technical Data."[33]

Exporters must be specific and are encouraged to attach additional material that thoroughly explains the product.

HELP WITH EXPORT ADMINISTRATION REGULATIONS

The Government Printing Office's Export Administration Regulation Web site at www. bis.doc.gov/policiesandregulations/index.htm, contains an up-to-date database of the entire Export Administration Regulations (EAR), including the Commerce Control List, the Commerce Country Chart, and a link to the Denied Persons List. EAR revisions are incorporated into this site within 48 to 72 hours and the EAR can be viewed, downloaded, and searched. This Web site also includes a table with all the Federal Register notices that revise the text of the EAR since its complete revision in 1996. In addition, users can subscribe to GPO's paper version of the EAR from this Web site. Finally, users can e-mail the Regulatory Policy Division directly from this Web site, to get answers to general questions about the EAR.[34]

> ## SPOTLIGHT ON GLOBAL TRADE 5.2:
> Summary of Steps to Take to Process Your Export
>
> > Verify that the export is under U.S. Department of Commerce jurisdiction.
> > Classify your item according to the Commerce Control List and the Export Control Classification Number (ECCN). Unlisted items, if still subject to USDOC jurisdiction, will be designated EAR99. The ECCN number will identify the reasons for control (see the polygraph example in text).
> > Cross-reference the ECCN controls against the Commerce Country Chart to see if a license is required. If yes, determine if a License Exception is available before applying for a license.
> > Check that no illegal or restricted end-users or end-uses are involved with your export transaction. If restricted end-users or end-uses are involved, determine if you can proceed with the transaction or must apply for a license.
> > Export your item using the correct ECCN and the appropriate symbol (NLR, license exception, or license number and expiration date) on your export documentation, such as Shipper's Export Declaration.

The **NTIS EAR Marketplace** Web site also offers an up-to-date searchable EAR database and files that are downloadable and viewable. In addition, the EAR Marketplace has a combined, downloadable and searchable version of the Denied Persons List, the Entity List, the Debarred List, and the Specially Designated Nationals List. Subscribers to the EAR on-line database are notified by email whenever a change occurs to any of these lists. The EAR Marketplace also includes a table with all the Federal Register notices that revise the text of the EAR since its complete revision in March 1996.[35]

BASIC EXPORT DOCUMENTS

Certain documents are commonly used in exporting; but which of them are necessary in a particular transaction depends on the requirements of the U.S. government and the government of the importing country. Documentation required for export shipments varies widely according to the country of destination and the type of product being shipped. Determining what additional documentation is necessary can be a frustrating process.

Exporters may want to consider having a reputable freight forwarder handle the formidable amount of paperwork that exporting requires, as forwarders are specialists in this process. Following are a list of common documents and information resources to help with this process:[36]

Shipper's Export Declaration (SED or Form 7525-V)

The **Shipper's Export Declaration (SED)** is a government-required document for every single export item over $2,500. It is available through the Government Printing Office and a number of other commercial outlets. As of September 30, 2008, the SED must be electronically filed using **AESDirect**, the U.S. Census Bureau's free, Internet-based system for filing SED information to the Automated Export System (AES). It is the electronic alternative to filing a paper SED, and can be used by U.S. Principal Parties in Interest (USP-PIs), forwarders, or anyone else responsible for export reporting. AESDirect significantly streamlines the export reporting process by reducing the paperwork burden on the trade community, reducing costly document handling and storage, and ensuring that export information is filed in a timely manner.

AESDirect improves the quality of the export trade statistics, helping the Census Bureau provide the government and the public more accurate information.

Commercial Invoice

A bill for the goods from the seller to the buyer is known as the **commercial invoice**. These invoices are often used by governments to determine the true value of goods when assessing customs duties. Governments that use the commercial invoice to control imports will often specify its form, content, number of copies, language to be used, and other characteristics.

Certificate of Origin

The **certificate of origin** is only required by some countries. In many cases, a statement of origin printed on company letterhead will suffice. Special certificates are needed for countries with which the United States has special trade agreements, such as Mexico, Canada, and Israel. NAFTA Certificate of Origin is needed for shipments to Mexico and Canada.

CE Mark Requirements

In order to market export products into the European Union (EU), goods must meet certain requirements that are identified by the CE Mark. Once a manufacturer has earned a CE Mark for its product, it may affix the CE Mark to its product, and then it can be marketed throughout the EU without having to undergo further modifications in each EU member country.

Exporter's Bill of Lading

The **exporter's bill of lading (B/L)** is a contract between the owner of the goods, usually the manufacturer/exporter and the carrier (as with domestic shipments). There are two types: a *straight bill of lading* which is non-negotiable and a *negotiable* or *shipper's order bill of lading*. The latter can be bought, sold, or traded while the goods are in transit. The customer usually needs an original B/L as proof of ownership to take possession of the goods. If the mode of transportation is via air, the bill of lading is called an air waybill. Air freight shipments can never be made in negotiable form.

Insurance Certificate

An **insurance certificate** is used to assure the buyer (consignee) that insurance will cover the loss of or damage to the cargo during transit. Policies can be obtained from freight forwarders or marine insurance providers.

Export Packing List

Considerably more detailed and informative than a standard domestic packing list, the **export packing list** is important as it itemizes the material in each individual package and indicates the type of shipping package, such as a box, crate, drum, or carton. Both commercial stationers and freight forwarders carry packing list forms.

Import License

Import licenses, if required, are the responsibility of the importer. Including a copy with the packet of export documentation, however, can sometimes help avoid problems with customs in the destination country.

Consular Invoice

A document that is required by some foreign countries, often in the language of the importing country, the **consular invoice** describes the shipment of goods and shows information such as the consignor (seller), consignee (buyer), and value of the shipment. If required, copies are available from the destination country's embassy or consulate in the U.S.

Inspection Certificate

An **inspection certificate** is required by some purchasers and countries in order to guarantee the specifications of the goods shipped are the same as originally ordered. This is usually performed by a third party and often obtained from independent testing organizations.

Dock Receipt and Warehouse Receipt

Documents that are used to transfer accountability when the export item is moved by the domestic carrier to the port of embarkation and left with the ship line for export are **dock receipts** and **warehouse receipts**.

Destination Control Statement

The **destination control statement** appears on the commercial invoice and ocean or air waybill of lading to notify the carrier and all foreign parties that the item can be exported only to certain destinations.

Export License

An **export license** is a U.S. Government document required for "dual use" exports (commercial items which could have military applications), or exports to embargoed countries. These licenses, granted by the BIS, are transaction-based—not based on the individual exporter, although they are the applicants to the license. As such, there is no such thing as an "exporter's license." However, most export transactions do not require specific approval from the U.S. Government, as they are classified as No License Required (NLR). Before shipping products, exporters should be sure they understand the concept of dual-use and the basic export control regulations.

In addition to the U.S. export control policy for dual-use items, the Bureau of Industry and Security is also charged with the development, implementation, and interpretation of the anti-boycott provisions of the Export Administration Act. The anti-boycott provisions encourage, and in some cases require, U.S. traders to refuse to participate in foreign boycotts that the United States does not sanction. They are also required to report receipt of boycott-related requests.[37]

SUMMARY

The U.S. Department of Commerce, Bureau of Industry and Security (BIS) is charged with the development, implementation and enforcement of the U.S. Export Administration Regulations (EAR). These regulations control the export and re-export of most, but not all commercial and non-commercial goods, services and technologies. Other U.S. government agencies, including the U.S. Departments of State, Homeland Security, Treasury, Defense, and Energy, also play critical roles in export control and nonproliferation activities both within the United States and outside its borders.

The primary reasons for export controls are national security, foreign policy, and short supply. The key questions to ask is determining whether or not a commerce export license is required are: What are you exporting? Where are your exports going? Who will receive your exports? And: What will be the end-use of your exports? Export authorization is determined by each transaction; there is no such license called an "Exporter's License."

Classification, by Export Control Classification Number (ECCN), as listed on the Commerce Control List (CCL), will describe the export controls placed on that item.

Most U.S. export controls pertain to *dual-use* commodities, software, and technology. Dual-use items are those that have predominantly commercial uses, but also have military or proliferation applications that make their export contrary to U.S. national security, foreign policy or economic interests.

Perhaps the easiest method of export application is the Simplified Network Application Process Redesign (SNAP-R).

One of three options must be selected and referenced on all export documentation: 1) No License Required (NLR); 2) license (required), and 3) license exception. Only the "license required" designation requires written authorization from the Commerce Department's Bureau of Industry and Security. NLR and License Exception are assumed grants of authority to export—but subject to commodity and country restrictions outlined in the EARs.

In March 2009, the U.S. government announced a series of new steps to ensure that dual-use export control policies and practices support the National Security Strategy while facilitating U.S. economic and technological leadership. The new program includes revised procedures concerning foreign end users, U.S. competitiveness, and transparency.

U.S. exporters cannot export to just anyone. A number of regulatory procedures prohibit this, including the Prohibitive Parties Lists, which includes the entity list; the Treasury Department's Specially Designated Nationals and Blocked Persons List; the Unverified List, and the Denied Persons List.

The U.S. export control agency for dual-use items, the Bureau of Industry and Security, is also charged with the development, implementation and interpretation of the anti-boycott provisions of the Export Administration Act.

Key Terms

- AESDirect
- Bureau of Industry and Security (BIS)
- Certificate of origin
- Commercial invoice
- Commerce Country Chart (CCC)
- Commerce Control List (CCL)
- Consular invoice
- Debarred list
- Denied Persons List
- Destination control statement
- Dock receipt
- Dual-use items
- EAR99
- End-use Violations
- Entity list
- Export Control Classification Number (ECCN)
- Export Enforcement Arm (EEA)
- Export license
- Export packing list
- Freight forwarder
- Import license
- Insurance certificate
- Inspection certificate
- License exception
- NTIS Ear Marketplace
- Office of Foreign Assets Control of the Treasury Department (OFAC)
- Shipper's Export Declaration (SED)
- System for Tracking Export License Applications (STELA)
- Treasury Department Specially Designated Nationals and Blocked Persons List
- Unverified list
- Voluntary self-disclosures (VSDs)
- Warehouse receipt

Review Questions

1. Describe the primary purpose for U.S. export controls.

2. What is meant by "dual-use items?"

3. What are the four questions that must be answered before determining the need for a commerce export license?

4. What are the functions of the Commerce Control List, the Export Control Classification Number, and the Commerce Country Chart?

5. Explain the three forms of export authorization and identify the only form that requires written authorization from the BIS.

6. Can U.S. individuals or firms export to whomever they wish? If not, what restrictions are imposed and are they consistent with our democratic system?

Discussion Questions and Activities

1. Go to the primary U.S. Government Web site for export controls, www.bis.doc.gov, and review the following brochures: "Don't Let This Happen to You," and "Introduction to the Commerce Department's Export Controls."

2. Debate the pros and cons of restricting U.S. firms from trading with countries designated as unfriendly to us or our allies or as harboring terrorists, while our competitors are not similarly restricted.

3. Think of an American product—one actually made in the U.S.A.—and go through the export classification process, starting with the CCL, to determine the ECCN, and then consult the CCC to determine the controls, if any, on your case study country. Do you think those controls are reasonable and fair to the exporter? Are they consistent with our free-enterprise economy?

References

1. Export Enforcement, Bureau of Industry and Security, U.S. Department of Commerce. "Don't Let this Happen to You: Actual Investigations of Export Control and Antiboycott Violations." July 2008 edition, p. 13. Retrieved on February 10, 2009, from www.bis.doc.gov/compliance andenforcement/dontletthis happentoyou-2008.pdf.

2. Ibid. p. 18

3. BIS Mission Statement. Retrieved on February 10, 2009, from www.bis.doc.gov/about/mission.htm.

4. "Adapting Dual-Use Controls to Address Evolving Economic Opportunities and Threats," Remarks of Acting Under Secretary Daniel O. Hill, Bureau of Industry and Security's Fourth Annual Export Control Forum, Newport Beach, California, March 16, 2009. Retrieved on March 30, 2009, from www.bis.doc.gov/news/2009/export_control_forum_speech.htm.

5. Op. cit., BIS, "Don't Let . . ."

6. Ibid.

7. Ibid.

8. "Update on Voluntary Self-Disclosures at the Bureau of Industry and Security." Retrieved on February 11, 2009, from http://bis.doc.gov/news/2007/cases/vsd.paper.pdf.

9. "Introduction to Commerce Department Export Controls," Bureau of Industry and Security, U.S. Department of Commerce. Retrieved on February 9, 2009, from http:// bis.doc.gov/licensing/exportingbasics.htm.

10. Ibid.

11. Ibid.

12. Ibid.

13. Ibid.

14. Op. cit., Export control Forum, speech by Daniel O. Hill

15. "Validated End User (VEU)." Retrieved on February 10, 2008, from www.bis.doc.gov/finalchina.html.

16. "Department of Commerce Publishers Antiboycott Penalty Guidelines." Retrieved on February 13, 2009, from www.bis.doc.gov/news.

17. Op. cit., Intro to Export Controls.

18. Ibid, pg. 2.

19. Ibid.

20. "ECCN: Questions and Answers." Retrieved on February 20, 2009, from www.bis.doc.gov/licensing/do_1_need aneccn.html.

21. "EAR99." Retrieved on February 20, 2009, from http://bis.doc.gov/exportlicensingqanda.htm.

22. "Embargoed export destinations," Office of Foreign Assets Control. Retrieved on February 19, 2009, from www.treas.gov/ofac.

23. "Commerce Country Chart." Retrieved on February 20, 2009, from www.bis.doc.gov/licensing/bis_exports.pdf.

24. "Export Licensing," Bureau of Industry and Security, U.S. Department of Commerce. Retrieved on February 20, 2009, from http://bis.doc.gov/licensing/exportingbasics.htm.

25. "The Entity List," Bureau of Industry and Security, U.S. Department of Commerce. Retrieved on February 20, 2009, from www.bis.doc.gov/entities/default.htm.

26. "Know Your Customer and Red Flags Guidance," Bureau of Industry and Security, U.S. Department of Commerce. Retrieved on February 20, 2009, from www.bis.doc.gov/complianceandenforcement/knowyourcustomerguidance.htm and www.bis.doc.gov/complianceandenforcement/redflagindicators.htm.

27. "The Denial List," Bureau of Industry and Security, U.S. Department of Commerce. Retrieved on February 20, 2009, from www.bis.doc.gov/dpl/thedeniallist.asp.

28. "Specially Designated Nationals List," Office of Foreign Assets control. Retrieved on February 21, 2009, from www .bis.doc.gov/licensing/bis_ exports.pdf.

29. "The Unverified List," Bureau of Industry and Security, U.S. Department of Commerce. Retrieved on February 20, 2009, from www.bis.doc.gov/ enforcement/unverifiedlist/ unverified_parties.html.

30. Op. cit. www.bis.doc.gov/ licensing/exportingbasics.htm, p. 6.

31. "Multipurpose Application form," at www.bis.doc.gov/ licensing/applying4lic.htm, and "SNAP-R," at www.bis.doc.gov/ snap/index.htm.

32. "System for Tracking Export License Applications (STELA)." Retrieved on February 20, 2009, from www.bis.doc.gov/ Licensing/STELA4U.htm.

33. "Export License Application Processing: How to Avoid Delays." Retrieved on February 20, 2009, from www.bis.doc.gov/ licensing/applying4lic.htm.

34. "U.S. Export Administration Regulations." Retrieved on February 20, 2009, from www .bis.doc.gov/policiesand regulations/index.htm.

35. "The NTIS EAT Marketplace." Retrieved on February 20, 2009, from www.bis.doc .gov/policiesandregulations/ index.htm.

36. "Global Trade Terms." Retrieved on February 21, 2009, from www.bis.doc.gov/ exportbasics/eg_main_017485 .asp, and http://export.gov/ logistics/eg_main_018121.asp.

37. "Antiboycott Compliance." Retrieved on February 21, 2009, from www.bis.doc.gov/ complianceandenforcement/ antiboycottcompliance.htm.

Importing
into the
United States

Part III

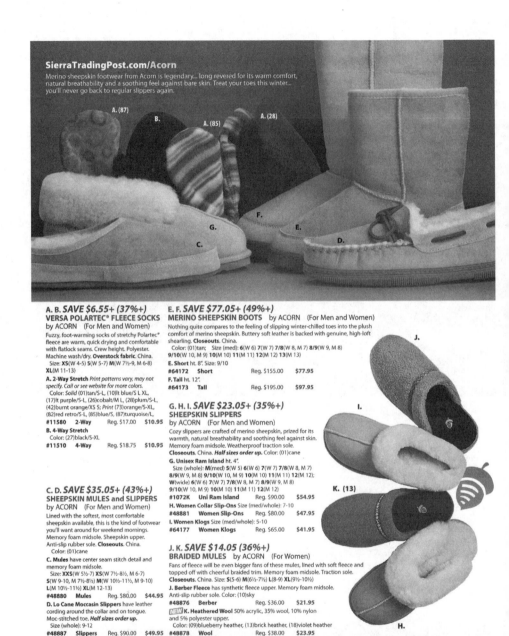

Figure 6.1 **The goods offered by retailers such as Sierra Trading Post come from throughout the world.**

● ● ● ● ● ●

6

BASICS OF IMPORTING INTO THE UNITED STATES

Adventure Edge is the name of just one of the catalogs of Sierra Trading Post, yet it captures the spirit of this outdoor and casual apparel, home furnishings, and active gear outlet retailer. Featuring clothing for men, women, and children, plus equipment for hiking, climbing, skiing, and fishing, the company has retail stores in Cheyenne and Cody, Wyoming, plus Reno, Nevada, and Meridian, Idaho. Through its many catalogs, Sierra Trading Post reaches customers throughout the world who then contact the retailer by telephone or through its online store, SierraTradingPost.com. Orders are received by some 200 telephone service representatives in two Cheyenne service centers.

hy is this in-home outlet retailer so popular? By buying closeouts, overstocks, and some irregular merchandise, Sierra Trading Post offers well-known brands such as Columbia Sportswear, The North Face, Rockport, Teva, and others at deep discount prices. And the sources for its goods read like a world map; in addition to the United States, Austria, Canada, China, Latvia, Laos, Peru, England, Vietnam, Sri Lanka, Thailand, Cambodia, the Philippines, Italy, Taiwan, Germany, and Korea are some of the nations whose factories provide the retailer with its goods.

How did Sierra Trading Post come to be a global importer? It all began with the faith and perseverance of its owner, Keith Richardson who had always wanted to be an entrepreneur. When asked to take a lesser job at Sportif, USA, where he had recently been made president, Keith decided that it was time to strike out on his own. The idea of Sierra Trading Post struck him as a viable concept, so he leased a warehouse and, with the help of his artist son, Ron, created the first catalog and mailed it to 100,000 people. The response was phenomenal. In a few years, the company had developed more specialized catalogs featuring women's clothing, shoes, outdoor, travel, and adventure gear, plus men's designer apparel. The retail stores also grew and the Web site was put in place. The strong faith and beliefs of founder Keith Richardson have created a company truly global in nature.[1]

IMPORTING IS A PRIVILEGE, NOT A RIGHT

The Internet has made it easy for anyone to find and purchase products or services from almost anywhere in the world. However, many individuals and businesses are discovering that getting a foreign-bought item successfully imported into the United States is much more complicated, time consuming—and expensive—than they ever imagined.

WHY IMPORTS?

If imports are time-consuming and possibly costly to bring into the country, why bother? A check of your closet is like a walk through a global marketplace. One of your jackets may have come from Italy; your shoes may be from Spain, and your denim jeans from Indonesia. Your living room sofa may be French-inspired while the floor it sits on is made from Brazilian cherry wood. Our clothes, homes, and daily lives are surrounded by imports.

As the world's largest consumer market, we are the target of producers of goods and services from virtually every country around the globe. Americans are acquisitive, and we seem to have an insatiable appetite for imports as well as domestic merchandise.

The United States imports over $2 trillion worth of products annually from more than 150 countries. U.S. Customs and Border Protection officials project that this amount will triple by 2015, as American consumers continue to demand foreign products.[2]

Figure 6.2 Import buyers have to make a number of decisions even before choosing goods on their buying trips.

....

[U.S IMPORT VALUE]

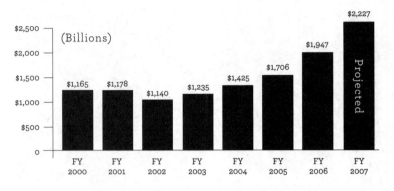

(Billions)

Source: U.S. Customs and Border Protection.

Figure 6.3a
**The growth
in U.S. imports
since 2003 was
steady and rapid,
until 2008.**

. . . .

[TOP FIVE IMPORTING COUNTRIES]

For all commodities in billions:

2006   2007   2008 (January to April)

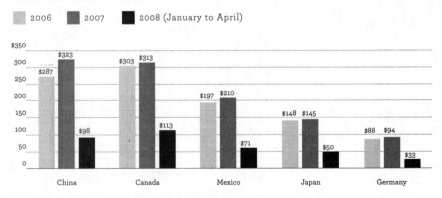

Figure 6.3b China is now challenging Canada as the number one source of U.S. Imports.
. . . .

Source: U.S. Department of Commerce; U.S. International Trade Commission.

Why is the United States the largest importing nation in the world? There are many reasons, but the primary one is the need to satisfy consumer demand; a second reason is that consumers have the capability to pay for all of these purchases. They seek out the unique and find it often in imported goods. And the demand for these goods appears in all price ranges from the designer level using fine fabrics and complex construction to the moderate and budget price ranges using less expensive materials and fabrication. Without imports in all price ranges, the fashion industry, including manufacturers, wholesalers, and retailers, could not survive because it could not serve the needs and wants of its markets.

Although price is still an important consideration in deciding on an import, today's customer is also looking for quality, value, uniqueness, and sustainability. Of course, the status appeal of a Rolex watch, Ferrari automobile, or Chanel handbag cannot be ignored, but American-made brands have come to challenge imports in fashion areas such as wines (consider Napa Valley), home furnishings (Baker, and Henredon), and apparel (Oscar de la Renta, Joseph Abboud, and St. John).

Although major trading partners and sources for U.S. imports remain Canada, China, Mexico, Japan, and Germany (see Figure 6.3b), shifts have also taken place in countries of origin for imports at both the high and low end. China, India, and Pakistan are replacing Japan as the source for high-tech electronics such as computers, while South Korea's Samsung is now one of the leading manufacturers of cell phones and television sets. Quality automobiles, stocked with many imported parts, now come from U.S.-based assembly plants owned by South Korean, German, Japanese, and—expected soon—Chinese and Indian companies. While much of the profit made selling cars to Americans heads back to the foreign owners (creating wealth overseas), the foreign car companies are investing in their U.S. plants at a high rate, hiring American workers and stimulating local economies.

Officials in Mississippi lured a $950 million Nissan plant with a $295 million subsidy deal. While the plant was still under construction, the company announced an expansion of the project that also involved an increase in the subsidy package to $363 million. State officials estimate that the Nissan factory in Grenada has spawned the creation of 25,000 supplier and support jobs that generate a combined $500 million in economic activity.[3]

RISKS TO IMPORTING

Like any business venture, purchasing goods from factories and suppliers thousands of miles away involves certain risks. The language may be unfamiliar, as are the sets of laws, and the forms of protection not afforded foreign traders. Global sourcing may add several weeks to the **lead time**, the amount of time between ordering goods and receiving the shipment from overseas. For fashion merchandise, importers must consider whether the goods will still be in demand when they reach the store. Slow or unpredictable delivery—often due to outdated transportation systems or infrastructure failures—can result in undue delivery delays. If goods cannot reach the retailer's shelves on time, retailers need to sever even long-standing relationships.

[IMPORTERS BY FREQUENCY OF SHIPMENTS - FY 2006]

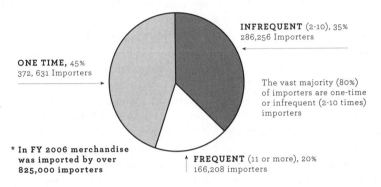

INFREQUENT (2-10), 35%
286,256 Importers

ONE TIME, 45%
372, 631 Importers

The vast majority (80%)
of importers are one-time
or infrequent (2-10 times)
importers

* In FY 2006 merchandise
was imported by over
825,000 importers

↑ **FREQUENT** (11 or more), 20%
166,208 importers

Figure 6.4 Over 825,000 importers brought shipments into the United States in FY 2006, through more than 300 seaports, land border crossings, postal facilities, and other ports of entry.
• • • • • • • •

Source: U.S. Customs and Border Protection.

Strict U.S. import controls imposed after the 2001 terrorist attacks can hold up entry of a shipment for weeks or months, depending on the country of origin, as the government is determined to inspect a greater percentage of the over 70,000 truck, rail, and sea containers that arrive in this country every day, at over 300 seaports, land border crossings, postal facilities, and other ports-of-entry. Over 825,000 importers brought shipments into the U.S. last year. Approximately 80 percent of these shipments are by one-time or infrequent importers.[4]

Chapter 7 will address the new controls and procedures that have impacted all importers, such as the **Container Security Initiative (CSI)** which focuses on the threat to border security and global trade posed by the potential for terrorist use of a maritime container to deliver a weapon. The plan is to station multidisciplinary teams of U.S. officers from both CPB and Immigration and Customs Enforcement (ICE) to work together with host foreign government counterparts.

REASONS FOR IMPORTING

Nevertheless, as you can tell from the chapter's opening vignette, Keith Richardson and other retailers have many reasons for searching out goods from other countries. These include: customer demand (the market); opportunity to offer a unique assortment of a variety of goods; and price.

THE MARKET

The first and most important step in deciding whether to import goods is to determine an existing demand for those goods in the United States. That demand is called a **market**, or a particular group of people, companies or other organizations that not only have the desire to buy goods but also have the means (money or credit) to pay for them. This chapter focuses on **import traders**, those who import goods for resale, as opposed to manufacturers who may import **components**, materials and parts that go into a finished good that is sold domestically.

Remember that the demand for any product or service depends upon the marketer's ability to satisfy the needs or wants of the target market consumer or industrial user—at a price each is willing to pay. Even though a potential import may be attractive for a number of reasons—price, quality, uniqueness, or design—the actual size of the market cannot be assessed accurately until you know how much the item will cost, delivered to the United States. In international trade, a company may quote a **first price**, the manufacturer's selling price in the factory showroom, but the importer must calculate the actual **landed cost**, which includes all shipping and entry costs and duty charges to the port of foreign entry.

Figure 6.5 The Port of Long Beach, California, is one of the world's busiest seaports and a leading gateway for trade between the United States and Asia. It supports millions of jobs nationally and provides consumers and businesses with billions of dollars in goods each year.

. . . .

The delivered-into-store cost plus delivery and insurance to reach the store and overhead expenses and profit margin, will determine the resale price of the imported goods. For example, the retail prices for fashion goods are often four or five times the price quoted in the foreign showroom. Figuring out the actual retail price should help to indicate the potential for sales and ultimate profit from your import.

Some Questions to Ask about the Market for an Imported Product

Before buying any foreign goods, here are some questions a potential importer needs to ask:
> Is there an existing domestic need and demand for the product?
> If yes, who are the major suppliers of these products and what are their market shares?
> Are the suppliers domestic or foreign companies?
> Is the market dominated by one or two large companies or is it divided among many small suppliers?
> What is the approximate size, in dollar amount, of the current market?
> Who are the current **end-users**, the final consumers or industrial users of a product, for this item?
> Where are they located?
> What is their average income?
> What is their disposable income?
> What are their spending habits?
> What advertising media are they exposed to?
> What kind of work do they do?
> Are they typically members of civic or religious organizations?
> What kind of message will they respond to?
> How much will they be prepared to buy?
> What will they be prepared to pay?
> How often will they buy?
> Which domestic or imported products compete with those you intend to import?
> How are these products distributed in the United States?
> What are their average manufactured, wholesale, and retail price points?
> As a category, how are they regarded in the market place—needed, wanted or neutral?
> What competitive advantage (design, warranties, and after-sales service) do existing domestic or imported products have in the current market?
> What competitive advantages would the new imports have?

Keeping in mind that the main objective in business is to make a profit, the best way to do that is to identify a substantial, lucrative, long-term market for the products you plan to import.

CONDUCTING A S.W.O.T. ANALYSIS

When a company considers importing, it should first review its own situation by conducting an assessment of its strengths, weaknesses, opportunities, and threats, known as a

[S.W.O.T. ANALYSIS]

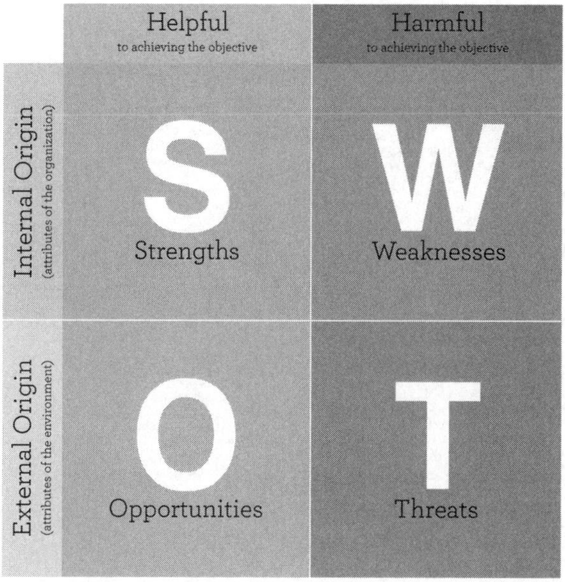

Figure 6.6
Armed with a
S.W.O.T. analysis,
a business can
more accurately
identify potentially
successful import
opportunities.

. . . .

S. W. O. T. analysis. The purpose is for the organization to realize its own major attributes (strengths); areas where it can improve (weaknesses); internal and external factors that can impede its progress (threats), and areas where it can capitalize on its strengths (opportunities). The goal of this exercise is for the company to maximize its opportunities while minimizing its risks.

Armed with a S.W.O.T. analysis, an organization is then prepared to analyze its domestic and international competitors in order to identify potentially profitable marketing opportunities.

Before trying to source goods from foreign countries, potential importers should first research suppliers in the United States to determine if the types of goods they are seeking are already being imported into the country and, if so, from which countries. The competitive research data provided by the S.W.O.T. analysis will reveal the strengths, weaknesses, opportunities, and threats—competitive or environmental—of those firms who may challenge your success.

Domestic suppliers can be identified by referring to trade association directories, manufacturers' indexes or industry journals. Very valuable research tools are the annual show issue of leading trade publications for specific industries. Usually available at industry trade association-sponsored shows and conventions, these special publications list all major manufacturers, wholesalers, distributors, manufacturer's representatives, and often leading retailers—a market researcher's dream come true.

The case for importing a certain product can be made much stronger if domestic suppliers can't match the quality, price, delivery or unique features of your potential import.

Personnel:

Executive Director: Elaine Strass

Membership Manager: Barbara Abbott

Meetings Manager: Suzy Brown

E-Mail: sbrown@genetics-gsa.org

Historical Note

Organized in 1931 in New Orleans as an outgrowth of the Genetics Section of the American Society of Zoologists and the Botanical Society of America. Incorporated in Maryland in 1984. Membership: $120/year (full member), $50/year (student).

Meetings/Conferences:

2008 – San Diego, CA(Town & Country Hotel)/Apr. 2-6

2009 – Chicago, IL(Sheraton Chicago Hotel & Towers)/March 4-8

2010 – Washington, DC(Marriott Wardman Park Hotel)/Apr. 7-10

2011 – San Diego, CA(Town & Country Hotel)/March 30-Apr. 3

Number of non-conference events/year: 3

Publications:

Genetics. monthly.

Membership Directory. biennially.

GSA Newsletter. quarterly.

Geochemical Society *(1955)*

Dept. of Earth and Planetary Sciences Washington Univ., One Brookings Dr., CB 1169

St. Louis, MO 63130-4899

Tel: (314)935-4131   *Fax:* (314)935-4121

E-Mail: gsoffice@geochemsoc.org

Web Site: www.geochemsoc.org

Members: 2800 individuals

Staff: 2

Annual Budget: $100-250,000

Personnel:

Manager, Business: Seth Davis

E-Mail: seth.davis@geochemsoc.org

Administrative Assistant: Kathryn Hall

E-Mail: kathryn.hall@geochemsoc.org

Historical Note

Founded November 7, 1955 and incorporated in the District of Columbia in 1956. Encourages the application of chemistry to the solution of geological and cosmological problems. Membership: $30/year (Professional); $10/year (Student); $12/year (Senior-above 65 years of age).

Meetings/Conferences:

Annual: Fall/1,600

2008 – Houston, TX/Oct. 5-9

Publications:

G3 – Geochemistry, Geophysics, Geosystems. Reviews in Mineralogy & Geochemistry. quarterly.

Geochemical News. quarterly. adv.

Geochimica et Cosmochimica Acta. semi-monthly.

Elements magazine. irregular. adv.

Geological Society of America *(1888)*

P.O Box 9140

Boulder, CO 80301-9140

Tel: (303)357-1000   *Fax:* (303)357-1074

Toll Free: (800)472 - 1988

E-Mail: gsa@geosociety.org

Web Site: www.geosociety.org

Members: 20000 individuals

Staff: 50

Annual Budget: $5-10,000,000

Personnel:

Executive Director: John W. Hess

E-Mail: jhess@geosociety.org

Senior Director, Information Technology: Todd Berggren

E-Mail: tberggren@geosociety.org

Director, Communications and Marketing: Ann Cairns

Director, Meetings: Melissa Cummiskey

Controller: Kay Dragon

E-Mail: kdragon@geosociety.org

Director, Membership: Pat Kilmer

Director, Education and Outreach: Gary Lewis

E-Mail: glewis@geosociety.org

Director, Strategic Initiatives: Deborah Nelson

Director, Publications: Jon Olsen

E-Mail: jolsen@geosociety.org

Historical Note

Founded in 1888 and incorporated in New York in 1929. GSA includes topical divisions, specializing in Archaeological Geology, Coal Geology, Engineering Geology, Geobiology/Geomicrobiology, Geology and Society, Geophysics, Geoscience Education, History of Geology, Hydrogeology, International Division, Limneology, Planetary Geology, Quaternary Geology and Geomorphology, Sedimentary Geology, and Structural Geology and Tectonics. GSA has six regional sections, each of which holds its own annual meeting in the spring. Also has 35 member, associated and allied societies. GSA is a member society of the American Geological Institute. Membership: $65/year (members/fellows).

Meetings/Conferences:

Annual Meetings: Fall

2008 – Chicago, IL/Oct. 26-30

2009 – Portland, OR/Oct. 18-21

2010 – Denver, CO/Oct. 31-Nov. 3

2011 – Minneapolis, MN(Minneapolis)/Oct. 9-12

Publications:

Geological Society of America Bulletin. irregular.

Environmental & Engineering Geoscience. quarterly.

GSA Today. monthly. adv.

Geology. monthly. adv.

Geoscience and Remote Sensing Society *(1962)*

445 Hoes Ln.

Piscataway, NJ 08854

Tel: (732)981-0060   *Fax:* (732)981-1721

Web Site: www.grss-ieee.org

Members: 2100 individuals

Tax Exempt Status: 501(c)(3)

Personnel:

President: Dr. Leung Tsang

E-Mail: tsang@ee.washington.edu

Communications and Informatin Policy Representative: Dr. David B. Kunkee

E-Mail: David.Kunkee@aero.org

Historical Note

A technical society of the Institute of Electrical and Electronics Engineers (IEEE). Membership in the Society, open only to IEEE members, includes a subscription to a technical periodical in the field published by IEEE. Has no paid officers or full-time staff.

Publications:

GRSS Newsletter. quarterly.

Transactions on Geoscience and Remote Sensing Journal. monthly.

JSTARS. quarterly.

Geoscience Information Society *(1965)*

3026 Shapiro Science Library, University of Michigan,

Ann Arbor, MI 48109-1185

Tel: (734)936-3079   *Fax:* (734)763-9813

E-Mail: pyocum@umich.edu

Web Site: www.geoinfo.org

Members: 200 individuals

Annual Budget: $10-25,000

Tax Exempt Status: 501(c)(3)

Personnel:

President: Patricia B. Yocum

E-Mail: pyocum@umich.edu

Chair, Membership: Miriam Kennard

Secretary: Andrea Twiss-Brooks

E-Mail: atbrooks@uchicago.edu

Historical Note

Founded in Kansas City, GIS was incorporated in the District of Columbia in 1966. Affiliated with the Geological Society of America and the American Geological Institute. GIS membership includes national and international representation from colleges and universities, business and industry, publishing, geological surveys, geological societies

and other aspects of the field. Membership: $45/year (individual); $100/year (institution); $20/year (student or retired); $135/year (sustaining).

Meetings/Conferences:

Annual Meetings: Fall

2008 – Houston, TX/Oct. 5-9

2009 – Portland, OR/Oct. 18-21

2010 – Denver, CO/Oct. 31-Nov. 3

2011 – Minneapolis, MN/Oct. 9-12

Number of non-conference events/year: 5

Publications:

GIS Newsletter. bi-monthly.

Proceedings. annually.

Membership Directory. annually.

Membership List Available to Non-members

Geospatial Information Technology Association *(1982)*

14456 E. Evans Ave.

Aurora, CO 80014

Tel: (303)337-0513   *Fax:* (303)337-1001

E-Mail: info@gita.org

Web Site: www.gita.org

Members: 244 organizations; 2200 individuals

Staff: 11

Annual Budget: $2-5,000,000

Personnel:

Executive Director: Robert M. Samborski

E-Mail: bsamborski@gita.org

Membership Services Manager: Lisa Connor

E-Mail: lconnor@gita.org

Education and Exhibits Coordinator: Julie Eckhart

E-Mail: jeckhart@gita.org

Manager, Marketing and Communications: Kathryn Henton

E-Mail: khenton@gita.org

Deputy Executive Director: Henry Rosales

E-Mail: hrosales@gita.org

Education Coordinator: James Sakamoto

E-Mail: jsakamoto@gita.org

Historical Note

GITA is a non-profit, educational association which fosters information exchange and educational opportunities and scientific research and development in the field of geospatial information technology. Membership: $125/year (individual).

Meetings/Conferences:

Conference Chair: Julie Eckhart

Annual Meetings: Spring/3,200

2008 – Seattle, WA/March 1-1

2008 – Houston, TX(Westchase Hotel)/Sept. 21-24

2009 – Tampa, FL(Tampa Convention Center)/Apr. 19-22

2009 – Houston, TX(Marriott Westchase Hotel)/Sept. 14-16

2010 – Phoenix, AZ(Phoenix Convention Center)/Apr. 25-28

Publications:

Geospatial Technology Report. annually.

GIS for Oil & Gas Conference Proceedings. annually.

GITA Networks. irregular. adv.

Conference Proceedings. annually.

Geosynthetic Materials Association

1801 County Rd. B.W

Roseville, MN 55113-4061

Tel: (651)225-6907   *Fax:* (651)631-9334

Toll Free: (800)636 - 5042

E-Mail: amaho@ifai.com

Web Site: www.gmanow.com

Personnel:

Managing Director: Andrew Aho

Historical Note

Promotes the technical and economic benefits of geosynthetics to the user community and, in turn, assists in building stronger civil infrastructures in a cost-efficient manner. GMA represents the entire geosynthetics industry, including manufacturers as well as companies that test or supply materials and offer services to the industry. Membership fee ranges from $500 to $16000.

Figure 6.7 The **NTPA Directory** is a comprehensive source of trade associations that sponsor national and international trade shows.

....

INTERNATIONAL FASHION FOCUS 6.1:
American Fashion Imports Are Global Business

The glamorous fashion weeks held in New York's Bryant Park occur several times a year. One main purpose is to give retail store fashion buyers a preview of upcoming fashion looks which the buyers then must translate for their customers at home. It used to be that Americans would opt for their own sportswear look which has become classic throughout the world. Thanks to the Internet, everywhere the casual apparel of Ralph Lauren, Liz Claiborne, or Tommy Hilfiger are clearly recognizable signs of American fashion. Perhaps too recognizable.

Current market weeks are showing more diverse looks, often ones that no longer can be identified with a single country. At a recent New York City Fashion Week, designers and their ideas hailed from across the globe, major European countries such as France and Italy, to be sure, but also the Asian nations of Thailand, Japan, and China, as well as Brazil and Turkey.

Vera Wang found inspiration from ancient Roman society, Diane von Furstenberg located bright flowery prints in Bali, while Tia Cibani, who designs for a Chinese line Ports 1961, gathered ideas from East African patterns and fabric treatments such as tie-dyeing. When asked about sources of global design inspiration, Lazaro Hernandez who, with Jack McCullogh, creates the Proenza Schouler label, admits that although the team does not have the money to travel extensively, they can travel in their heads. Hernandez believes that, "with technology, you can go anywhere on the Internet."

In addition to the fact that the fashion industry requires a new season four or five times a year, each possessing its own unique qualities, the designers of luxury fashion goods want to stay ahead of moderate price manufacturers who are quick to copy any new look that catches on. So top-level designers search continuously for special qualities that characterize their styles as luxe, whether it is the addition of couture embroidery for an evening gown, a hand-rolled hem on an Hermès scarf, or tiny gems hand-sewn on a blouse. Inspired by designers, affluent fashion consumers seek out what is new that sets them apart for a while from the rest of the world. Often that element is provided by an import, one that can soon be produced at a lower price.

Adapted from Kate Betts, "Geography Lesson: The coolest designers redefine the idea for American style in an increasingly global business," *Time*, September 2007, p. 61.

LOCATING FOREIGN SUPPLIERS

Once opportunities are confirmed, the next step is to find a number of international supply sources. There are many ways to do this. First, identify a country or group of countries where the product may be available. In addition to the Internet, many organizations can help in the process of supplier identification. Some are located overseas but many are here. For example:

Overseas

> government trade promotion agencies or departments of commerce;
> foreign chambers of commerce;
> industry associations' export programs, and
> city government export promotion agencies.

In the United States:

> foreign embassies;
> foreign consulates;
> trade commissioners, and
> bi-national chambers of commerce.

Other sources of information about overseas suppliers include:

> industry trade journals;
> trade fairs and exhibitions;
> other importers;
> ethnic community organizations;
> foreign banks' U.S. branches;
> freight forwarders;
> customs brokers, and
> the Internet.

The next step is to contact prospective suppliers and ask for their catalogs and price lists. You will need to introduce yourself and provide a brief description of your international trade qualifications. Most foreign manufacturers or distributors are eager to export to the United States or to sell their goods to U.S. importers, due to the size of this market—the largest in the world. However, they may hesitate to do business with an entrepreneur or very small business—at least until a personal working relationship can be established. It is for that reason potential—and current—American importers should attend foreign trade shows where they can meet future suppliers face-to-face to start building a relationship. For example, the growing number of Islamic residents in the United States may prompt U.S. importers to visit fashion shows in Islamic countries (Figure 6.9).

Many international trade associations, or their trade publications, foreign chambers of commerce, the U.S. Commercial Service of the U.S. International Trade Administration, and foreign embassies and consulates can provide information on profiles, dates, and locations of foreign trade shows for industries across the board.

Figure 6.8 **U.S. import buyers select goods from markets throughout the world, to satisfy consumer demands.**

· · · · · · · ·

While foreign travel may not be practical for the start-up company, some potential importers visit major trade shows in the U.S., where foreign country pavilions and individual foreign exhibits and booths increase dramatically each year. Many of these companies are seeking U.S. distributors or venture partners. The *National Trade and Professional Trade Association Directory*, published by Columbia Books, features detailed contact and background information on more than 8,100 trade associations, professional societies, technical organizations, labor unions, and their more than 14,000 key executives in the United States. It lists U.S. trade shows and annual conventions for most of these organizations. Other trade publications frequently list trade shows and exhibitions, by industry or by state and city.

Convention centers that typically host international trade shows offer enough floor area to accommodate several thousand attendees. The largest in the United States is McCormick

Figure 6.9 Located only minutes away from downtown Chicago, McCormick Place is North America's premier convention center, attracting over 3 million visitors annually.
••••••••

Place in Chicago, Illinois, with over 2.7 million square feet of exhibit space. Over 3 million people visit each year, many seeking foreign customers for their exports or looking for foreign-exhibited products they can import.[5]

The major trade shows for the fashion industry are held in New York City, such as those the 7th on Sixth organization produces during Fashion Week. The MAGIC apparel trade shows for men, women, and children are held at the Las Vegas Convention Center in Las Vegas, Nevada, also one of the world's largest in terms of exhibit space. The Orange County Convention Center (OCCC) in Orlando, Florida, is also a significant trade show location. The OCCC currently ranks as the second largest convention center in the United States, with 2.2 million square feet of exhibition space.[6] Other trade shows are held in Dallas, Miami, and Seattle, among U.S. cities.

Without U.S. and foreign trade shows, the business of exporting and importing would be much more difficult and costly. Where else could exhibitors—and attendees—research global markets for their export products or find new sources for their imports, in one location, over a concentrated time frame of several days? Since many manufacturers and marketers of consumer products are dispersed all over the world, often in remote locations, it would not

be cost or time effective to visit them individually. The trade show brings all the key charac-
ters of an industry together—to meet, greet, and compete.

IMPORT PENETRATION

Since the flood of imports began in the 1970s, they have become an integral part of American
life. Japanese electronics and later their automobile manufacturers were pioneers in giving
American consumers new choices of quality products at lower prices than available domestically. Manufacturers from other countries, notably South Korea, Taiwan, and Hong Kong,
quickly followed Japan into the lucrative U.S. market. Government attempts at **protectionism**, or restraining trade between nations, through methods such as tariffs, quotas, and
anti-dumping laws, selling products in foreign countries at prices less than wholesale in their
originating country, did not diminish the American consumer's demand for imported goods.
Even when **currency revaluation**, the government-initiated official changes in the value of a
country's currency relative to other currencies, increased the cost of Japanese and European
imports, the better quality and distinctive styles seemed to justify the higher prices.

During the past two decades, the growth rate of world trade has grown much faster than
world output. In 2006, for example, real merchandise export growth was about 8 percent, almost two percentage points faster than in 2005, and well above the average expansion of the
decade 1996-2006. The expansion of real trade—imports and exports of goods and services—
exceeded global output growth by more than four percentage points.[7]

Real GDP and Trade Growth of OECD Countries, 2007–08
(Percentage change on a year to year basis)

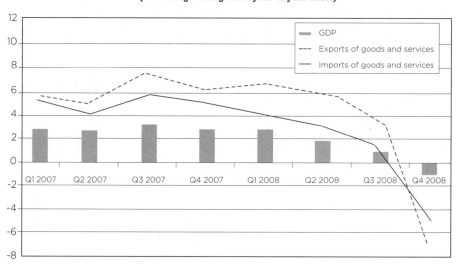

Figure 6.10 World economic output and trade growth became a victim of the global financial
crisis that began in the second half of 2008 and continued through most of 2009, as illustrated
in this chart.
....
Source: OECD National Accounts.

A major contributor to that growth has been the explosion of **e-commerce**, the buying and selling of products or services over electronic systems such as the Internet and other computer networks. Companies can now offer their products to markets anywhere in the world and consumers can now import products from suppliers in virtually any country (as permitted by their import laws).

INTERNATIONAL FASHION FOCUS 6.2:
Neiman Marcus Imports Anti-Aging Cream for 100th Birthday

To celebrate the company's 100th anniversary, Neiman Marcus is importing from Orlane, a renowned Paris beauty and cosmetics firm, a new anti-aging product called Crème Royale. Although the prestigious retailer is bearing its years exceedingly well, apparently, management thinks some of its customers could stand some help.

The day and night cream, exclusive to Neiman's, makes use of ancient Chinese medicines and 24-karat liquid gold. Made from a honey ingredient labeled Royale Gelée, which scientists have not yet been able to recreate, its origin is supposed to be a substance made by worker bees for their queen bee to enable her to live longer. "The average bee lives six weeks, but this honey allows the queen bee to live up to seven years," says Naz Touloui, a vice president at Orlane. The 24-karat gold ingredient adds anti-wrinkle, firming and antioxidant qualities. Also, acacia Senegal and coco glycerides from coconut and fruit sugar are added for skin nourishment. The target customers, people 35 years and older will be asked to pay $650 for a 1.7 ounce jar. However, the demand is there: even in its introductory year Orlane estimates that revenues from Crème Royale can range between $3 to $5 million.

Source: Michell Edgar, "Orlane Does New Cream for Neiman's," *Women's Wear Daily*, October 12, 2007, p. 9.

IMPORTING BY E-TAILERS AND RETAILERS

Retailers have been a major force in fashion importing since the introduction of **global sourcing**, the process of purchasing imported goods from markets around the world. Now, with Internet shopping malls and retailers online Web sites supplementing their bricks-and-mortar stores, consumers are exposed to more imports now than ever before.

The E-tailing Explosion

According to a Shop.org study conducted by Forrester Research (*The State of Retailing Online 2009*), retail executives regarded 2008 as one of the worst years ever, but they do acknowledge that online retailing divisions grew by about 18 percent that year.[8] In 2009, many **E-tailers** have made it easier for consumers to buy clothes online by adding extra incentives, such as free shipping on orders over certain minimums and on returns and exchanges. Many retailers are now operating their own Web sites, offering consumers the convenience of ordering online from their home or office computers without visiting traditional store locations. They are integrating new technologies onto their Web sites, allowing customers to zoom and rotate merchandise or view items in a selection of colors before ordering.

Sourcing Options for Retailers

Fashion retailers have the option to purchase imported garments ready-made, for direct sale to the final end user, or to buy all or part of their raw materials abroad and import them into the U.S. for domestic production. With global sourcing, a single apparel item may even include components from as many as five countries. Retailers who produce their own private labels (to be discussed in the next section) now use **off-shore production**, having their garments entirely made in a part of the world other than the country in which the retailer is headquartered.

Figure 6.11 Workers at a Chinese textile factory in Zhengzhou, Central China's Henan Province.

. . . .

A majority of U.S. offshore apparel manufacturing is in China, where all foreign direct investment totaled a record $63 billion in 2007. Foreign manufacturers had more than 300,000 factories, producing a wide range of products, in China by the end of 2006, according to a report by HSBC Holdings economist Qu Hongbin in Hong Kong. Illinois-based Caterpillar Inc., the world's largest maker of earthmoving equipment, recently opened a plant in the southern Jiangsu province. China's ballooning trade surplus is entirely due to the nation's role as a final assembly point for manufacturers, Qu wrote. About 80 percent of the assembly factories are foreign-owned, he said.[9]

According to the report, "World Textile and Apparel Trade and Production Trends: China, Hong Kong, Japan, South Korea and Taiwan," available at http://www.reportbuyer.com/go/TXI00081, Chinese textile and clothing exports were down by 11 percent in the first six months of 2009 after growing by 8.2 percent in 2008 and 18.9 percent in 2007. In the U.S. market, in contrast to the general trend, sales of Chinese textiles and clothing in the first half of 2009 advanced by 3.9 percent.[10] Other options for retailers seeking foreign fashion sources include:

> Foreign fashion markets and trade shows. One of the best known trade shows is the French prêt-à-porter show held in March and October and featuring the ready-to-wear of designer such as Karl Lagerfeld, Sonia Rykiel, and Jean-Paul Gaultier. Lower-priced ready-to-wear is shown at another venue around the same time. Showings in Italy and Britain also draw buyers for those goods.

> Direct assistance from importers. There are independent American companies who import goods for retail buyers and often show these at domestic markets in New York and Las Vegas.

> Store-owned buying offices. Large chain retailers such as Macy's, Sears, Neiman Marcus, and JCPenney have access to company-owned buying offices located in fashion centers such as Paris, Milan, London, and Tokyo. Local store buyers may visit these offices during market weeks, and the buying office buyers may purchase goods for the stores in between markets.

> Independent agents, known as commissionaires in the fashion industry, and found in the major fashion cities, assist retail buyers not affiliated with an overseas buying office. They facilitate buying and expedite delivery and for this service are paid a fee.

IMPORTING BY MANUFACTURERS

Manufacturers who import raw materials as well as finished products are another major segment of the American import industry. This group also includes chain retailers such as the Gap, Wal-Mart, and Coldwater Creek who produce their own private labels. Their objective is to offer good value and quality—but in the least expensive way, which usually requires foreign sourcing. Using the apparel industry as an example, domestic production with domestic materials is still the standard against which all other production methods are compared, but newer options have emerged with the growth of global sourcing.

The cost of producing clothing is largely determined by two components—the costs of labor and materials. Clothing production is therefore likely to relocate to countries where labor costs are lower—but laws concerning working conditions and child labor are more often violated.

The U.S. Department of Labor, Bureau of International Labor Affairs, has commented on the effect that increasing competition has had on working conditions in the mass segment of the market:

> . . . the competition between an increasing number of developing countries to win contracts has a downward effect on wages and working conditions in enterprises specialized in providing low-range articles—for which the production cost must be as low as possible. Only by filling a slot in the market for higher-range goods can these enterprises break out of this vicious circle in which production costs must be compressed for them to remain competitive.[11]

Significant changes have occurred in the apparel industry in recent decades. Once concentrated in the United States and other industrialized countries, this industry has gradually spread to countries with lower production costs, becoming globalized with its geographical distribution constantly changing.

A number of factors have contributed to this globalization. Many developing countries have based or are basing their industrialization on labor-intensive export sectors, particularly the apparel sector. Developing countries have almost doubled their share of world clothing exports since the early 1970s to account for more than half of all exports today. At the same time, companies in the U.S. and other industrialized countries have adopted strategies to relocate certain labor-intensive activities, such as clothing assembly, to low-wage countries through direct investment or outsourcing. Thus, according to the International Labour Organization (ILO), the industrialized countries have "promoted the expansion of the clothing industry in the developing countries and participated actively in the growing globalization of the sector."

Intense competition in the U.S. retail sector has resulted in significant restructuring of the apparel industry in recent years. Contributing to this trend has been the rise of mass marketing stores and discount retailers with low overhead costs and low prices. These non-traditional retailers have displaced a significant share of the sales of traditional apparel retailers such as department and specialty stores. There have been a growing number of bankruptcies and consolidations, such as the Macy's acquisition of the renowned Marshall Field & Company in Chicago, as well as other well-known regional or local favorites in the retail sector, resulting in an increased concentration of large firms at the retail level.

Many experts point to changes in consumer attitudes as a driving force behind the restructuring that is occurring in the retailing industry. Not only have consumers become more cautious in their buying habits, but they have been reducing the portion of their disposable income that they spend on non-electronic merchandise, or soft goods, such as apparel. Consumers are increasingly demanding quality goods at low prices. Retailers have often been forced to sell merchandise permanently at sale prices, with promotions occurring throughout the year.

Economists and sociologists have attributed the increasingly volatile consumer demand to growing numbers of new products, the rise of fashion-consciousness for even the lowest-cost apparel, and selling seasons, and more recently to the state of the economy. In response, retailers are increasingly utilizing new technology to facilitate communication with suppliers and speed the distribution of goods. Apparel manufacturers who wish to remain competitive must reduce cycle times for apparel design, manufacture, and delivery. Many manufacturers have adopted **Quick Response** replenishment systems that allow retailers to trim inventory, respond more quickly to changes in consumer preferences, restock almost instantly, and offer a wider choice of clothing styles.

The recent slowdown in the U.S. economy has resulted in weakened consumer demand and when combined with higher raw-material costs, has placed increased pressures on apparel manufacturers. Unable to pass higher costs onto consumers in a market with excess supply, both apparel manufacturers and retailers have been squeezed by lower margins. Since retailers have gained growing bargaining power through consolidations, apparel manufacturers have had to absorb higher costs and cope with lower profit margins in order to maintain production.

In this increasingly competitive environment, the lines between apparel retailers and manufacturers are being blurred as each takes on new roles and enters new aspects of the garment industry. Many retailers, for example, have entered product development and manufacturing as they develop their own private labels. In some cases, department stores and other retailers are directly contracting goods from the same foreign factories used by the brand-name producers from which they buy.

Apparel and other merchandise manufacturers and retailers increasingly turn to imports from lower-cost producers to retain their competitive edge in the U.S. market. Retailers are developing global sourcing alliances with suppliers and directly sourcing brand-name and private-label merchandise domestically and internationally. Many of the largest retailers, such as Wal-Mart, also have become the largest importers of general merchandise and apparel.

Domestic Production—Foreign Materials

Many products, including fashion and home furnishings, can be produced in the U.S. using foreign raw materials or components. This method is popular with American firms who specialize in using unique or unusual materials. Manufacturers can offer a wider range of products than they would if they were buying all materials and components domestically. Designers such as Donna Karan, Calvin Klein, and Oscar de la Renta make great use of fine imported fabrics.

Foreign Production—Foreign Materials

Sometimes a private label fashion buyer cannot find exactly what customers want, such as a certain style of Scottish cashmere sweater to coordinate with an Italian woolen skirt. In this case, the buyer may go to a factory in Scotland and one in Italy with the croquis (sketches) of the designs to be made. This is called **specification buying**; the domestic private label company (J. Crew or Talbot's) has designed the product, even the entire product line, and the foreign manufacturer creates it using local materials at the buyer's directions.

Complete foreign production can mean smaller, more specialized runs that are an advantage to smaller and mid-sized manufacturers, but large manufacturers, such as Ford Motor Company, also are producing goods overseas that eventually may show up as imports in the U.S.

Figure 6.12 **Ford's foreign auto production may be a preview of auto imports from China.**
. . . .

The elimination of all textile and apparel quotas, limits on the amount of specific goods from certain countries, has opened the door to this option, especially apparel goods from China and India. The Agreement on Textiles and Clothing provided for the gradual dismantling of the quotas that existed under the Multifiber Arrangement (MFA). This process was completed in January, 2005, but large tariffs remain in place on selected textile products by Presidential action taken after textile and clothing exports from China to the U.S. and Europe grew by 100 percent or more in 2005. The U.S. and EU cited China's WTO accession agreement allowing them to restrict the rate of growth to 7.5 percent per year until 2008. In June 2005, China agreed with the EU to limit the rate to 10 percent for three years. No agreement was reached with China, so the U.S. imposed its own import growth quotas of 7.5 percent instead.

Foreign Production—Domestic Materials

A third option gives U.S. manufacturers control over their raw materials, while saving production costs by going offshore to Mexico or Canada, under the NAFTA trade agreement (1994) or the Caribbean Basin Initiative (CBI).

Initially launched in 1983 through the Caribbean Basin Economic Recovery Act (CBERA), and substantially expanded in 2000 through the U.S.-Caribbean Basin Trade Partnership Act (CBTPA), the CBI currently provides 19 beneficiary countries with duty-free access to the U.S. market for most goods. Referred to as 9802 production, this program permits some phase of production, usually assembly, to be done outside the United States, then brought into the country with the tariff, or import tax, paid only on the value-added portion of the item.

A disadvantage of these programs is the extra time it takes for sending domestic raw materials to the foreign production site. Because of favorable regulations, some domestic jeans producers have the denim manufactured here and the garments cut and sewn in Mexico or Caribbean countries.

Manufacturer-owned Foreign Production

American apparel manufacturers and retailers are also increasingly turning to low-cost suppliers abroad to supplement their U.S. production. In some cases, manufacturers contract out apparel assembly operations to overseas contractors. In other cases, U.S. apparel manufacturers have shifted production abroad to take advantage of lower costs and, in some cases, preferential trade programs. In fact, U.S. executives are more likely to invest in China and India than at any time since 1998.[12]

Competing manufacturers and labor unions are critical of this option, as it leads to **outsourcing** of American jobs, the delegation of non-core operations from internal production to an external entity specializing in the management of that operation.

THE IMPORT DEBATE

During 2007, the quality and safety of imports from China seemed to be a weekly controversy, as food products, toys and even toothpaste were found to be tainted with dangerous toxins or lead, in the case of the toys. Strong public and congressional reaction called for more vigilance in allowing these items to enter this country. The Web site, "Made (Deadly) in China," reports that the U.S. agencies charged with monitoring the safety of imported food and food ingredients, drugs and drug ingredients, toys, and other children's products, have not been able to keep pace with import growth in recent years. On the Web site, Maureen Keene reported that it is not only Chinese imports that customs needs to inspect, but also those from India and other countries. She notes that 20 percent of generic and over-the-counter drugs, and more than 40 percent of active ingredients for drugs made in the U.S., come from India and China. It's predicted that within 15 years, 80 percent of key ingredients will come from those countries.[13]

SPOTLIGHT ON GLOBAL TRADE 6.1: AN IMPORT PLANNING GUIDE

How do you manage to import goods?
The following suggestions can be useful:

1. Evaluate Market Demand—is there a viable market demand for the goods you wish to import into the United States? Whether consumer goods or manufacturing components, imports must present not only a price advantage but a long-term source of satisfaction for the American end-users.

2. Locate Foreign Suppliers—The absence of domestic suppliers offering products at the price, quality and features consumers demand, is rationale for foreign sourcing. Consult trade publications and directories, manufacturing associations, and foreign government agencies to connect with potential suppliers. Attend trade shows overseas as well as in the U.S. for direct contact with potential distributors and manufacturers. Facilitators of the export-import trade process, such as freight forwarders, customs brokers, international banks, chambers of commerce, and the Internet can provide recommendations and references on reliable suppliers.

3. Review Import Regulations—Requirements for importing specific commodities, from certain countries, depend upon a wide variety of variables, such as quota restrictions, duty rates or restrictions due to an embargoed country of origin. These regulations can be determined only if you know the item's Harmonized Tariff Schedule classification HTSUS number. After obtaining the proper HTSUS classification number for your type of intended import from the U.S. International Trade Commission (dataweb. usitc.gov), research current import regulations to identify any government-imposed barriers to importing the type of goods you wish to bring in from the country or countries you have selected. Current U.S. tariffs, which are maintained and published by the USITC as a statutory responsibility, can be accessed via the USITC Dataweb.

The United States technically regulates all imports according to the HTSUS classification system. Some items from certain countries are totally banned, due to primary boycotts; others are subject to quotas or tariffs; while still others are prohibited due to non-tariff barriers to trade. Individuals may make their own customs clearance of goods imported for personal or business use. The U.S. Customs and Border Protection Agency does not require an importer to have a license or permit, but other agencies may, such as the U.S. Department of Agriculture, Department of State, and U.S. Treasury, depending on what is being imported. The Federal Trade Commission, for example, is responsible for enforcing import regulations on apparel and textiles.

Since customs tariff and trade laws are very complex and the entry procedures time-sensitive, the use of a customs broker is highly recommended.

"Buy American" policies can also create barriers for importers. For example, one of the biggest markets in the U.S. is the government procurement sector. It includes the General Services Administration (GSA) and Department of Defense (DOD), as well as state procurement agencies. These organizations are mandated to "Buy American" whenever possible.

4. Pricing Your Imports—the next step is to contact your supplier to get a quotation for the goods you wish to buy. Your suppliers should provide by letter, fax or e-mail exactly what their requirements are regarding price, quantity available—in what time frame, trade and payment terms, packaging, and delivery details. Approximate freight and insurance charges, if not included in the price, need to be calculated prior to your sending a firm purchase order.

The quotation you receive from the foreign exporter constitutes a formal offer for the sale of goods. Your acceptance of this offer, either verbally or in writing, will establish a contract that is legally binding on both parties.

5. Comply with U.S. Customs Policies and Procedures—To speed Customs clearance, the import community and Customs and Border Protection have created the Customs Automated Commercial System (ACS), which electronically receives and processes entry documentation and provides cargo disposition information from importers who intend to file their own entry documentation. Importers of merchandise for their own use or for commercial transactions can use a customs broker who will use the Automated Broker Interface (ABI) in combination with ACS.

Once documentation is presented, customs officials determine whether or not it is necessary to examine your shipment. If they determine that no legal or regulatory violations have occurred and all duties, if applicable, have been paid, liquidation, or release of the goods to the importer will take place.

You can expect U.S. Customs and Border Protection to do the following:
> determine the value of the goods for customs purposes and to apply any applicable duties;
> check the shipment for country of origin marks and special markings;
> review the shipment for prohibited articles;
> determine if the goods are correctly invoiced;
> see if the goods are in excess or shortage of the quantities invoiced, and
> examine the shipment for illegal narcotics or nuclear, biological, or chemical weapons. (WMD).

6. Learn Basic Vocabulary—Every industry has its own vocabulary of terms and the import business is no exception. It's important to understand exactly what your supplier is offering and how you should respond in accepting or rejecting the proposal.

Established by the International Chamber of Commerce (ICC), **Incoterms** are internationally recognized and most widely used rules for the interpretation of import-export terms. They indicate to the buyer what is—and what is not—included in the selling price. They also indicate when the exporter's responsibility ends and when the importer's begins—usually referred to as "transfer of title" to the goods.

For a list of basic international trade terms, see the Glossary of Terms in Appendix A.

The American Congress and general public was shocked to learn that the U.S. Food and Drug Administration (FDA) normally inspects less than 1 percent of all food and food ingredients entering the U.S. and tests only 0.5 percent. "Only 20 percent of food imports appear in FDA's food import computer system for review by the inspection force," stated David Nelson, an investigator for the House Committee on Energy and Commerce. [14]

Customs inspections have been decreasing for two reasons. First, food imports have grown dramatically, from $45 billion in 2003 to $64 billion in 2006. Second, food oversight activities have been reduced due to lack of funding. Shaun Kennedy of the National Center for Food Protection and Defense said no country is increasing its food exports faster than China. [15]

"China has increased overall its food sales to the United States by over 20 percent in the last year alone," Kennedy says. "Going back three years, we have doubled our agricultural inputs from China," Kennedy stated.

The safety issue of whether or not the United States should import, added to the political issue of exporting American jobs to manufacture goods in other countries has been the subject of an ongoing debate between protectionists and free trade proponents—on both sides of Congress. The advocates of **isolationism**, limiting international trade—frequently labor union officials or legislators from strong union-influential states—call for import restrictions, such as quotas or tariffs, to be imposed, in an effort to create a level playing field, to protect domestic manufacturers from unfair competition caused by cheaper labor or government subsidies in many foreign countries.

Those who believe in free trade advocate international trade with no or very few limitations. They stress that U.S. manufacturers should learn to compete with foreign businesses or concentrate on other industries in which they may have a competitive or technological edge. They also point out that any protectionist action by the U.S. may be matched by its trade partners, with the possibility of a trade war, to the detriment of all societies involved.

In recent years, discussions have centered on the issues of Free Trade versus Fair Trade. Adherents to **fair trade** believe in forms of international trade that provide for human rights including fair wages for workers; safe, clean places to work and live, and protection for the environment. An increasing number of trade agreements incorporate fair trade provisions.

Proponents of **free trade** argue that voluntary exchange meets the demands of justice because each party to the trade leaves the trade richer than he or she was before. Johan Norberg writes in his book *In Defense of Global Capitalism* that, "it may seem odd that the world's prosperity can be augmented by swapping things with each other, but every time you go shopping you realize, subconsciously, how exchange augments wealth. You pay a dollar for a bottle of milk because you would rather have the milk than your dollar. The shop sells it at that price because they would rather have your dollar than keep the milk. Both parties are satisfied with the deal, otherwise it would never have taken place. Both emerge from the transaction feeling that you have made a good exchange, your needs have been provided for."

In any case, the impact of global trade, whether importing or exporting, means more markets for businesses and more choices for consumers, as globalization has created an interdependent, linked global market.

SUMMARY

Although most Americans use imported clothing, autos, food, or appliances, few people stop to think about the various processes necessary to actually import items. Nevertheless, today's consumer is the best informed, most technologically savvy, and best equipped to find the widest variety of products, with the lowest price tags, thanks to importing and e-commerce.

The number one reason for importing is to satisfy customer demand. Therefore, the first and most important step in deciding whether to import goods or services is to determine the size of the potential market. Some importers resell their goods to wholesalers or retailers, others import components, or materials and parts that go into finished goods that are ultimately sold to consumers in the domestic marketplace. Most consumers don't know how complicated it can be to source goods in distant countries; negotiate in a language or with business customs that are unfamiliar; then transport the purchases thousands of miles; clear customs entry; and finally, to distribute them in the United States.

Potential importers need to assess their own company's strengths, weaknesses, opportunities, and threats by conducting a S.W.O.T. analysis. This competitive analysis then will aid in evaluating sourcing costs, domestic suppliers, and other competitors as well as the size and value of the current market. Information on current end-users' demographics and psychographics must preclude any import buying. The main business objective is to make a profit and the best way to do that is to identify a substantial, long-term need for the product you plan to import.

Once marketing opportunities are confirmed, the next step is to find a number of qualified international supply sources. Foreign government (non-U.S.) Departments of Commerce, or chambers of commerce, located here or overseas, as well as apparel-textile trade magazines, exhibit shows, and associations, are good sources for suppliers' names and e-mail addresses, if no Internet home page is available.

If foreign travel is not economically feasible at the start, potential importers should visit major trade shows in the U.S.—but marketing plans should include foreign show visits, as soon as possible.

With U.S. imports of over $2.5 trillion worth of goods and services, in 2008, the rationale for importing is obvious. More choices at better prices which result in more sales and profits, with the added advantage of diversified sourcing or manufacturing, give more reasons for importing.

Those businesses new to importing should also consider the risks to importing. Foreign sourcing can add weeks to lead times; slow or unpredictable delivery, quality control issues, and infrastructure failures can be costly or even terminal for long-term domestic relationships.

Strict U.S. government import controls, in the wake of the 2001 terrorist attacks, can be overwhelming to the smaller firm or individual importer. Import tariffs, or duties—taxes on goods or services coming into the United States—as well as non-tariff barriers to trade, such as quotas, can be strong dis-incentives for those wishing to import.

Both manufacturers and retailers engage in importing into the United States. The elimination of textile and apparel quotas, provided by the Agreement on Textiles and Clothing in January, 2005, has opened the door to more imports—especially from China and India. The safety of imports, especially from China, made the headlines for months during 2007, sparking debate from both Republican and Democratic members of Congress, as well as the administration, calling for stricter U.S. customs' controls, quality and safety checks, and even the prospect of more tariffs or quotas to protect American consumers from unsafe imports.

Key Terms

> Anti-dumping
> Components
> Container Security
   Initiative (CSI)
> Currency revaluation
> E-commerce
> End-users
> E-tailers
> Fair trade
> First price
> Free trade
> Global sourcing

> Import traders
> Incoterms
> Isolationism
> Landed cost
> Lead time
> Market
> Off-shore production
> Outsourcing
> Protectionism
> Quick Response
> Specification buying
> S. W. O. T. analysis

Review Questions

1. Why are imported goods appealing to American consumers, and what are some of the risks of importing?

2 What are the delivered-into-store merchandise costs an importer incurs?

3. State three or four questions a potential importer needs to pose before buying foreign goods.

4. Identify four ways fashion retailers can buy goods overseas.

5. Describe the major issues in the import debate: Fair Trade versus Free Trade.

Discussion Questions and Activities

1. How does the U.S. government's tariffs, quotas, or other restrictions on imported products that may compete with domestically-produced items violate the rights of U.S. importers, individuals, or businesses, in the pursuit of free-enterprise?

2. In what ways do imports create the export of American jobs? How do imports contribute to American employment?

3. What measures can be taken to protect American jobs without becoming a protectionist, anti-trade nation?

4. Discuss the positive and negative effects of the U.S. presidential action to reimpose quotas on China's exports of textile and clothing exports to the United States, soon after the 2005 Agreement on Textiles and Clothing had suspended quotas on these items and imports jumped by over 100 percent.

5. The Buy American Act (41 USC 10a-10d), passed in 1933, mandates preferences for the purchase of domestically-produced goods in direct procurements by the United States government. State your views on "Buy American" legislation that would require state or federal government procurement be from U.S. suppliers—unless these items were not available from domestic companies. What could be the possible fallout from such policies, should they become a reality in our country?

References

1. Sierra Trading Post, www.sierratradingpost.com

2. The Interagency Working Group on Import Safety, *Protecting American Consumers Every Step of the Way: A strategic framework for continual improvement in import safety*, A Report to the President, September 10, 2007. Retrieved on December 28, 2007, from www.importsafety.gov/report/report.pdf.

3. "The Good News About America's Auto Industry," *Business Week*, February 13, 2006.

4. Report to the President, op.cit. p. 5.

5. McCormick Place *Facilities*, Retrieved on December 28, 2007, from www.mccormick place.com/facilities/facilities_01.html.

6. Trade Fair & Runway Shows: exhibitions for the Apparel & Textile Industry. Retrieved on December 22, 2007, from www.apparelsearch.com/trade_show.htm.

7. "Real Merchandise Trade Developments and Output in 2006," WTO Press Release, *World Trade 2006; Prospects for 2007*, April 12, 2007, p. 5. Retrieved on December 22, 2007, from www.wto.org/english/news_e/pres.07.

8. "The State of Retailing Online 2009: Profitability, Economy, and Multichannel," a Shop.org study conducted by Forrester Research. Retrieved on November 18, 2009, from www.shop.org/soro08.

9. "China Industrial Output Rises 17.4% On Exports," China Daily.Com. Retrieved on December 27, 2007, from http://www.chinadaily.com.cn/china/2007-05/16/content_873878.htm.

10. "World Textile and Apparel Trade Production Trends: China, Hong Kong, Japan, South Korea, and Taiwan." Retrieved on November 18, 2009, from http://www.reportbuyer.com/go/TXI00081.

11. "Codes of Conduct in the U.S. Apparel Industry," U.S. Department of Labor, Bureau of International Labor Affairs. Retrieved on December 28, 2007, from http://www.dol/gov/ilab/media/reports/iclp/apparel/2c.htm.

12. Mark Bernstein, "The Smart Way to Invest Overseas," *World Trade Magazine*, October, 2006, pp. 70 and 71.

13. Maureen Keene, "Get the Facts," Made (Deadly) in China, July 25, 2007. Retrieved on December 20, 2007, from http://www.madedeadlyin china.com/get-the-facts/.

14. Stephen J. Hedges, "How Imports Swamp the FDA, *Chicago Tribune*, September 2, 2007, pp. 1 and 20.

15. Shaun Kennedy, Deputy Director, National Center for Food Protection and Defense, "Terrorist Threats to our Food Supply; Food Protection and Defense-Science, Ethics & Law," April 21, 2006, University of Minnesota.

16. Johan Norberg, *In Defense of Capitalism*, 2003, the Cato Institute, pp. 28–30.

Chapter 7

Entering
the Import
Business

Figure 7.1
Every import shipment is subject to detention and examination by U.S. Customs officers to insure compliance with all U.S. import laws and regulations.

• • • • •

7

Guess what? Individuals or companies of any size don't need to invest millions of dollars to enter the import business. Using eBay, Yahoo, Amazon, or other Web sites, importers are bringing goods into the United States from throughout the world, without a major investment or even an importer's license.

Although the **U.S. Customs and Border Protection (CBP)**, known as **Customs**, is the primary agency controlling all imports into the United States, it does not demand that importers have a license or permit; other government agencies may require a permit, license, or other certification, depending on the specific import. Customs entry forms do require an importer's number, which is either an IRS business registration number, Federal Employer Identification Number (FEIN), or personal Social Security number.

B usinesses interested in importing foreign goods (as well as individuals importing for personal use) need to understand and comply with the basic U.S. import requirements of the Customs Territory of the United States, the District of Columbia, and Puerto Rico. They must follow certain procedures governed by the CBP, whose primary mandate is to help expedite the movement of imported goods, known as **entry**, that is the presentation of required documents declaring the shipment's origin and value. Every import shipment is subject to detention and examination by Customs officers, to insure compliance with all U.S. import laws and regulations.

FIVE STEPS TO IMPORTING

Before deciding to allocate any time and money resources to a transaction, first-time importers will find it useful to proceed through a series of steps that may yield the answers as to whether or not their venture might be profitable. Their first call should be to the nearest U.S. Customs and Border Protection office. The number can be found online or in the local telephone directory. Ask for a *commodity control specialist* in charge of the basic product or category description of the intended import. Then follow these steps:

Step One: Determine Customs Classification

Determine the WCO/HTS Classification Number(s). All intended imports must be classified according to this schedule. The **World Customs Organization (WCO)** represents 171 Customs administrations around the world that together process 98 percent of the world's trade. The **Harmonized Tariff Schedule of the United States (HTSUS)**, issued by the United States International Trade Commission, has been combined with the WCO to create the WCO HTS schedule which numerically classifies merchandise by type of product, such as textile fibers and textile products, animal and vegetable products.[1]

These steps need to be taken prior to any price quoting to management or offers of sale to prospective customers, as duty changes can alter purchase costs and profit projections, as well as your selling price.

Customs Automated Commercial System

To speed customs clearance, the import community and the Customs Service have created the Customs **Automated Commercial System (ACS)**, which electronically receives and processes entry documentation and provides cargo disposition information. Cargo carriers, customs brokers, and individual importers may use the system, which reduces clearance time from days to hours or even minutes. Importers who file their own entry documentation with Customs find this method to be very efficient.[2]

INTERNATIONAL FASHION FOCUS 7.1:
Loomstate, Rogan, and Edun: Import Duties and Quotas Negotiated in Many Countries while Fair Trade Prevails

Just about every fashion organization around, huge companies such as JCPenney Company Inc., Wal-Mart, and the Target Corporation, and smaller ones such as Loomstate, Rogan, and Edun import apparel, accessories, home furnishings, and other goods to offer American consumers wider selections. The last three companies are a bit different from the rest, however. They offer high fashion, and in the case of Edun, high-price merchandise carried by stores such as Barneys and Nordstrom and manufactured under fair trade standards.

Loomstate, Rogan, and Edun were started by designer Rogan Gregory with his partner Scott Hahn. Like the managers at Patagonia, Gap, Nike, and a few others with a social conscience, Rogan and Scott wanted to be certain that their goods are manufactured according to fair trade rules, meaning that the factory workers receive fair pay, suitable working conditions, and are not otherwise exploited. One day, Ali Hewson saw the Edun line, and she thought her husband might be interested. Hewson's husband happened to be U2's Bono, and indeed he was interested. Through Bono's efforts in Africa, Edun was able to expand and develop more factories where fair wages and working conditions result in superior products.

While some of the apparel for Loomstate, Rogan, and Edun, is manufactured in the United States, other sources include Peru, Turkey, India, and the African nations of Lesotho and Tunisia. Negotiating Customs regulations in a number of countries is mind-boggling. For example, to make the garments, Turkey levies a duty but Africa does not unless the fabric originates in another country. For entry into the United States, a shirt in a Chinese factory may carry a "Made in Bangladesh" label if the garment was sewn there but sent to China for finishing (including collars and cuffs).

Since duties and quotas are the laws of each government, they must be strictly followed in order for goods to flow smoothly to customers. To do this and to be sure that goods are made under fair trade standards takes even more effort, but the owners sleep well at night.

Sources: Rachel Louise Snyder, *Fugitive Denim, A Moving Story of People and Pants in the Borderless World of Global Trade*, New York: W.W. Norton Company, 2008. *Wallpaper**, April 18, 2004. www.wallpaper.com. Retrieved on February 13, 2008.

Automated Broker Interface

Those individuals or companies importing merchandise either for their own use or for commercial transactions may decide to use a **customs broker,** an independent business, licensed by the U.S. Treasury Department, engaged in clearing goods through U.S. Customs. Brokers commonly use the **Automated Broker Interface (ABI)**, an integral part of ACS that permits qualified participants to file import data electronically with Customs. ABI is a voluntary program available to brokers, importers, carriers, port authorities, and independent service centers. Currently, over 96 percent of all U.S. import entries are filed through the ABI. Additional information on ACS and ABI can be found on the Customs Web site at www.cbp.gov.[3]

The WCO HTS updates apply to the ACI and ABI, as of February, 2007.[4] An importer who is unsure of the proper way to classify an item may submit a request, in writing, for a binding classification ruling to the National Commodity Specialist Division, U.S. Customs, Attn: Classification Ruling Requests, New York, New York 10048. The rulings will be binding at all ports of entry unless revoked by the Headquarters' Office of Regulations and Rulings.

Importers who are not satisfied with the binding ruling received from New York can appeal it to the Headquarters' Office of Regulations and Rulings, Washington, D.C. 20229. Import specialists can give advisory rulings orally but the classification-related opinions or advice of Customs Service personnel at one port are not binding for other Customs ports. Oral inquiries may be made to Customs offices regarding existing binding rulings that might cover a specific importation. Binding rulings may also be researched on the Customs Web site at www.cbp.gov.[5]

Figure 7.2
A CBP officer checks for specific chemicals arriving in cargo from another country.

••••••••

Step Two: Calculate Customs Quotas and Duties

The WCO HTS number also indicates the amount of Customs duties and/or quotas that may be applicable upon entry into the United States. In some instances Customs quotas and duties can be complex, difficult, and time consuming. As worldwide trade increases, steps to lower or eliminate these requirements have become more favorable to exporters and importers. For example, the NAFTA agreement has worked to eliminate most duties and quotas among the U.S., Canada and Mexico. Here's how quotas and duties work in today's economy.

Import Quotas

An **import quota** is a quantity limit on imported merchandise for a specific period of time. Quotas are established by legislation, by directives, and by proclamations issued under the authority contained in specific legislation. The majority of import quotas are administered by CBP. The Commissioner of CBP controls the importation of quota merchandise but has no authority to change or modify any quota.

U.S. import quotas may be divided into two types: **absolute quotas**, specific quantities of certain products that may be permitted entry during a quota period, and **tariff-rate quotas**, that provide for the entry of a specified quantity of the quota product at a reduced rate of duty during a given period. Under the North American Free Trade Agreement (NAFTA), there are **tariff preference levels (TPLs)**, which are administered like tariff-rate quotas.[6]

For tariff-rate quotas, there is no limitation on the amount of the product that may be entered during the quota period, but quantities entered in excess of the quota for the period are subject to higher duty rates. In most cases, products of Communist-controlled areas are not entitled to the benefits of tariff-rate quotas.

Some absolute quotas are global, while others are allocated to specified foreign countries. Imports in excess of a specified quota may be held for the opening of the next quota period by placing them in a foreign trade zone, stored in a warehouse, or they may be exported or destroyed under CBP supervision.

The import of textiles and apparel has special quota requirements. CBP administers import controls on certain cotton, wool, man-made fiber, silk blend, and other vegetable-fiber articles manufactured or produced in designated countries. CBP administers the Special Access Program and the Andean Trade Preference Act on certain products which are made of U.S. formed-and-cut fabric. These controls are imposed on the basis of directives issued to the Commissioner of CBP by the Chairman of the Committee for the Implementation of Textile Agreements.[7]

For example, a **textile visa**, an endorsement in the form of a stamp on an invoice or export control license which is executed by a foreign government, is used to control the exportation of textiles and textile products to the United States and to prohibit the unauthorized entry of the merchandise into this country.[8]

Figure 7.3 CBP laboratory personnel check textiles imported into the United States.
. . . .

The visa system is the most effective way to prevent illegal *trans-shipments*, (goods produced in one country such as China, but labeled as originating in another, such as Thailand) and quota fraud. It also ensures that both the foreign government and the United States count merchandise and charge quotas in the same way so that over shipments, incorrect quota charges, and embargo infractions can be avoided. If a visa cites an incorrect category, quantity, or contains other incorrect or missing data, or a shipment arrives without a visa, the entry is rejected and the merchandise is not released until the importer reports the discrepancy to the foreign government and receives a new visa or visa waiver from the government.

However, a visa does not guarantee entry of the merchandise into the U.S. If the quota closes between the time the visa is issued in the foreign country and the shipment's arrival in the U.S, the goods will not be released to the importer until the quota opens again. To avoid expensive warehousing costs, or even the loss of a perishable shipment, importers must advise their foreign source the status of any applicable quotas or other restrictions that might delay entry. In other words, don't ship the goods unless certain entry will take place without extensive delays.

When a shipment arrives at a port in the United States, the Customs import specialist reviews the visa documents for accuracy and completeness prior to release of the merchandise. The review ensures that the category number, quantity, signature, date, and visa number are correct and match the shipment. Only after this action is completed and the merchandise is charged to the quota (if required) is the shipment released to the importer.

Goods brought in for the importer's personal use and not for resale, regardless of value, whether or not accompanying the traveler, (except for custom-made suits from Hong Kong), are exempt from quota, visa, and exempt certification requirements.[9]

Quotas are product-and country-specific and are usually for a one-year period. Information concerning current and specific import controls may be obtained from the Commissioner of CBP. Information concerning the textile program may be obtained from the Committee for the Implementation of Textile Agreements, U.S. Department of Commerce, in Washington, D.C.

Import Duties

Another possible challenge to profitable import trade is **customs duties**, also known as **tariffs**, or taxes, on certain goods brought into the country. Most industry professionals use the terms duty and tariff interchangeably-both refer to the tax placed on imports, according to duty rates established by Congress.[10]

Using the example of an import of women's wool car coats, let's examine the HTS classification number procedure to determine this item's duty rate:

1. On the Internet, go to the homepage of the U.S. International Trade Commission at: www.usitc.gov.
2. On the left-side menu, click the link: *Tariff Information Center (TIC).* If you are new to the import business, read the HTS background information to better understand the U.S. classification system.
3. From the home page of the TIC, click on the left-side menu link: *Official Harmonized Schedule.*
4. After reading the HTS coding explanation, click (at the bottom of the page) the link for the current year *HTSA Basic-by-Chapter.*
5. Scroll down through the chapter-by-chapter listings until you find a description of your import category; in our example, we find women's coats in Chapter 62, titled: "Articles of Apparel and Clothing Accessories, Not Knitted or Crocheted." Click on the chapter listing (in blue type.)
6. Enlarge the page and scroll past the Chapter 62 notes (which may apply to your imports, in some cases, but not our example) until you find the listing for women's coats, which is on page 10.

So the heading for our example is Chapter **62** ("women's or girls' overcoats, carcoats, capes, cloaks, anoraks . . ."), with a subheading of **11**, for "of wool or fine animal hair." The HTS number is **6202.11.00** (see Figure 7.4).[11]

Harmonized Tariff Schedule of the United States (2008) Supplement 1 (Rev. 1)
Annotated for Statistical Reporting Purposes

XI
62-10

Heading/ Subheading	Stat. Suf- fix	Article Description	Unit of Quantity	Rates of Duty		
				1		2
				General	Special	
6202		Women's or girls' overcoats, carcoats, capes, cloaks, anoraks (including ski-jackets), windbreakers and similar articles (including padded, sleeveless jackets), other than those of heading 6204:				
		Overcoats, carcoats, capes, cloaks and similar coats:				
6202.11.00		Of wool or fine animal hair	. . . .	41¢/kg + 16.3%	Free (BH,CA, CL,IL,JO,MX, P,SG) 12.4¢/kg + 5% (MA) 15.5% (AU)	46.3¢/kg + 58.5%
	10	Women's (435)	doz. kg			
	20	Girls' (435)	doz. kg			
6202.12		Of cotton:				
6202.12.10	00	Containing 15 percent or more by weight of down and waterfowl plumage and of which down comprises 35 percent or more by weight; containing 10 percent or more by weight of down (354)	doz. . . . . . kg	4.4%	Free (BH,CA, CL,IL,JO,MX, P,SG) 1.3% (MA) 3.9% (AU)	60%
6202.12.20		Other	. . . .	8.9%	Free (BH,CA, CL,IL,JO,MX, P,SG) 2.7% (MA) 8% (AU)	90%
		Raincoats:				
	10	Women's (335)	doz. kg			
	20	Girls' (335)	doz. kg			
		Other:				
		Corduroy:				
	25	Women's (335)	doz. kg			
	35	Girls' (335)	doz. kg			
		Other:				
	50	Women's (335)	doz. kg			
	60	Girls' (335)	doz. kg			

Figure 7.4 Potential importers can go online, at www.usitc.gov, to find their product's HTS number, which will determine importability as well as any applicable duty rates.

. . . .

7. Note the two columns under the title "rates of duty." Column one is subdivided into "General" and "Special." The general duty rate is for imports of countries that have general, or **normal trade relations (NTR)**, the most common and lowest duty rate, (except for "special") with the United States at the time of the import transaction. Rates in the "special" column are for countries with active U.S. Free Trade Agreements or other special tariff treatment.[12]

    Column two rates apply to products, whether imported directly or indirectly, of certain countries that are controlled by Trade Act laws, or by action taken by the President of the United States. As of this writing, products from the countries of Cuba and North Korea were listed, but import restrictions will be applied to any country, in accordance with U.S. international trade policies and the embargoes and sanctions in place at the time of import entry.[13]

8. In the case of our wool car coats, HTS number 6202.11.00, the duty rate is $ .41/kg + 16.3 percent, assessed on the customs value, if imported from a country under a column one "general" classification.[14]

Using the eight steps above, import duty rates can be calculated by individuals or businesses sourcing goods from certain foreign countries. However, since tariff rates and country restrictions change frequently, it is always wise to confirm duty rates with a U.S. Customs Commodity Specialist at a local Customs and Border Protection office or with national offices accessed via the Internet. Professional customs brokers can also assist, but expect a sales pitch for your import transportation business.

Duties are generally assessed at **ad valorem rates**, a percentage of the value of the goods when clearing customs that is added as a tax to the import price. Thus, an ad valorem duty-assessed imported designer raincoats would be the same percentage, say nine percent, (but obviously far higher in terms of the dollar amount) as that of a lower-priced imported raincoat. Some articles, however, are dutiable at a **specific rate**, for example, per piece, liter, or kilo; leather boots might be levied a specific rate of $3 per pair. Other products are assessed at a **compound rate** of duty, which is a combination of both ad valorem and specific rates. Women's woolen cardigans might be assigned an ad valorem rate of 15 percent plus a specific rate of $.35 per kilogram.[15]

It is the responsibility of the importer—not Customs—to declare the **dutiable value**, the value of a shipment that will be subject to import duties. The final appraisal, however, is fixed by Customs at the time of entry. Several methods are used to arrive at the official customs value. The **transaction value**, the price actually paid or payable by the buyer to the seller for the goods when sold for exportation to the United States, is the primary basis of appraisal. The European Union (EU) employs the term **CIF (cost, insurance, and freight) values** to sum up the elements in the transaction value.

a. Raf Simons

b. Junya Watanabe

c. Comme des Garçons

d. Dries Van Noten

Figure 7.5a–d Importers of fashion follow trends from all over the world.

● ● ● ● ● ●

Other factors may also add to the dutiable value of merchandise, such as packing costs, any selling commission incurred by the buyer, any royalty or license fee that the buyer is required to pay, directly or indirectly, as a condition of the sale and the proceeds of any subsequent resale, and disposal, or use of the imported merchandise that accrue, directly or indirectly, to the seller.[16]

When the transaction value cannot be determined, then the value of the imported goods being appraised is the transaction value of identical merchandise. If merchandise identical to the imported goods cannot be found or an acceptable transaction value for such merchandise does not exist, then the value is the transaction value of similar merchandise. Merchandise that is produced in the same country and by the same organization as the merchandise being appraised, would qualify as similar merchandise. It must be commercially interchangeable with that merchandise. Also, identical or similar merchandise must have been exported to the United States at or about the same time the merchandise being appraised.[17]

In addition to duties, processing fees may also be applicable, according to Customs' final determination of the correct tariff rate. Tariffs are intended to level the playing field, or protect domestic producers from imports made with foreign government subsidies or with very low wages in underdeveloped countries. The duty rate of an item is tied to its classification number.

The United States is one of the most open countries in the world with regard to import duties and regulations. Over 95 percent of the import categories have zero duty rates and no quotas. However, the collection of duties is the second highest revenue source for the U.S. Treasury; only the Internal Revenue Service's collection of Income Taxes contributes more.

Where imported items are placed on the Tariff System determines their value. In accordance with the **Customs Modernization Act (Mod Act)**, the 1996 legislation declared it is the responsibility of the importer of record to use "reasonable care to enter, classify and value the goods and provide any other information necessary to enable Customs to properly assess duties, collect accurate statistics, and determine if all other applicable legal requirements have been met."[18]

Step Three: Find Out Special Customs Regulations

Another type of import restriction, **Non-Tariff Barriers to Trade (NTBs)**, can also be imposed, but it does not involve the payment of taxes or penalties. NTBs can be in the form of manufacturing standards or safety requirements; or even how an animal is caught or the use of endangered species in the production process. If the imports don't meet NTB requirements, they will be denied access. Some are applied only in special circumstances, which can spark controversy, as they border on **protectionism** or the government's protection of

Figure 7.6 CBP officer at the Port of Long Beach inspects a child's toy to see that it meets the requirements for lawful entry into the United States.

. . . .

domestic business by restricting or regulating foreign trade. An example would be import quotas, introduced in step two, that technically qualify as NTBs, since they are government-sponsored import restrictions on amounts of specific items from certain countries, but do not involve the assessment of taxes.

If the NTBs are too costly or difficult to comply with, importers may decide to cancel efforts to bring the items into this country. For a more in-depth discussion of NTBs, go to the following Web site: research.stlouisfed.org/publications/review/89/01/Trade_Jan_Feb1989 .pdf for an excellent article published by the Federal Reserve Bank of St. Louis.[19]

New importers should ask their local Customs commodity control specialist for tips on the most common problems or mistakes related to labeling, packaging or marking, experienced by other importers, for the same types of goods. Clarification of specific NTBs, such as industry standards or safety certifications, can usually be obtained by contacting the U.S. trade association for the industry in which the imported products would be included.

Figure 7.7 The Federal Trade Commission (FTC) Web site, www.ftc.gov, offers a guide to compliance with federal labeling requirements for textile, wool, and fur products.

••••••

Textiles and Apparel Import Regulations

The Federal Trade Commission (FTC) Web site, www.ftc.gov, offers a guide to compliance with federal labeling requirements for textile, wool and fur products. The law requires that textile and wool products have a label listing: the fiber content, the country of origin, and the identity of the manufacturer or another business responsible for marketing or handling the item. Labels for fur products are required under a separate statute and rule. [20]

Care labels for wearing apparel also are required by FTC rule, and information about preparing labels can be found in the FTC publication: *Writing a Care Label: How to Comply with the Care Labeling Rule*, which can also be found on the following Web site: www.ftc.gov/os/statutes/textilejump.shtm.[21]

Another example of textile import restriction applies to the fabric itself. "Any article of wearing apparel, fabric, or interior furnishing cannot be imported into the United States if it fails to conform to an applicable flammability standard issued under the Flammable Fabrics Act. These flammability standards cover:

> general wearing apparel,
> children's sleepwear,
> mattresses,
> mattress pads, including futons, and
> carpets and rugs.

Certain products can be imported into the United States, as provided in Section 11(c) of the Act, in order to finish or process them to render these products less highly flammable and thus less dangerous when worn by individuals. In such cases, the exporter must state on the invoice or other paper relating to the shipment that the shipment is being made for that purpose."[22]

Who's Covered and Who's Not

Those businesses that manufacture, import, sell, offer to sell, distribute, or advertise products covered by the Textile and Wool Acts must comply with the labeling requirements. The labeling requirements do not apply until the products are ready for sale to consumers. Items shipped or delivered in an intermediate stage of production, and not labeled with the required information, must include an invoice disclosing the fiber, country of origin, manufacturer or dealer identity, and the name and address of the person or company issuing the invoice. If the manufacturing or processing of the goods is substantially complete, they are considered to be ready for sale to consumers. Even if small details have not been finished—such as hemming, cuffing, or attaching buttons to garments—the products must be labeled.[23]

INTERNATIONAL FASHION FOCUS 7.2:
Halston Net à Porter Requires Swift Entry for Imports

During the 1970s and 1980s, Roy Halston Frowick lit fashion fires throughout the world. Born in Des Moines, Iowa, growing up in Indiana, and attending the School of the Art Institute in Chicago, he first designed hats and then total outfits for a myriad of clients such as Liza Minelli. Known for his minimalist styles, use of cashmere, silk, and Ultrasuede textiles, (his Ultrasuede shirtwaist dress alone sold 60,000 copies), and the disciplined colors of black, ivory, and red, his fashion looks were sought out by consumers everywhere.

After his relatively early death in 1990, a number of designers (John David Ridge, Randolph Duke, and Bradley Bayou) and companies (Beatrice, Revlon, Borghese) tried to capture the spirit of his work and revive his label. Recently, 35-year old Marco Zanini undertook to create a Halston look that has meaning to fashion enthusiasts in the twenty-first century. His training and previous work at Versace and Dolce & Gabbana place him in the center of the times today. And his backers have fashion know-how plus financial expertise. They include Tamara Mellon who founded Jimmy Choo, and Hollywood producer Harvey Weinstein, husband of Georgina Chapman, a designer for Marchesa.

Zanini's work for Halston depended on the prompt availability of his imported goods. The clothes are manufactured in Italy, using Italian wools, cashmere, and jersey, as well as French silk. His first season colors included combinations of burnt orange, mauve, cream, blue, and purple gray. Wrap and tailored blouses and cashmere coats are simple and smart, in the Halston manner, without cloning specific styles.

In order to carry out the company's innovative merchandising policy, the Halston line needs to clear Customs swiftly, for the plan was truly a first for the designer price level: to have the actual garments in New York and available to customers immediately after the fashion showings, truly net à porter. Zanini has since left Halston to return to Europe as a design for the French fashion house of Rochas.

Sources: Cathy Horyn, "Will 6 Be a Lucky Number for Halston?" The *New York Times*, Sunday Styles, February 3, 2008, Section ST, pp.1 and 8. Richard Martin, *The St. James Fashion Encylopedia*, Detroit: Visible Ink Press. 1997, pp. 158–161. Blog posts tagged "Marco Zanini" from *New York* magazine. Retrieved April 16, 2009, nymag.com/tags/marco%20zanini-38K.

Step Four: Obtain Outside Agency Approvals

Importers must determine—before issuing a purchase order—what outside agency approvals or certificates might be necessary and how much they could add to the import price of each item. For example, the Department of Agriculture is concerned with the importation of certain food products. Once applicable agencies are identified, direct contact should be made to determine whether or not specific imports are subject to testing, specific modifications or certificates—and how much they may cost. Ask agency officials what were the most common problems or mistakes made by other firms importing the same category or type of product, including documentation errors, standards or prototype requirements. If certification is too costly or time-consuming, it may not be practical to import the intended products.

Step Five: Follow Sampling Procedures

Check with Customs to determine how they define a sample of the intended import. An apparel item, for example, imported as a sample—not for sale—may require a 4 inch diameter hole in the center of the garment to prevent its sale without paying any duties. Check for an explanation of the proper documentation required from Customs for this type of sample.[24]

Since one country's import is another country's export, the laws governing a single international trade transaction may differ considerably. Firms exporting to the United States will have to conform to laws of their country, as well as to U.S. import laws. Therefore, potential importers should obtain specific import information from a Customs officer at the port nearest their business or home and then share that information with foreign trading partners. A list of U.S. ports of entry is on the Internet, at www.cbp.gov.

SUMMARY

Going into the importing business does not mean that it is necessary to invest a great deal of money. It does mean, however, that in order to bring goods into the country successfully, a business needs to operate within the U.S. government's Customs system. To assist in determining the eventual profitability of bringing in goods from foreign sources, potential importers will want to consider these five steps:

1. Determine the Customs classification of the intended imports according to the Harmonized Tariff Schedule of the United States (HTSUS). All goods are classified in this schedule which also includes applicable duties and quotas.
2. Ascertain Customs Quotas and Duties when applicable. Some goods may be brought in under a quota system. There are two types: absolute quotas, meaning no additional goods may be imported during that time period; and tariff rate quotas, meaning that additional goods may be brought in at a higher tariff rate. Duties or tariffs are classified as ad valorem, a percentage of the value of an item; specific, per a measured amount such as a kilo; or compound, a combination of ad valorem and specific duties.
3. Find Out Special Customs Requirements. Some goods such as textiles have special requirements that importers need in order to secure their goods.
4. Obtain Outside Agency Approval. Some goods must be cleared with other agencies; certain food items need the approval of the Department of Agriculture.
5. Follow Sampling Procedures. If a garment is brought in as a sample, in order not to be liable for duties it must have a 4-inch hole in the center.

A list of specific Customs information is available from all Customs offices.

Key Terms

- Absolute quotas
- Ad valorem rates
- Automated Broker Interface (ABI)
- Automated Commercial System (ACS)
- Compound rate
- Cost, insurance, and freight values (CIFs)
- Customs (see U.S. Customs and Border Protection)
- Customs broker
- Customs duties
- Customs Modernization Act (Mod Act)
- Dutiable value
- Entry
- Harmonized Tariff Schedule of the United States (HTSUS)
- Import quota
- Non-Tariff Barriers to Trade (NTBs)
- Normal trade relations (NTR)
- Specific rate
- Tariff preference level (TPL)
- Tariff-rate quota
- Textile visa
- Transaction value
- U.S. Customs and Border Protection (CBP)
- World Customs Organization (WCO)

Review Questions

1. Describe the five steps that are necessary for first-time importers to follow before bringing in goods from other countries.

2. Why is it important for potential importers to understand the requirements of the five steps before deciding whether or not to enter the business?

3. What factors contribute to the *dutiable value* of a shipment that will be subject to import duties?

4. Barriers to importing into the United States are either tariff or non-tariff (NTBs); explain how they differ.

5. For many industries, including apparel, the use of samples is routine for showing a new line before taking future production orders. Should these samples be imported duty-free? What steps need to be taken to ensure they are not sold without proper duties being paid?

Discussion Questions and Activities

1. Identify class members who think the United States should limit imports (to save American jobs as one reason) and members who think all trade should be liberalized, and debate the following questions: Why does this nation need to import foreign goods? Does it produce everything needed here? If not, why can't it? Do import restrictions deprive the American consumer of foreign goods or services?

2. Discuss whether or not you think American consumers will be willing to spend more—maybe 10 percent or more on each purchase—to inspect all imports and ensure, to of their best ability, that our imports are safe.

3. Using the WCO HTS classification system, found on the USITC.gov Web site, determine the tariff rate for several common import items that may be found in your closet or dresser drawers.

References

1. World Customs Organization, www.wcoomd.org/home.htm, p. 1. Retrieved on February 13, 2008.

2. Customs and Border Protection, www.cbp.gov/automated_systems/acs/addtl_capabilities.xml, p.1. Retrieved on February. 14, 2008.

3. Customs and Border Protection, www.cbp.gov/xp/cgov/import/operations_support/automated _systems/abi/. Retrieved on February 14, 2008.

4. Customs and Border Protection, www.cbp.gov/xp/cgov/import/communications_to_trade/world_customs org/wco_hts.xml, pg. 1. Retrieved on February 15, 2008.

5. *Importing into the United States: A Guide for Commercial Importers, 2003 ed.*, p. 61. Retrieved on February 15, 2008, from www.usitc.gov/trade_remedy/731_ad_701_cvd/investigations/customs_importation_guidelines.pdf.

6. *Importing into the United States: A Guide for Commercial Importers*, Revised ed., Nov. 2006, p.143. Retrieved on February 2, 2008 from www.cbp.gov/linkhandler/cgov/toolbox/publications/trade/iius.ctt/iius.doc.

7. Ibid. p.144. Retrieved on February 10, 2008.

8. Ibid. pp. 147 and 148. Retrieved on February 11, 2008.

9. Ibid. p. 21. Retrieved on February 11, 2008.

10. Op. Cit. *Importing into . . . , 2003 ed.*, Chapter 13, pp. 59–61. Retrieved on February 6, 2008.

11. *Harmonized Tariff Schedule of the United States (2008)*, Chapter 62, p.10. Retrieved on February 7, 2008, from http://hotdocs.usitc.gov/docs/tata/hts/bychapter/.

12. Ibid., *General Notes*, p. 3. Retrieved on February 7, 2008.

13. Ibid. p. 6. Retrieved on February 7, 2008.

14. Ibid. p. 10. Retrieved on February 7, 2008.

15. Op.cit., *Importing into the United States . . .* pp. 59–61. Retrieved on February 8, 2008.

16. Customs and Border Protection, tcc.export.gov/Trade_Agreements/Exporters_Guides/List_All_Guides/exp_005458.asp unstats.un.org/. p. 3. Retrieved on February 8, 2008.

17. Ibid. p.4. Retrieved on February 8, 2008.

18. Export.gov, https://www.cbp.gov/linkhandler/cgov/toolbox/publications/trade/iius.ctt/iius.pdf. Retrieved on February 2, 2008.

19. FedEx, www.fedex.com/us/services/ftn/consulting.html?link=2, p.1. Retrieved on February 3, 2008.

20. Cletus C. Coughlin and Geoffrey E. Wood, "An Introduction to Non-Tariff Barriers to Trade," *Federal Reserve Bank of St. Louis*, Jan.–Feb., 1989, p.32. Retrieved on February 20, 2008, from research.stlouisfed.org/publications/review/89/01/Trade_Jan_Feb1989.pdf.

21. Op.cit. *Importing into the United States: A Guide for Commercial Importers*, Chapter 31, pp. 141 and 142. Retrieved on February 6, 2008.

22. Federal Trade Commission, *Writing a Care Label: How to Comply with the Care Labeling Rule*. Retrieved on February 21, 2008, from www.ftc.gov/bcp/conline/pubs/buspubs/thread.shtm.

23. Federal Trade Commission, *Writing a Care Label: How to Comply with the Care Labeling Rule*. Retrieved on February 21, 2008, from www.ftc.gov/bcp/conline/pubs/buspubs/thread.shtm.

24. Op. cit., *Textile and Wool Acts*, p.116. Retrieved on February 21, 2008, from www.ftc.gov/os/statutes/textilejump.shtm.

25. Op. cit., *Importing into the United States: A Guide for Commercial Importers*, pp.141 and 142. Retrieved on February 21, 2008.

Chapter 8

Navigating the Maze of Import Controls

Figure 8.1 During the night of December 16, 1773, in Boston Harbor, three ships carrying tea were boarded by Massachusetts colonists, and 45 tons of tea were tossed overboad in retaliation to oppressive British taxes on the colonies.

••••••

8

NAVIGATING THE MAZE OF IMPORT CONTROLS The early settlers in colonies such as Virginia and Massachusetts began importing goods when they first arrived nearly 400 years ago. But the import taxes that the colonies were forced to pay the British government (for their goods ranging from sugar to newspapers and playing cards, and later paint and paper) became the fuel of the revolution to come. By 1773, as a reaction to excessive taxation plus an attempted British monopoly on the sale of tea, Bostonians dressed as indigenous Americans and dumped hundreds of chests of it into Boston Harbor in what became known as the Boston Tea Party. That action ignited the flames that would burn in the war for Independence three years later.

acing a chaotic treasury burdened by the heavy debt of the Revolutionary War, a primary interest of Alexander Hamilton, the first Secretary of the Treasury, when he took office was the repayment of the war debt in full. "The debt of the United States . . . was the price of liberty," Hamilton affirmed, and the idea of regulating imports as a source of income seemed natural. He devised a revenue system based on *customs duties* and *excise taxes*. Hamilton's attack on the debt helped secure the confidence and respect of foreign nations.[1]

Shortly after the United States Constitution was ratified in 1788, President George Washington signed into law the **Hamilton Tariff Act**. Enacted on July 4, 1789, it was the first substantive legislation passed by the first Congress and is often called, "the second Declaration of Independence" by the news media of that era. Set up as a way to both protect trade and raise money for the federal government, the Act authorized the collection of **customs duties**, or taxes, on imported goods. Geographic entry points were determined shortly after, and everyone—citizens and visitors—coming into the country had to account to the new government for goods they shipped or carried into the United States.[2]

Most of the rates of the tariff (duties) were between 5 and 10 percent, depending on the value of the item. As Secretary of the Treasury, Alexander Hamilton was eager to establish the tariff as a regular source of revenue for the government and as a protection of domestic manufacturers. In economic terms, the government at that time embraced the principle of protectionism, the policy of restricting trade among nations through such barriers as tariffs, or taxes, on imported goods, quotas, and a limit on the amount of imports (by commodity and by country) within a given time period and other government regulations designed to discourage imports. The Hamilton Act is closely aligned with today's anti-globalization sentiment, a contrast to that of free trade (where no artificial barriers exist to the entry or exit of goods and services in international business), and a persistent political dispute that remains more than 200 years later.[3]

The act authorized the collection of taxes on imported goods, primarily from England. For more than a century, Customs' collections supported virtually the entire government and its **infrastructure** (bridges, communications, and transportation). Later, President Jefferson's purchase of the Louisiana territory stretching to the Pacific Ocean, the accession of Florida and Alaska, and the Transcontinental Railroad were financed by import duties. Customs revenues built the city of Washington, D.C., many of the nation's lighthouses, and the U.S. military and naval academies, and had, by 1835, reduced the national debt to zero.[4]

Import duties were the number one income source for the U.S. government until the Internal Revenue Act was enacted in 1913, when the 16th Amendment to the Constitution made the income tax a permanent fixture in the U.S. tax system.

HISTORY OF U.S. CUSTOMS

The history of the United States Customs Service goes back to the same month and year of the Hamilton Trade Act, which established duties on imports. The Fifth Act of the First Congress, signed by President Washington on July 31, 1789, created the first agency of the federal government: U.S. Customs, a field organization of collectors, "to regulate the collection of duties imposed by law on the tonnage of ships or vessels and on goods, wares, and merchandises imported into the United States."[5]

As the nation developed into a world power, the role and importance of the U.S. Customs Service grew with it. They assumed more extensive and complex role responsibilities to protect and provide revenues for this country. For over 125 years, the primary responsibility of the U.S. Customs Service was to administer the tariff acts, designed to protect the nation's revenue by assessing and collecting duties or taxes and fees related to the international trade. In more recent years, Customs' responsibilities grew, with the need to control narcotics trafficking and imports of counterfeit goods, and more recently to protect the United States from terrorists and other security threats.[6]

IMPORT CONTROLS

Today, import controls still exist—in every sovereign nation—because governments want to have the option of protecting their domestic industries, by imposing import duties or non-tariff barriers to trade. They also have the right to know *what* is coming into their countries. They want a count of products coming in, to measure imports against exports, and to help determine the economic health, strength and competitiveness of their economies versus those of other countries. In addition, each government wants to assure that imported goods are in compliance with its laws, for example, those concerning consumer protection, safety and health. Today, the United States Customs and Border Protection (CBP) agency is responsible for the legal movement of imported goods into the country.[7]

U.S. Customs and Border Protection (CBP)

In March, 2003, the U.S. Customs Service became the U.S. Customs and Border Protection (CBP), as a result of the merger of the functions of Customs, Immigration and Naturalization Service, Border Patrol, and the Animal and Plant Health Inspection Service. Now an agency of the Department of Homeland Security, CBP's priority mission is to secure U.S. nation's boundaries by detecting, deterring, and preventing terrorists and their weapons from entering the United States.[8]

SPOTLIGHT ON GLOBAL TRADE 8.1:
A Day in the Life of CBP

On a typical day, U.S. Customs and Border Protection Agency:

Processes:
> 1,087,069 passengers and pedestrians;
> 256,897 incoming international air passengers;
> 43,188 passengers/crew arriving by ship;
> 786,984 incoming land travelers;
> 331,347 incoming privately owned vehicles;
> 70,451 truck, rail and sea containers.

Executes:
> 73 arrests of criminals at ports of entry;
> 2,796 apprehensions at and in between the ports for illegal entry;
> 614 refusals of entry at our ports of entry.

Seizes:
> 7,621 pounds of drugs;
> $295,829 in undeclared or illicit currency;
> 4,125 prohibited meat, plant materials, or animal products, including:
> > 435 agricultural pests at ports of entry.

Refuses entry of:
> 844 aliens (found inadmissible or withdrew application to enter) at our ports of entry, and
> 395 criminal aliens attempting to enter the United States between the ports of entry (estimated).

Intercepts:
> 76 fraudulent documents;
> 1 for terrorism/national security concerns.

Rescues:
> 3 illegal crossers in distress or dangerous conditions between ports of entry.

Deploys:
> 1,275 canine enforcement teams;
> 18,276 vehicles, 275 aircraft, 181 watercraft, and 252 horse patrols.

Protects more than:
> 5,000 miles of border with Canada;
> 1,900 miles of border with Mexico, and
> 95,000 miles of shoreline.

Employs approximately:
> 51,553 employees, including:
>> 19,726 officers;
>> 17,499 Border Patrol agents;
>> 2,277 agriculture specialists.
> 1,088 Air and Marine agents including:
>> 140 Air Enforcement officers;
>> 769 Air Interdiction agents;
>> 171 Marine Interdiction agents.

Manages:
> 327 ports of entry;
> 144 Border Patrol stations within 20 sectors, with 35 permanent checkpoints.

Uses the following technology:
> non-intrusive inspection equipment that allows rapid screening of incoming vehicles and vessels, including radiation portal monitors that screen for terrorist weapons;
> integrated automated fingerprint identification system that allows CBP officers to quickly check national fingerprint databases to identify wanted criminals, and
> unmanned aerial systems that allow for efficient monitoring of desolate areas and quick resolution of alarms on the border.

Based on statistics gathered during the period October 1, 2007 through September 30, 2008. Source: U.S. Customs and Border Protection.

It is a big job and a daunting responsibility. The U.S. shares a 5,252-mile border with Canada and a 1,989-mile border with Mexico, with a combined total of more than 300 international land-based ports of entry. Intertwined with the borders is a maritime system that includes 95,000 miles of coastline and navigable waterways, and a global transportation network—over 300 seaports, 429 commercial airports, and several hundred thousand miles of highways and railroads—that offer access to almost every community in America. CBP includes more than 44,000 employees including officers, canine enforcement officers, Border Patrol agents, aircraft pilots, trade specialists, and mission support staff. The challenges to homeland security are immense.[9]

Seizing Counterfeit Trademarked Goods

The new agency continues in its role of assessing and collecting duties and narcotics import interdiction, as well as other former activities, such as the intervention of illegal imports of counterfeit branded merchandise. One example of Customs' vigilance is the seizure of imported goods for federal violation of merchandise bearing a counterfeit trademark. For two consecutive weeks in August 2008, U.S. Customs and Border Protection officers at Los Angeles-Long Beach seaport seized over $1 million worth of counterfeit handbags and footwear. If legitimate, the items would have been valued at over $24 million. CBP officers and import specialists intercepted a **shipment manifest**—official papers filed and sworn to as being accurate—as electronic appliances arriving from China. CBP officers examined the container and discovered 59,198 counterfeit Coach and Fendi handbags and 17,400 pairs of fake Coach footwear. The items had counterfeit trademarks, a U.S. federal violation. The merchandise was not claimed by the importer; violations of these laws may subject the importers to civil penalties and/or criminal prosecution.[10]

Figure 8.2 **Counterfeit children's toys are seized as violations of intellectual property rights.**

• • • • • •

The agency also maintains an aggressive and comprehensive enforcement program that devotes substantial resources to combating trade in counterfeit goods at United States borders and around the world. The U.S. Department of Homeland Security (DHS), the CBP's parent agency, announced that it had seized counterfeit or pirated merchandise worth approximately $200 million in domestic value for FY 2007. Activities marked a significant upward trend in the value of seizures, exceeding FY 2006 by 27 percent. According to the CBP, these criminal organizations are not only stealing the trademarks of U.S. businesses, they are siphoning millions of dollars from the American economy and are often deceiving an unsuspecting public.[11]

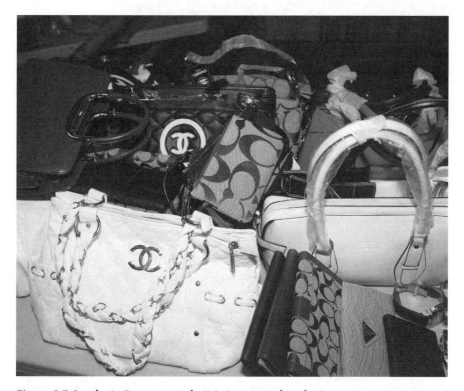

Figure 8.3 One day in August 2008, the U.S. Customs and Border Protection agency seized what would have amounted legitimately to $24 million worth of fake Coach and Fendi handbags and Coach footwear at Long Angeles–Long Beach seaport.

• • • • • •

The CBP increases compliance with domestic and international customs laws and regulations. These activities are aimed at keeping U.S. imports free from terrorist or other malicious interference, such as tampering or corruption of containers or commodities.

Figure 8.4 On Canal Street in New York many counterfeit items, such as these fake watches, are available to shoppers.

• • • • • •

Container Security Initiative (CSI)

CBP is also in charge of the Container Security Initiative (CSI), a joint program with host-nation counterparts to identify and prescreen containers that pose a risk at the foreign port of departure before they are loaded on board vessels bound for the U.S. It is now operating at ports in North America, Europe, Asia, Africa, the Middle East, and Latin and Central America. CBP's 58 operational CSI ports now prescreen approximately 90 percent of all transatlantic and transpacific cargo imported into the United States. CBP has stationed multidisciplinary teams of U.S. officers from both CBP and Immigration and Customs Enforcement (ICE) to work together with host foreign government counterparts. Their mission is not only to target and prescreen containers but also to develop additional investigative leads related to any terrorist threat to cargo destined for the United States.[12]

U.S. import trade and tariff laws are enforced by CBP import and entry specialists and other trade compliance personnel. This helps to ensure that industry operates in a fair and competitive trade environment.

Trade-related activities include:

Figure 8.5 Checking cargo coming into the United States by ship calls for thorough planning and organizing.

• • • • • •

> protecting U.S. businesses from theft of intellectual property and unfair trade practices;
> collecting import duties, taxes and fees;
> enforcing trade laws related to admissibility;
> regulating trade practices to collect the appropriate revenue;
> maintaining export controls, and
> protecting U.S. agricultural resources via inspection activities at the ports of entry.[13]

CBP further facilitates trade through partnership programs such as Importer Self-Assessment as well as account management, which helps frontline personnel facilitate the movement of legitimate, compliant trade and allows the organizations to focus on those shipments that may present a risk to the United States.

Import Safety

In the United States, import safety is a public-private responsibility, and some agencies and private individuals (brokers and importers) are working to develop a more preventative system here. In 2007, government agencies, including the departments of Commerce, Transportation, Defense, and Agriculture among others, produced an interagency report to the President titled, *Protecting American Consumers Every Step of the Way: A strategic frame-*

FORM APPROVED OMB NO. 1651-0014 Exp. 01-31-2010

DEPARTMENT OF HOMELAND SECURITY
U.S. Customs and Border Protection

**DECLARATION FOR FREE ENTRY
OF UNACCOMPANIED ARTICLES**

19 CFR 148.6, 148.52, 148.53, 148.77
Any text that scrolls will not print

PAPERWORK REDUCTION ACT NOTICE: This request is in accordance with the Paperwork Reduction Act. We ask for the information in order to carry out the laws and regulations administered by CBP. These regulations and forms apply to importers to ensure that they are complying with the law and to allow us to figure, collect, or refund the right amount of duty and tax. It is mandatory. The estimated average burden associated with this collection of information is 10 minutes per respondent depending on individual circumstances. Comments concerning the accuracy of this burden estimate and suggestions for reducing this burden should be directed to U.S. Customs and Border Protection, Information Services Branch, Washington, DC 20229, and to the Office of Management and Budget. Paperwork Reduction Reducation Project (1651-0014), Washington, DC 20503.

PART I -- TO BE COMPLETED BY ALL PERSONS SEEKING FREE ENTRY OF ARTICLES (Please consult with the CBP official for additional information or assistance. REMEMBER--All of your statements are subject to verification. False declarations or failure to declare articles could result in penalties.)

1. IMPORTER'S NAME (Last, first and middle)	2. IMPORTER'S DATE OF BIRTH	3. IMPORTER'S DATE OF ARRIVAL
4. IMPORTER'S U.S. ADDRESS	5. IMPORTER'S PORT OF ARRIVAL	
	6. NAME OF ARRIVING VESSEL CARRIER AND FLIGHT/TRAIN	

7. NAME(S) OF ACCOMPANYING HOUSEHOLD MEMBERS (wife, husband, minor children, etc.)

8. THE ARTICLES FOR WHICH FREE ENTRY IS CLAIMED BELONG TO ME AND/OR MY FAMILY AND WERE IMPORTED ▶	A. DATE	B. NAME OF VESSEL/CARRIER	C. FROM (Country)	D. B/L OR AWB OR I.T. NO.
E. NUMBER AND KINDS OF CONTAINERS	F. MARKS AND NUMBERS			

PART II -- TO BE COMPLETED BY ALL PERSONS EXCEPT U.S. PERSONNEL AND EVACUEES

9. RESIDENCY ("X" appropriate box) I declare that my place of residence abroad ☐ is ☐ was	A. NAME OF COUNTRY	B. LENGTH OF TIME Yr. Mo.

C. RESIDENCY STATUS UPON MY/OUR ARRIVAL ("X" One)

☐ (1) Returning resident of the U.S.   (2) Nonresident: ☐ a. Emigrating to the U.S.   ☐ b. Visiting the U.S.

10. STATEMENT(S) OF ELIGIBILITY FOR FREE ENTRY OF ARTICLES
I the undersigned further declare that ("X" all applicable items and submit packing list) :

A. Applicable to RESIDENT and NONRESIDENT

☐ (1) All household effects acquired abroad for which free entry is sought were used abroad for at least one year by me or my family in a household of which I or my family was a resident member during such period of use, and are not intended for any other person or for sale. (9804.00.05, HTSUSA)

☐ (2) All instruments, implements, or tools of trade, occupation or employment, and all professional books for which free entry is sought were taken abroad by me or for my account or I am an emigrant who owned and used them abroad. (9804.00.10,9804.00.15, HTSUSA)

B. Applicable to RESIDENT ONLY

☐ All personal effects for which free entry is sought were taken abroad by me or for my account. (9804.00.45, HTSUSA)

C. Applicable to NONRESIDENT ONLY

☐ (1) All household effects acquired abroad for which free entry is sought were used abroad for at least one year by me or my family in a household of which I or my family was a resident member during such period of use, and are not intended for any other person or for sale. (9804.00.05, HTSUSA)

☐ (2) Any vehicles, trailers, bicycles or other means of conveyance being imported are for the transport of me and my family and such incidental carriage of articles as are appropriate to my personal use of the conveyance. (9804.00.35, HTSUSA)

PART III -- TO BE COMPLETED BY U.S. PERSONNEL AND EVACUEES ONLY

I, the undersigned, the owner, importer, or agent of the personal and household effects for which free enty is claimed, hereby certify that they were in direct personal possession of the importer, or of a member of the importer's family residing with the importer, while abroad, and that they were imported into the United States because of the termination of assignment to extended duty (as defined in section 148.74(d) of the Customs Regulations) at a post or station outside the United States and the CBP Territory of the United States, or because of Government orders or instructions evacuating the importer to the United States; and that they are not imported for sale or for the account of any other person and that they do not include any alcoholic beverages or cigars. Free entry for these effects is claimed under Subheading No. 9805.00.50, Harmonized Tariff Schedule of the United States.

1. DATE OF IMPORTER'S LAST DEPARTURE FROM THE U.S.	2. A COPY OF THE IMPORTER'S TRAVEL ORDERS IS ATTACHED AND THE ORDERS WERE ISSUED ON:

PART IV -- TO BE COMPLETED BY ALL PERSONS SEEKING FREE ENTRY OF ARTICLES (Certain articles may be subject to duty and/or other requirements and must be specifically declared herein. Please check all applicable items and list them separately in item D on the reverse.)

A. For U.S. Personnel, Evacuees, Residents and Non-Residents

☐ (1) Articles for the account of other person.
☐ (2) Articles for sale or commercial use.
☐ (3) Firearms and/or ammunition.
☐ (4) Alcoholic articles of all types or tobacco products.
☐ (5) Fruits, plants, seeds, meats, or birds.
☐ (6) Fish, wildlife, animal products thereof.

B. For Residents and Non-Residents ONLY

☐ (7) Foreign household effects acquired abroad and used less than one year.
☐ (8) Foreign household effects acquired abroad and used more than one year.

C. For Resident ONLY

☐ (9) Personal effects acquired abroad.
☐ (10) Foreign made articles acquired in the United States and taken abroad on this trip or acquired abroad on another trip that was previously declared to CBP.
☐ (11) Articles taken abroad for which alterations or repairs were performed abroad.

CBP Form 3299 (10/95)

Figure 8.6 This Declaration for Free Entry of Unaccompanied Articles is one of the forms that the CBP may ask importers to fill out.

• • • • • •

work for continual improvement in import safety. The report outlines efforts to improve the safety of imported products while facilitating trade.[14]

Noting that approximately $2.5 trillion of imported products entered the United States economy in 2008, and projections are for that amount to triple by 2015, the report concludes that the U.S. Federal government cannot physically inspect every product entering the United States. Doing so would not only bring international trade to a standstill, but would also divert limited resources away from those imported goods (and importers) posing the greatest risk.[15]

Figure 8.7 A Customs and Border Patrol laboratory inspector checks foreign shrimp brought into the United States.

• • • • • •

Several recent incidents involving dangerous imports of apparel, pet foods, seafood, and toys with high lead in their painted parts, highlighted the need for the U.S. import system to keep pace with a changing world and to continue meeting the expectations of the American people. The volume and value of U.S. imports continue to grow due to increasing demand by American consumers for goods that come from global markets.

U.S. departments of State, Treasury, Justice, Agriculture, Commerce, Transportation, Homeland Security, and the Office of the United States Trade Representative, the Environmental Protection Agency, and the Consumer Product Safety Commission are the lead agencies entrusted with strengthening our import system to promote security, safety, and trade for the benefit of all American consumers.[16]

There are two primary goals of the CBP: preventing terrorists and terrorist weapons from entering the United States, and facilitating the flow of legitimate trade and travel.

CBP uses multiple strategies and employs the latest technology to accomplish its dual goals. Its initiatives are designed for domestic protection against acts of extreme violence, and reduce the vulnerability to potential terrorist acts through a multilevel inspection process.

Textiles Designated a Priority Trade Issue

U.S. Customs and Border Protection maintains a priority trade enforcement program to ensure compliance with laws and regulations governing all imports. Due to the high-risk nature of imports of textile and apparel products, CBP has designated the industry a priority trade issue since 2008.[17]

Figure 8.8 Dogs, trained by canine officers to sniff out bombs, regularly inspect the contents of goods held in a warehouse.

••••••

There are numerous requirements placed on textile products entering the United States under various free trade agreements and legislative preference programs. In addition, the United States maintains quantitative limits—or quotas—on the amount of textile products that may enter the United States from China. Approximately 42 percent of all duties collected by CBP are from textile imports. Many different schemes are used to evade duty or quotas on imported goods being brought into the country. Some importers try to avoid quotas by transshipping goods through another country that they falsely claim as the official country of origin of their goods. Others use false documents or labels or provide incorrect descriptions of the merchandise.

CBP uses a multifaceted, but complementary approach, consisting of trade pattern analysis, on-site verification, review of production records, audits, and laboratory analysis to enforce U.S. trade laws and to ensure that appropriate revenue is collected.

Import specialists at CBP with specialized commodity knowledge analyze and review textile imports for possible violations. Focusing on textile violations has paid off with seizures of major illegal shipments. CBP has seized more than $100 million in goods since the beginning of calendar year 2006 and close to $50 million in 2008 for violations of the China quota agreement. In addition, CBP issued 68 penalty actions valued at $4 million. More than 11,000 physical examinations were performed, 1,677 fiber samples analyzed by the laboratories, and 40 audits conducted.[18]

One of the enforcement tools being used is on-site verification of manufacturers. CBP Textile Production Verification teams travel to foreign factories to review and verify that wearing apparel [that is] shipped to the U.S. is produced at those facilities. As a result of these site visits, CBP import specialists will target shipments that are in violation. Sites are selected after extensive trade analysis. The Textile Production Verification Team visited 15 countries in FY 2008. Approximately 427 factories were visited, a 57 percent increase in the numbers over the previous year.[19]

CBP has initiated operations to address the intentional false descriptions of merchandise to achieve much lower import duty rates. CBP's import specialists have identified many of these cases and have seized millions in misdescribed goods. In recent textile enforcement operations, illegally classified goods worth over $12 million were confiscated. In addition, CBP import specialists have identified significant **Intellectual Property Rights (IPR)** violations. In 2007, goods worth about $27 million were seized for violating IPR laws involving textile products.[20]

Figure 8.9 Border patrol agents regularly search trains entering the United States from Canada or Mexico.

• • • • • •

If Customs determines that the goods are different from the entered descriptions in quantity or value, that the classification of the goods is incorrect, or that a different rate of duty than the one indicated by the importer applies, it may assess an increase in duties. Should Customs determine that the importer has deliberately failed to properly classify and value the goods, a court may assess a fine or even criminal penalties.[21]

Import Procedures

The U.S. Customs Service does *not* require an importer to have a license or permit. Other agencies may require a permit, license, or other certification, depending upon what is being imported. However, Customs must authorize entry and delivery of the merchandise before any goods can legally enter the United States. An individual may make their own Customs clearance of goods imported for personal use or business. This is normally accomplished by filing the appropriate documents, either by the importer or by the importer's agent. To expedite this process, Customs entry papers may be presented before the merchandise arrives, but official entry will not take place until the merchandise arrives within the port limits.

INTERNATIONAL FASHION FOCUS 8.1:

An Importer's Responsibilities: Kathryn Kerrigan

Being able to combine importing with entrepreneurship can produce not only independence, but also considerable profits for individuals or small businesses.

Kathryn Kerrigan is a Chicago-area fashion business owner who fits that profile. She loves shoes and fashions, yet as a teenager she would often want to skip special occasions because she couldn't find a suitable size 11 dressy shoe to fit her 6-foot frame.

After an exhausting shoe shopping trip to six malls with her father, he suggested that she might want to start her own business. She thought about it for a while, earned an MBA, and then made up her mind to give it a try. After developing a business plan, she secured a bank loan, and began to talk with experienced wholesale shoe representatives to seek out sources. First, she looked at manufacturers in China, but was not impressed by the samples she saw. She then turned to Italy, renowned for its leather goods, including shoes.

In Pisa, Italy, she located a group of skilled shoemakers who helped guide her choices as she selected the materials, designed the style, and chose the heel. Her shoes take 10 days to hand craft, passing through the operations of 10 experienced craftsmen. The final product is more expensive than many of the shoes carried by stores such as Nordstrom, but these are hand-made and last for decades. Popular styles include ballet slippers, pumps, as well as glamorous evening looks in silks and sequins.

One of the reasons for Kerrigan's success is that she carefully chose her niche target market—tall women. Offering shoes in sizes 6 to 15, she refers to her line as "shoes for women who stand tall." Another reason is that she proceeded gradually. Early on, representing her collection at trade shows, she was greeted by skeptical boutique owners and buyers who balked at her prices. They soon came to realize, however, that their own store customers were looking for fashionable, well-made, larger shoes and were eager to pay the price. After selling to boutiques, Kerrigan decided to open her own store in Libertyville, Illinois, and is now considering another. Recently, *Inc.* Magazine named her one of the nation's top five business people under 30 years old, and was the only woman in that group.

As Kathryn Kerrigan found out, it is the importer's responsibility to ensure that the imported goods meet admissibility requirements--that means proper marking and safety standards have been met and the proper permits obtained in advance of the goods arriving in the country. (See section on Informed Compliance later in this chapter.)

Christine Verstraete, "Shoes, glorious shoes:heels, pumps, sandals in big sizes bring fame to entrepreneur," *Winnetka Talk*, Glenview, Illinois: Pioneer Press, September 27, 2007, Section A, pp. 3 and 4.

The Customs Service does *not* notify the importer of the arrival of the shipment. However, the carrier of the goods or, sometimes the entry port authority, will notify the importer that the goods have arrived. Importers or their Customs brokers should be aware of estimated arrival dates, so entry papers can be filed in advance and delays in obtaining the goods avoided.[22]

Kathryn Kerrigan (see "International Fashion Focus: An Importer's Responsibilities") learned through trial and error that the Customs tracking number for each delivery needed to be picked up in person at the Customs House in Chicago while her shipments were brought into O'Hare airport, nearly 20 miles away.

Customs Entry

The Customs Service defines "**entry**" not merely as the arrival of goods at a port, but as the process of presenting documentation for clearing goods through Customs. Imported merchandise not entered through Customs in a timely manner (within 15 calendar days of arrival) is sent by Customs to a general order warehouse to be held as unclaimed. The importer is responsible for paying storage charges while unclaimed merchandise is held at the warehouse. If it remains unclaimed at the end of six months, the merchandise is sold at auction.[23]

Customs Examination of Goods

In simple cases involving small shipments or certain classes of goods such as bulk shipments, for example boxes of socks or underwear, examination may be made on the docks, at container stations, cargo terminals, or the importer's premises. The goods are then released to the importer.[24]

Sometimes, when navigating through the maze of Customs requirements, it's useful for an importer to have an enduring sense of humor. This was the case for Kerrigan, when, before taking possession of one shipment, she found she had to deal with the factory-printed word "snake" on the outside of the container. She needed to explain to U.S. Customs that the term referred only to a type of leather, but her description was not looked on favorably by the authorities. Customs called in the U.S. Fish and Wildlife agency which wanted to know the type of snake she was importing: was it alive or dead, and where was her import license for the snake? Next, the Illinois Department of Natural Resources paid her a visit to inspect her state import license for snakes. Eventually, she was able to straighten out the confusion, but in the interim, she encountered some hefty storage costs. No wonder she has subsequently decided to use the services of a Customs broker![25]

U.S. Customs and Border Protection Declarations

All shipments of foreign goods into the United States require accompanying official U.S. documentation, including the **U.S. Customs and Border Protection Declaration Form**. This full and accurate description of the merchandise, should be securely attached to the outside of each shipment (just as the "snake" label had been attached to that shipment for Kathryn Kerrigan). Declaration forms vary from country to country, and they don't all ask for the information required by the U.S. Customs and Border Protection.[26]

Entry Requirements

When imported merchandise enters the Customs territory of the United States, a process known as entry, it is under the control of U.S. Customs and Border Protection.

The importer assumes control of the goods only after complying with certain entry regulations. As a general rule, the entry process has six requirements:[27]

> Evidence of right to make entry
> Filing of entry
> Filing of entry summary
> Evidence of surety (bond)
> Formal versus informal entry
> Other types of entry

Many importers are not aware that an entry form is required for every import, whether the merchandise is duty free or dutiable, regardless of value, unless exempted specifically by law. Some types of Customs entry declarations must be made at the first port of arrival.

Ordinarily entry is made for one of the following reasons: consumption, for entry into a bonded warehouse, or for transportation in bond to another port where a consumption or warehouse entry will be made.

Importers, particularly small businesses, may find the effort needed to gain delivery clearance too time-consuming. Their alternative is to hire a Customs broker who, for a fee, acts as the importer's agent in shepherding shipments through Customs. It is understandable that after the snake incident plus other time-consuming encounters with Customs, Kerrigan realized that in her situation the services of a Customs broker would be worth the cost and effort. Now she finds shipments arriving smoothly right to her door. A list of Customs brokers may be obtained from the local U.S. Customs office or found on the Internet or in the local telephone directory.[28]

In the case of a single noncommercial shipment, a relative or other designated individual may act as the importer's agent for customs purposes. This person must know the facts pertaining to the shipment and must be authorized in writing to act for the importer.

The law prohibits Customs employees from performing entry tasks for importers; however, they will advise and give information about Customs requirements.[29]

Formal versus Informal Entry

Formal entries are generally commercial shipments supported by a surety bond to ensure payment of duties and compliance with Customs requirements. A port director can require a formal entry for any import deemed necessary for the payment of the tax revenue or for the protection of the general public.[30]

Informal entries cover personal shipments, commercial shipments, and mail shipments that are being entered for consumption, that is, for use or sale. In most cases informal entry will work if the merchandise is valued at $2,000 or less. There are some exceptions such as textiles, certain types of footwear, and other goods subject to quota/visa restrictions. Personal shipments valued over $2,000 will also require a formal entry.

Goods admitted as informal entries do not require the posting of a bond and goods are liquidated on the spot. The difference between an informal entry and a formal entry is the bond requirement and the liquidation process. **Liquidation** is the final computation of duties or *duty drawback* (refund) and is the final step in the entry process.

After the importer receives notification of the arrival of merchandise from the carrier

Figure 8.10 The locomotive and all of the cars in the train are x-rayed as they enter the United States to seek out any illegal weapons and other potential hazards.

••••••

and it is determined that all shipping charges are satisfied, an invoice is presented to Customs. When clearing an informal entry, the inspector, not the importer, is responsible for determining the classification number of the goods being imported. The inspector also completes the Customs forms used for informal entry.[31]

Other Types of Entry

Imported goods may be sent in-bond from the first port of arrival to another Customs port. **In-bond entries**, when the duties have not yet been paid, postpone final Customs formalities including payment of duty and processing fees, until the goods arrive at the final port. Arrangements for in-bond shipments need to be made before the goods leave the country of export.

When all the information has been acquired, including the report of the Customs import specialist as to the customs value of the goods, and the laboratory report, if required, a final determination of duty is made, the entry is liquidated, and the goods are turned over to the importer. At this time, any overpayment of duty is returned or under-payment billed.[32]

Figure 8.11 Cargo is unloaded from a ship recently docked at the Port of Los Angeles/ Long Beach, the largest port in the United States.

••••••

Documents for Entry of Goods

To make or file a **consumption entry** (for imported goods going directly into the commerce of the United States without any time or use restrictions placed on them) the following documents are generally required:

> Bill of lading
> Air waybill
> Commercial invoice
> Entry manifest
> Packing lists

When a **consumption entry**, such as for perishable goods, is filed, the importer indicates the tariff classification and pays any estimated duty and processing fee. A surety bond may also be required.

PROTEST

Within 90 days after the date of liquidation or other decision, an importer or consignee may **protest** the decision and receive an administrative review. The protest is filed with the port director whose decision is being protested. At the time the initial protest is filed, the importer or consignee must make a request for further review if one is desired. Review of the port director's decision by the Customs Service Center or headquarters is then automatic. Notice of the denial of all or part of the protest will be mailed to the person filing the protest or to their agent. Any person whose protest is denied may contest the denial by filing a civil action in the United States Court of International Trade.[33]

MAIL SHIPMENTS

Shipments by mail which do not exceed $2,000 in value, whether commercial or noncommercial importations (except for commercial shipments of textiles from all countries and made-to-measure suits from Hong Kong, regardless of value), are entered under a mail entry prepared by a Customs officer after the Postal Service submits the package for Customs examination.

The parcel is delivered (to the addressee) by the U.S. Postal Service and is released upon the payment of duty, which is shown on the mail entry accompanying the package. A postal handling fee is also due at the time the package is delivered. This handling fee is not charged on packages sent through military mail channels.[34]

A formal entry is required for any mail shipment exceeding $2,000 in value. Formal entry is also required, regardless of value, for commercial shipments of textiles from all countries and made-to-measure suits from Hong Kong. Certain other articles valued over $250 require a formal entry (billfolds, footwear, fur, gloves, handbags, leather, luggage, plastics, rubber, textiles, toys, games, and sports equipment, etc.).

If formal entry is required on a package, it is held at the Customs international mail branch and notice is sent to the addressee of the package's arrival. The addressee can then go to the nearest Customs office to file the formal entry on the package. An entry must be filed in the same manner as for shipments arriving by vessel or airfreight. Once the mail branch has been notified that entry has been filed, the package will be released to the Postal Service and forwarded to its final destination.[35]

FOREIGN ASSETS CONTROL

U.S. trade sanctions administered by the Office of Foreign Assets Control (OFAC) generally prohibit the importation into the United States (including U.S. territories), either directly or indirectly, of most goods, technology, or services (except information and informational materials) from, or which originated from Cuba, Iran, North Korea, Serbia (except Kosovo), or Sudan; from foreign persons designated by the Secretary of State as having promoted the proliferation of highly destructive weapons; named Foreign Terrorist Organizations; designated terrorists and narcotics traffickers; or from the Taliban, and areas of Afghanistan controlled by the Taliban. Vessels and aircraft under the registry, ownership, or control of sanctions targets may not import merchandise into the United States. The importation of Cuban cigars or Iranian carpets is subject to certain restrictions. Diamonds may not be imported from Angola without a certificate of origin or other documentation that demonstrates to Customs authorities that they were legally imported with the approval of the Angola Government of Unity and National Reconciliation. Contact your local Customs office for further information.

Import restrictions imposed against sanctions targets vary by program. Contact the Office of Foreign Assets Control at (202) 622-2490 with specific questions or concerns or visit OFAC's Web site at www.treas.gov/ofac.[36]

COMPLIANCE ASSESSMENT AND MEASUREMENT

The international trade community actively promotes **compliance assessment**, the systematic evaluation of importers' systems supporting their CBP-related activities. The assessment includes testing import and financial transactions, reviewing the adequacy of an importer's internal controls, and determining their compliance levels in key areas. Companies whose systems are noncompliant will be asked to formulate, in cooperation with CBP advisors, a compliance improvement plan or corrective actions. Serious violations of law or regulations may result in CBP referring the company for a formal investigation or other enforcement actions.

Compliance measurement is the primary tool CBP uses to assess the accuracy of port-of-entry transactions and to determine the compliance rate for all commercial importations. Compliance not only ensures the collection of import revenues legally owed the United States government, but also helps CBP protect this country from illegal shipments by terrorist organizations, including nuclear, chemical or biological weapons.[37]

SUMMARY

U.S. taxes and controls on imports are older than the country itself. Early colonists were forced to pay the British government for a range of goods sent to the new settlers, necessities such as sugar, paper, and paint. When the new nation came into being, the second act passed under George Washington's presidency, the Hamilton Act, established duties for goods brought into the country. The Act authorized the collecting of customs duties to raise revenue for the government. In fact, duties remained the government's number one source of revenue until the early twentieth century when it was replaced by the income tax.

Controlling imports is important not only as a continuing source of revenue, but also as a measure of protection, ensuring safe products for U.S. consumers. A number of government departments including State, Commerce, Agriculture, Treasury, and Homeland Security cooperate in incentives to strengthen our import system and its security.

In March 2003, the U.S. Customs Service (along with employees from other organizations like the U.S. Border Patrol) became U.S. Customs and Border Protection, an agency of the Department of Homeland Security. Today the U.S. Customs and Border Protection agency is responsible for ensuring that all imports and exports are legal and comply with U.S. laws and regulations, and for collecting revenues associated with the enforcement of those laws. The agency also:

> Seizes contraband, including illegal drugs and narcotics, and arrests people engaged in smuggling or other fraudulent behavior with the intent to get around customs laws.

> Processes people, luggage, cargo and mail.

> Protects U.S. business and intellectual property rights by enforcing laws aimed at preventing illegal trade practices.

> Protects the general welfare and security of the U.S. by enforcing import and export prohibitions and restrictions, including money laundering and the export of data essential to the production of mass weapons of warfare.

> Gathers import and export data for the purpose of compiling international trade statistics.

> Enforces over 400 provisions of law—many related to quality of life issues, such as pollution and health—for approximately 40 other agencies.

> Provides, under the Mod Act, **informed compliance** programs and public information concerning the trade community's rights and responsibilities under customs regulations and related laws. Both the importers and CBP share responsibility for carrying out these requirements.

Key Terms

> Compliance assessment
> Consumption entry
> Formal entries
> Hamilton Tariff Act
> In-bond entries
> Informed compliance
> Informal entries
> Infrastructure

> Intellectual Property
  Rights (IPR)
> Liquidation
> Protest
> Shipment manifest
> U.S. Customs and
  Border Protection
  Declaration Form

Review Questions

1. What did the Hamilton Tariff Act of 1789 authorize, and for what purpose? How is the act related to ideas on international trade today?

2. Why do governments establish controls on imports?

3. Why doesn't the United States government physically inspect every shipment coming into the country?

4. To which government department does the U.S. Customs and Border Protection (CBP) belong and what are its main duties?

5. As part of the importing process, according to what documented criteria are goods classified, and who is responsible for classifying them and determining their dutiable value?

6. Since the Customs Service does not notify an importer of the arrival of shipped goods to U.S. ports, how does that importer learn that a shipment is ready to proceed through Customs?

7. What are the two kinds of the entry process, and when may the goods be released?

8. List the documents necessary for the formal entry process.

Discussion Questions and Activities

1. When a batch of Chinese-made ingredients for the popular drug Heparin was found to be tainted, causing hundreds of people to have allergic reactions, and the deaths of at least four people, it was revealed that the U.S. Food and Drug Administration (FDA) was inspecting only 7 percent of the foreign factories (in 2008) producing pharmaceutical components. Discuss who should bear the blame for this unfortunate incident and who should be responsible for future safeguarding of our imports of drugs? The foreign factory? The U.S. pharmaceutical company that imports the drug compounds? Or the U.S. Food and Drug Administration agency?

2. Why should counterfeit goods be prohibited from entering the United States? If they serve consumers looking for the prestige brand while paying much less for the fake goods, why should they be confiscated at the points of entry?

3. Discuss the role of American unions in fighting liberalization of imports and the answers to their positions, by free-trade advocates.

References

1. U.S. Treasury-Biography of Secretary Alexander Hamilton. Retrieved on March 3, 2008, from http://www.treas.gov/education/history/secretaries/ahamilton.shtml.

2. "Tariff Act of 1789," Information from Answers.com. Retrieved on March 3, 2008, from http://www.answers.com/topic/tariff-act-of-1789.

3. Douglas A. Irwin, "Historical Aspects of U.S. Trade Policy," *NBER Reporter: Research Summary*, Summer 2006. Retrieved on March 4, 2008, from www.nber.org/reporter/summer06/irwin.html.

4. "U.S. Customs Service—Over 200 Years of History," U.S. Customs and Border Protection. Retrieved on March 3, 2008, from www.cbp.gov/xp/cgov/about/history/history2.xml.

5. Anne Saba, "The U.S. Customs Service: *Always there . . . ready to serve*," Customs Archives, Office of Information and Technology, U.S. Customs TODAY, The U.S. Customs Service, February, 2003, p. 1. Retrieved on March 4, 2008, from http://www.cbp.gov/xp/CustomsToday/2003/February/always.xml.

6. Ibid. p. 2

7. Op. cit., U.S. Customs Service-Over 200 Years of History, p. 1.

8. "The Future is Now," *U.S. Customs TODAY*, The U.S. Customs Service, February, 2003, p.1. Retrieved on March 4, 2008, from www.cbp.gov/xp/CustomsToday/2003/February/future.xml.

9. "Snapshot: A Summary of CBP Facts and Figures," U.S. Customs and Border Protection, February 2008. Retrieved on March 5, 2008, from www.cbp.gov/linkhandler/cgov/newsroom/fact_sheets/cbp_overview/snapshot_final.ctt/cbp_snapshot_final.pdf.

10. "CBP on a Roll Seizing Fake Handbags, Footwear Again in California," CBP news release, August 28, 2008. Retrieved on September 2, 2008, from www.cbp.gov/xp/cgov/newsroom/news_releases/08282008_8.xml.

11. Ibid. p.2

12. "CSI In Brief," CBP.gov. release of March 20, 2008. Retrieved on March 26, 2008, from www.cbp.gov/xp/cgov/trade/cargo_security/csi/csi_in_brief.xml.

13. Op. cit., Snapshot, p. 2.

14. "Protecting American Consumers Every Step of the Way: A strategic framework for Continual improvement in import safety," *A Report to the President*, Interagency Working Group on Import Safety, September 10, 2007. Retrieved on March 2, 2008, from www.importsafety.gov/report/report.pdg.

15. Ibid. p. 1.

16. Ibid. Letter to the President, p. 1.

17-21. "Textiles Designated a Priority Trade Issue," CBP Press Release, April 2009. Retrieved on September 26, 2009, from www.cbp.gov/xp/cgov/newsroom/fact_sheets/trade/textiles_priority.xml.

22-24. "U.S. Import Requirements—American Importers Association," by U.S. Customs Service. Retrieved on March 10, 2008, from www.americanimporters.org/pages/marketing/USimportrequirements.html.

25. Interview with Kathryn Kerrigan, January 20, 2008.

26-36. Op. cit. American Importers Association.

37. Export and Import Compliance Programs: *Designing, Implementing and Updating Systems to Comply with U.S. Export and Import Laws.* Retrieved on April 1, 2008, from www.medey.com/pdf%20export%20andimport%20compliance%20programs.pdf.

Rewards and
Challenges
of Export-
Import Trade

Part IV

Figure 9.1 The Dubai Mall of more than 12 million feet contains stores from many nations, a huge aquarium, restaurants, and an ice rink, all next to an Armani Hotel.

9

**EXPORTING
AMERICA'S
FASHION
GOODS
AROUND
THE WORLD**

"Years back fashion was somewhat segregated. The French wore French fashions, Italians wore Italian fashions ... Now we're living in a global community, certainly sharing ideas about not only fashion, but all sorts of products...There are very few boundaries to doing business. People in Japan are as interested in fashion as people in Argentina or Russia or Dubai."

—TOMMY HILFIGER, *WOMEN'S WEAR DAILY*, APRIL 22, 2008, P. 22.

Along with other successful fashion goods marketers, Tommy Hilfiger is acutely aware of consumers' need for appealing apparel, accessories, and home furnishings. While the Hilfiger organization sells its apparel line exclusively to the Macy's department stores in the United States, Hilfiger also runs six free-standing full-price stores throughout the world.[1]

P eople's desire for new and interesting fashions and designed goods is universal today. Through instant worldwide Internet communication, consumers everywhere are able to view and obtain the newest trends. The trends then become global, exposing the world to and perhaps uniting it through fashion.[2]

REASONS FOR EXPORTING

Since the demand for fashion goods exists around the globe, designers and marketers from businesses of all sizes reach out to anticipate and fulfill consumer desires in more and more ways. As you saw in Chapter 4, the reasons for companies to export are attractive: successful exporting increases total sales; it helps balance seasonal and business cycle sales figures—summer in the northern hemisphere is winter in the south, a sales slump in one region may be counterbalanced by a rise in another area, and seasonal goods such as swim suits and après ski wear can sell globally year-round. Entering overseas markets also may bring demand for new products, leading to company growth and diversification. And finally, an international presence contributes an enhanced dimension to the company image.

The global fashion market is truly competitive. A stroll in an American, European, or Asian shopping district reveals well-known fashion names from all over the globe: Ferragamo (Italy); Chanel (France); H&M and Ikea (Sweden); Uniqlo (Japan); George Jensen (Denmark); Waterford (Ireland); and Zara (Spain) are just a few foreign organizations whose products are found worldwide. For foreign travelers, the opportunity to purchase fashion exports en route has created international airport bazaars. For example, London's Heathrow Airport houses branches of Coach, Tiffany, Harrod's, Prada, and Mulberry, as well as vendors offering an assortment of British, French, and American cosmetics and fragrances, tobaccos, and other rare goods. Charles de Gaulle Airport in Paris contains the jewelry stores Van Cleef & Arpels and Cartier; the department store Printemps; and an Yves Saint Laurent boutique.[3] And these airports are just two in Europe. Think of similar sites in the rest of the world, Africa, the Middle East, Asia, and Australia!

Notice, too, that most of these fashion names are not American. The United States vies for customers with many global competitors, and the world economy which used to be formed by the U.S., Europe, and Japan, now faces competition from China, India, Brazil, and other emerging nations. According to the *World Competitiveness Yearbook 2008*, middle-class growth in China, India, Russia, and Central Europe, and the Middle-Eastern oil countries, has already reached 600 million, and these people spend some $4 trillion annually on consumer products including fashion goods and luxury items. Demand for fashion goods, as well as competition among fashion producers, is on the upswing.[4]

Figure 9.2 This Paul Smith boutique at London's Heathrow Airport offers British menswear to global travelers.

....

SPOTLIGHT ON GLOBAL TRADE 9.1:
Exporting Retail Expansion—Where to Go?

With domestic markets well-saturated by U.S. retail organizations, many fashion marketers such as Coach, Guess, and Polo Ralph Lauren (and more recently retailers such as Macy's) are looking overseas for expansion opportunities. The A.T. Kearney organization, a management consulting firm, through its Retail Apparel Index, rates developing countries according to their investment attractiveness for fashion retailers. Factors such as market attractiveness, existing competition, and risk are cited. "This study identifies where windows of opportunity are opening up for global retailers, and also for local and regional retailers," said Mike Moriarty, Kearney partner in charge of consumer industries and retail practice. According to the study, the top emerging countries for overseas retail expansion are:

1. **Brazil.** Consumers are fashion-conscious and already spending significant amounts on apparel. Domestic manufacturing is important. More than half of the population is under age 29, and some international retailers such as Spain's Zara are there already.

2. **China.** According to Moriarty, "China is a dynamic market right now, but if you're looking to enter the region, you have to have a more unique format, a more sophisticated approach, or you have to enter second- or third-tier cities, because the very best opportunities have been snagged up." Also, the Chinese have a different sense of color and design, but care for brand names and are willing to pay for them.

3. **India.** With a rising middle class that includes women, the attitudes toward apparel are changing. Many women now have the means and interest in fashion, including western fashions for work. The Italian firms Ferragamo, Gucci, and Bottega Veneta, among others, are already in Mumbai.

4. **Turkey.** Coach, Prada, and Jimmy Choo are among the organizations that have recently opened retail stores in Istanbul where the luxury market holds great appeal for the expanding middle class.

5. **Chile.** In the capital, Santiago, one of the most popular malls is Parque Arauco which contains stores such as Polo Ralph Lauren, Versace, and Zara. Brooks Brothers is also located in the city. Vitacura, Chile's version of Rodeo Drive, offers unique international shops featuring apparel and accessories, home decorating and household goods, and furniture.

6 through 10. (6) Romania. Although it accounts for lower spending than many European countries, it has a tremendous growth potential. (7) Argentina. Although still recovering from an earlier financial crisis, contains stores offering well-known designer brands such as Chanel, Gucci, and Valentino. (8) Thailand's capital, Bangkok, draws great interest among retailers considering expansion. Some famous brands already entrenched are Christian Dior, Fendi, and Louis Vuitton. (9) Russia. Although costly to open a store in Moscow, the city already contains two Polo Ralph Lauren stores, as well as stores bearing the names of a number of European brands. (10) The United Arab Emirates, burgeoning due to oil, is promoting industrial and retail expansion in Dubai and Abu Dhabi. Among the well-known brands there are French Connection, Ralph Lauren, and Carolina Herrera.

Source: Cecily Hall, "The WWD List: Ripe for Retail, The top emerging countries for global apparel retail expansion," *Women's Wear Daily*, June 5, 2008, p. 16.

EXPORTING BY ENTREPRENEURS AND YOUNG DESIGNERS

As stated earlier, one of the most immediate ways global consumers seek to satisfy desires for fashion goods is through the Internet. They reach out to small and large fashion organizations through net surfing and online buying, and the pace of Internet buying throughout the world is on the upswing. Many retail stores, for example, realize that in order to serve customers efficiently, and at the same time increase sales, an Internet presence is a necessary and welcome addition to their **bricks-and-mortar store** or physical presence.

Smaller Fashion Businesses

By no means is the province of exporting exclusive to large businesses. A company, large or small, through its Web site, has access to consumers worldwide. For example, Illinois shoe retailer Kathryn Kerrigan (whom you met in Chapter 8), receives inquiries on her company Web site from Canada, the United Kingdom, Australia, Serbia, the Middle East, Africa, and elsewhere. The wives of dignitaries in various overseas locations purchase from Kerrigan's site fashionable dress shoes for important events. On occasion, Kerrigan says, an inquiry appears suspicious, whereupon she asks for payment in the form of a wire transfer or U.S. bank certified check. If potential fraud seems in the offing, the so-called customer learns the bluff has been called, Kerrigan notes, and does not contact the Web site again.[5]

In addition to selling online, Kathryn Kerrigan is successfully expanding her retail stores. Other boutique owners, however, are finding that sales from their Web sites are driving business sufficiently to make closing their boutiques advantageous. Natalie Barber, owner of the former Wicker Park (Chicago) apparel and accessories boutique, Language, who decided to devote her energies exclusively to the Internet, commented, "I spend 100 percent of my money and time on the store, and get so much more return online." From her Web site, shoplanguage.com, her customers order from New York and California, but also from Canada, France, Great Britain, and Australia. Another fashion-oriented retailer, Active Endeavors, closed its boutiques in Chicago and the North Shore, concentrating on its Web site, activeendeavors.com, with 20 percent of customer orders originating from overseas. "If you have an interesting product and it appeals to certain segments but not enough of them can produce the volume of a retail store, you can do it on an Internet site and create a market that you can't with a store," states retail consultants McMillan-Doolitle's senior partner Will Anderson.[6]

Tory Burch

Young designers are among the first to realize the value of an overseas presence. One of these is 2008 Council of Fashion Designers award recipient, apparel and accessories designer Tory Burch who (like a number of celebrities) attracted attention through an appearance on *Oprah*. Someone had given Oprah Winfrey one of Burch's caftans as a gift, and she was impressed enough to invite Tory Burch to appear on her show. The next day there were 8 million "hits" on the Tory Burch Web site. Burch maintains that her inspiration comes from famous designers like Balenciaga and Lanvin and her experience includes work with Ralph Lauren and Vera Wang. She has her own upscale preppy-chic look which she is starting to distribute in Europe through offices in Milan as well as through a number of shops in the United States.[7] Her company's latest expansion is into Japan and South Korea.

a)   b)

Figure 9.3a & 9.3b Phillip Lim and his Tokyo store appeal to Japanese consumers' willingness to experiment with new fashion looks.

....

Phillip Lim

Brought up in Orange County, California, in a Cambodian family of Chinese descent, Phillip Lim, according to his elders, was supposed to have been a doctor or a businessman. Lim, rebelling when he learned that for him the sight of blood was an authentic turn off, soon discovered that his turn-on was studying fashion. Before long, he became known in the industry for his svelte tailored jackets and feminine dresses. Moving to New York, he launched fashion lines for women, men, and children, opened a store there, and before long won a Council of Fashion Designers award.

Next, Lim decided to expand his own stores to Japan. Already familiar with the Japanese market through his wholesale business there which had brought his 3.1 line (so named because he started it at age 31) into some 85 department and specialty stores, Lim believed a logical step should be a free-standing Tokyo **flagship store**, a large company retail presence in a busy major city, featuring his main lines. With his joint venture Japanese partner, Lim is now investigating additional retail locations in Japan, including Kyoto and Osaka, plus, further out, stores in Hong Kong and mainland China. One of the factors influencing Lim's presence in Japan is the interest among customers there to try new fashion looks. "They'll buy it and wear it so religiously and it's nice because as a young designer . . . the worst is to have your ideas diluted into pieces." Lim believes it is important to diversify a business geographically, particularly if, when sales are soft in one area, they may be compensated for in other parts of the world. To maintain appeal, Lim keeps **markup**—the amount the retailer adds to the cost of goods—at a minimum and saves transportation costs by having goods produced in China. One reason he decided on opening the Tokyo flagship store was to have more control over product distribution, but he intends to maintain his wholesale operation in Japan for the time being.[8]

EXPORTING BY RETAILERS

While some U.S. retailers such as Saks and Wal-Mart have been operating in other countries for a while, others are beginning to see the value in looking for expansion outside of the United States where the market is well-saturated. One of these stores is the specialty retailer Lord & Taylor.

Lord & Taylor

An historically recognized name in apparel retailing, Lord & Taylor, years ago, was the first New York store to install an elevator. Also it is renowned for its window displays at Christmastime, as well as for being the first sizeable fashion retailer to be headed by a woman. Purchased by Federated Stores (now Macy's) in the early 2000s, Lord & Taylor was acquired by NRDC Equity Partners. NRDC's management began extensive fashion promotions such as obtaining a wider selection of American brand names, like Juicy Couture for contemporary women's apparel; refurbishing its stores and expanding the fashions in its home furnishings

INTERNATIONAL FASHION FOCUS 9.1:
Barbara Turf Oversees Crate & Barrel Expansion

A leading purveyor of international household goods and home accessories, Crate & Barrel got its start in Chicago in 1962 by offering in its single tiny store imported goods displayed on the crates that had transported them and promoted with hand-written signs. This marketing tactic of founder Gordon Segal and his wife has parlayed the company into more than 150 stores with 7,000 employees across the United States and Canada. Known for its buildings of steel and glass revealing a sleek and modern assortment of furniture and household items, Crate & Barrel has become a destination shopping bazaar for many consumers.

In 1988, the German catalog Otto Group (GmbH & Co. KG) purchased a major part of Crate & Barrel, soon leading to expanded catalog and Internet operations. In May 2008, after 46 years of running the organization, Segal decided to turn over the management to Barbara Turf, no stranger to the company's strategies and operations. Starting as a part-time sales associate in 1968, she later was named store manager. In 1972, she moved to corporate headquarters and three years later headed the merchandising division, later on rising to executive vice president of merchandising and marketing. In 1996, Segal named her president of Crate & Barrel, her current title.

As top executive, Turf's goals for the company include continuing the strategy of sustainability and "going green." Increasingly, its furniture features sturdier construction than its original bamboo, and some of its dinnerware is made from recycled glass. "To be successful, you have to have something unique," says Turf. "Our mission is to have the product stand on its own."

Another major company goal after Canada is expansion overseas. Dubai, in the Middle East, is among the locations under consideration.

Sources: Sandra M. Jones, "Crate & Barrel keeps pulse on the Environment," www.chicagotribune. com. March 24, 2008. Retrieved on June 18, 2008. otto group, http://212.162.143/index.php?L=O&id=482. Retrieved 6/18/08. www.yorkdale.com/imgs_07/crateBarrel.pdf.

Figure 9.4 Lord & Taylor's management seeks overseas expansion opportunities.

....

Figure 9.5 An entrance to the Dubai Mall's 1,000 stores.

....

departments; for seeking out potential store locations in nearby Mexico and Canada, and subsequently considering retail outlets in Asia.[9, 10]

Macy's and Bloomingdale's

Owned by the same parent corporation, Macy's, Inc., executives of Macy's and Bloomingdale's stores, are actively looking for possible overseas retail sites. Facing a mature domestic market for consumer fashion goods, Macy's top management recently named one of its executives to a corporate position for international retail development, responsible for researching and analyzing opportunities for overseas stores for both Macy's and Bloomingdale's.[11] At this point it looks as though Bloomingdale's may have the corporation's first overseas branch, most likely in the Dubai Mall (United Arab Emirates), scheduled for completion in 2010 as the largest shopping mall in the world. The Mall is expected to hold the world's tallest building with more than 200 floors and an Armani Hotel at its base. One thousand stores are to include brands, in addition to Armani, such as Coach, Bulgari, Gucci, and Yves Saint Laurent.[12]

Other locations Macy's executives are considering are in the Middle East, for example Kuwait, and in Asia, possibly China.

Saks, Incorporated

Saks, Incorporated, the owner of around 50 Saks Fifth Avenue stores in the United

States, (as well as several others throughout the Middle East and Asia) under a licensing agreement with a subsidiary of the Mexican conglomerate Grupo Sanborns, has recently opened a Saks Fifth Avenue store in Mexico City. Known for its designer collections of apparel for men and women, emphasizing European brands such as Chanel, Dolce and Gabbana, Hermès, Prada, and Ermenegildo Zegna, (rather than American brands for which Lord & Taylor prides itself) Saks Fifth Avenue had established itself in the Middle East earlier in this century.[13] In 2001, a full-line Saks Fifth Avenue store opened in Riyadh, Saudi Arabia, and another opened in 2004 in Dubai's (U.A.E.) Bur Jaman Centre, where a branch exclusively for men is also located. Subsequently, in November 2007, the corporation looked closer to home and created the arrangement described for its full-line Mexico City store. Other locations Saks is considering for its stores include Shanghai and other markets in Asia and the Middle East, as well as another Saudi store, in Jeddah.[14]

Figure 9.6 **A leader in fashion retailing overseas, Saks drew customers early on by offering global designer brands.**

. . . .

Figure 9.7 **Wal-Mart around the world.**

....

Wal-Mart

With sales of $405 billion in 2009, and more than $100 billion of that coming from its stores overseas, Wal-Mart maintains its lead by far as the world's largest retailer. While known mainly for hard lines and food, Wal-Mart also offers apparel and home furnishings. A few of its brands include Disney and Limited Too for children, Cuisinart and Kitchen Aid household appliances, and Hart Schaffner and Marx apparel for men, and Samsung and Panasonic home theaters and other electronics.

When Wal-Mart decided to open stores outside of the United States, it ventured into neighboring Mexico in 1991. Today, out of its more than 7,000 stores, over 1,000 branches are in that country. Still sticking close to home, Wal-Mart entered Puerto Rico the next year. Now it has more than 50 stores on the island. Canada was third on Wal-Mart's expansion list; today, over 300 stores carry the name there.

Wal-Mart's first overseas venture was into Germany, known to be Western Europe's largest market; however, this effort did not work out well for the retail giant. Consumers in Germany did not take to Wal-Mart's way of doing business. For example, food prices at German discount stores were already lower than the prices Wal-Mart could offer. Also, some of Wal-Mart's business practices struck a sour note in the German culture, as when Wal-Mart staff smiled at customers, German men thought the employees were flirting. In both Germany (after trying for 10 years and opening 85 stores) as well as South Korea (with just 16 stores and no Wal-Mart name recognition), sales performance did not measure up to management expectations and so the company pulled out of both countries.

Brazil also offered some challenges with stiff competition, but Wal-Mart learned here that holding on to its corporate name was not a plus when it could purchase successful local companies with familiar names and reputations. And so, over time, in various parts of the world, Wal-Mart stores became known under names such as ASDA (Britain), Seiyu (Japan), Bompreço (Brazil), and Carchochain (Central America).[15]

With Brazil and the United Kingdom as two of Wal-Mart's leading countries, and a vast presence in China with more than 200 stores, the company is expanding into India with a local partner, opening up three small supermarkets and an 85,000 square foot distribution center in Punjab and more stores later.[16] Another market Wal-Mart is considering, to the point of naming an executive to explore the potential, is Russia. Both Moscow and St. Petersburg have few supermarkets, and Russians are favorably disposed toward one-stop shopping.[17]

TABLE 9.1 WAL-MART GLOBAL DATA SHEET FEBRUARY 1, 2008

Retail Units Worldwide	7,262
US Retail Units	4,141 Wal-Mart Stores 971 Supercenters 2,447 SAM'S CLUBs 591 Neighborhood Market 132

International Retail Units	3,065		
	COUNTRY	RETAIL UNITS	DATE OF ENTRY
	Mexico	1,023	November 1991
	Puerto Rico	54	August 1992
	Canada	305	November 1994
	Argentina	21	November 1995
	Brazil	313	May 1995
	China(*)	202	August 1996
	United Kingdom	352	July 1999
	Japan	394	March 2002
	Costa Rica	149	September 2005
	El Salvador	70	September 2005
	Guatemala	145	September 2005
	Honduras	47	September 2005
	Nicaragua	46	September 2005

(*) Inclues a 35% interest in Trust-Mart, which operates 101 stores in 34 cities in China

Company History	First Wal-Mart Store opened in 1962 (Rogers, AR) First SAM'S CLUB opened in 1983 (Midwest City, OK) First Supercenter opened in 1988 (Washington, MO) First International unit opened in 1991 (Mexico City) First Neighborhood Market opened in 1998 (Bentonville, AR)
Company Trade Territory	Wal-Mart serves more than 176 million customers weekly in 14 countries worldwide including Argentina, Brazil, Canada, China, Costa Rica, El Salvador, Guatemala, Honduras, Japan, Mexico, Nicaragua, Puerto Rico, United Kingdom and United States.
Sales	FYE 1/31/07: $344.9 billion United States—more than 1.36 million Internationally—more than 550,000
Total Associates	Total Associates—more than 1.9 million worldwide

Wal-Mart is a classic example of an American retailer serving not only the domestic market, but also millions of customers in 14 countries around the world.

EXPORTING BY FASHION MARKETING ORGANIZATIONS

A number of fashion businesses, known as **fashion marketing organizations**, own or have continuing long-term connections beginning with product design and continuing through manufacturing and distribution, right to the customer through retail stores, catalogs, and/or the Internet. Some of these are apparel companies such as Abercrombie & Fitch; others market home furnishings such as Williams Sonoma, and still others are part of the beauty aids industry such as Estée Lauder. While a few of these have been operating in other countries for quite a while, others are just beginning to think in terms of an international presence. The following companies represent just a few of the many fashion marketers engaged in global marketing today.

Figure 9.8 Russians are favorably disposed toward one-stop shopping.
....

Abercrombie & Fitch

Highly popular yet controversial, Abercrombie & Fitch is the first teen retailer to open stores in Europe. Its London flagship store is said to produce sales at the rate of $4,500 per square foot, equal to that of the New York flagship. Founded in 1892, as an elite outdoor sporting goods retailer for rich men, Abercrombie's focus today has turned to marketing upscale jeans and T-shirts to 18-to-22 year-olds. The company also consists of an Abercrombie children's segment; Hollister for preteens; and Gilly Hicks for lingerie. With its various brands, Abercrombie & Fitch operates about 1,035 stores worldwide, plus individual Web sites. Located in the United States, Canada, and the United Kingdom, Abercrombie's next ventures are planned to include Paris, Copenhagen, and Milan.[18] In Tokyo's fashionable Ginza shopping district, Abercrombie & Fitch is creating an 11-story building, opening in 2009. "Tokyo's young, fashion-conscious consumers make the city an ideal location for our first Asian store," states Michael Jeffries, the company's chairman and chief executive officer. Abercrombie's long-range overseas expansion plans are aimed eventually toward creating other flagship stores in Italy, France, Germany, Spain, Denmark, Sweden, and the United Kingdom.[19]

GUESS, Inc.

One fashion marketing organization to expand most successfully overseas to date is GUESS, a designer and marketer of sportswear and accessories for men, women, and children. Some of the company's brands include: GUESS, GUESS? GUESS kids, baby GUESS, and GUESS by Marciano.

Figure 9.9 This view of the Casablanca, Morocco, store is typical of the GUESS retail look overseas.
....

Led by the brothers Maurice and Paul Marciano, GUESS has developed a collection of apparel based on both contemporary American lifestyle and European sensibilities. Operating some 579 stores in 65 countries in 2008, the company plans to double that number shortly. In addition to its stores in Canada and the United States, GUESS recently opened a European headquarters in Lugano, Switzerland, to oversee its many interests in Italy, England, France, Spain, and Germany. Its European division was responsible for half of the company's $1.75 billion revenue in a recent year. It is also planning e-commerce sites in Europe similar to those already running in the United States and Canada. In addition to its stores, GUESS has licensing agreements for handbags, watches, and shoes, which it sells through retailers as well as in its own stores.

The company's next area for future investment is Asia. Already GUESS operates 46 stores in South Korea, and has opened 21 stores in China, including Shanghai, Beijing, Macau, and Hong Kong. It maintains a **sourcing office**, a buying office to find regional suppliers, in Hong Kong. It is not hard to understand why the Marciano brothers' credo is "the world is our field."[20, 21]

Estée Lauder Companies, Inc.

Many people agree that the best-known cosmetics names worldwide belong to the Estée Lauder organization. In addition to the Estée Lauder brand, others under the company umbrella include Clinique, Aramis, Bobbi Brown, MAC, and Jo Malone, to mention a few, plus licensing agreements (mainly for fragrances) with design organizations such as Donna Karan, Coach, Tom Ford, Sean Jean, Michael Kors, and others. The company manufactures, markets, and sells skin care products, cosmetics, and fragrances (creams, lotions, makeup foundations, mascara, lipsticks, scents, and the like) through department stores, fragrance boutiques, on Web sites, and through duty-free stores.

Headquartered in New York, Lauder brands have long been represented throughout the United States in department and specialty stores, and in European stores such as Au Printemps and Galeries Lafayette in Paris, and Harrod's in London, among other internationally recognized retailers. Indeed, Lauder lines are found in more than 18,000 locations in some 135 countries throughout the U.S., Europe, Russia, the Middle East, and Asia.

Figure 9.10 This Lauder Mumbai boutique focuses on individualized service which appeals to Indian consumers.
....

Current plans for expansion are focused on Asia, and India in particular. Brands such as Lauder's are considered luxury items, and with India's emerging middle class, the demand for such goods is accelerating. The first of a possible 20 Lauder locations in India opened in Mumbai, in a single Lauder "jewel box" store located in a shopping area near other luxury shops such as Gucci, Bottega Veneta, and Jimmy Choo. A MAC store in Mumbai had already paved the way—with high sales records—for more Lauder openings in the city. Breaking its historic mold of maintaining a shop within a department store (as in the United States), Lauder decided to try freestanding boutiques and benefit from company research which had revealed that Indian women are attracted by high-quality products and dedicated customer service. The company realized that the best way to provide these is in an intimate store setting. "We wanted to enter the market with a freestanding store. Our goal is a consistent brand image with some local adaptation," comments Sonia Michon-Flochlay, Lauder's vice president regional director for Europe, the Middle East, and Africa. "Luxury is a service. Every woman can be our customer," she adds.

All of the locations will carry the company's best-selling global products, backed by advertising using local models, plus signature campaigns featuring celebrities such as Elizabeth

Figure 9.11 Levi's global fashion looks are available on its Web site and in its stores on four continents.

....

Hurley, Gwyneth Paltrow, and Hilary Rhoda. The company believes the luxury market for Lauder in India is growing beyond Mumbai and Delhi, to cities such as Hyderabad, Bangalore, and Chennai, among others.[22]

A more recent acquisition by Estée Lauder is part ownership in an Indian hair, skin, and body care firm, Forest Essentials, whose products are based on the ancient Hindu system of using fresh herbs and other plants as ingredients for scrubs, creams, and lotions. The ingredients are harvested high in the Himalayan Mountains, and the products are marketed in freestanding stores such as the one in Select Citywalk Mall in Delhi. Some 500 million Indian consumers provide a substantial customer base for Lauder, which already does more than half of its business outside of the United States and is aiming to have 70 percent of its sales come from other countries in 10 years.[23]

Levi Strauss & Co.

Although Levi Strauss built its reputation on 501 jeans and Dockers pants, the company's latest thrust in worldwide markets is a total look: tops, boots and shoes, accessories, and jackets. Referring to planned sales results from tops and pants, Australian John Anderson, Levi's CEO and president, said, "I think the mix should be 50/50. The real opportunity for us is in tops and other categories. We need to put those (tops) in front of more consumers." Other plans Anderson has for the company include improving both product quality and price points, refurbishing the Dockers brand marketed internationally, expanding the number of company operated and franchised retail stores, and improving the women's business. Currently, products for men account for 72 percent of company sales.

Management believes that the best way for Levi Strauss & Co. to display its products is through retail stores. It has around 200 company-owned stores, with some 45 full-price stores, 14 outlets, and a small number of Dockers stores in the U.S. One of the most exciting is the Levi's store, right in the heart of New York City's Times Square, which opened in May 2008.

Internationally, Levi's distributes its products through some 1,700 dedicated stores, mainly operated through franchise and licensing agreements. Approximately 50 percent of the company's revenue is generated internationally, and Anderson expects to see that figure rise in the next decade. He points out that the middle class in China is as large as, if not larger, than the middle class in the United States. "We are already the number-one jeans brand in China, India, and Indonesia. So these are the markets of the future," Anderson states. Indeed, sales overseas have helped counteract a recent slump in U.S. revenues. Sales in Europe (including Turkey, the Middle East, and Africa) and sales in Japan both grew while sales in North, Central, and South America were off slightly, he reported.

One sustained promotional effort, according to Anderson, will be a higher quality and price for the iconic 501 button-fly jeans which continue in worldwide appeal. "In the end, it's all about product, product, product," Anderson comments. "As long as consumers can see the value in a product, they'll pay the extra price . . . so when the consumer comes in, he says, 'Wow, I really want to buy something.'"[24]

Nike, International

Publicly held and **vertically integrated**, that is controlling the entire manufacturing and distribution process of its products, Nike, International is the world's leading supplier of athletic shoes, apparel, and equipment for sports such as basketball, baseball, golf, tennis, and football and more. Nike's worldwide revenues for 2007 amounted to more than $16 billion. Holding contractual agreements with some 700 factories in Indonesia, China, India, the Philippines and elsewhere, Nike maintains 45 regional offices to connect it with some 25,000 retailers in the United States and 160 other countries.

The company, now headquartered in Beaverton, Oregon, was the idea of Phillip Knight who sought the appropriate athletic gear in the early 1960's. In 1964, Knight was joined by his former coach, William Bauerman, who began designing athletic footwear. The business began to grow, offering shoes and equipment for jogging, running, and other sports. Its outlets spread in the United States and, in 1972, entered Canada. Along with maintaining its own stores and selling to other retailers, Nike created the Niketown store concept, part store, part sports arena (claiming an in-store basketball court), part training locale for Nike sales representatives, and part museum (with shoes and gear of athletes and real and virtual celebrities like Batman). Niketown stores became drawing cards in several U.S. cities including Chicago and Atlanta.

In 1981, when Nike management saw that U.S. consumers were not spending much on athletic gear, it decided to go international, (change its name accordingly), and establish retail connections in Europe, Japan and other Asian nations, Latin America, and Africa. The company opened a factory in Ireland to manufacture for the European market; Nike also broke off with its distributors there in order to gain greater control of its total marketing and distribution activities. To maintain visibility among consumers, Nike developed promotional agreements with star athletes, among them Michael Jordan and Tiger Woods. Along the way, the company acquired other businesses: Converse shoes and Cole Haan dress and casual footwear, among them.[25] More recently, Nike was named China's supplier of uniforms for the Beijing Olympics, creating apparel for China's basketball team, swim teams, cyclists, and track and field competitors, plus others. No wonder: Nike's goods are found in retail stores in some 300 Chinese cities, and the company has built its popularity by targeting brand-loyal Chinese teens. Among participants and followers of athletics, as well as much of the general public, the Nike "swoosh" is truly a global symbol.[26]

Williams-Sonoma, Incorporated

In the early 1950s, Sonoma County, California contractor Chuck Williams and his friends spent much of their leisure time cooking meals and eating together. One year, Williams traveled to France where he learned about French food and some of the special utensils, such as soufflé pans, used by French cooks. Around the same time, Francophile chef Julia Child was writing French cook books for Americans and later began giving French cooking demonstrations on her television program, "The French Chef." People started asking Williams (then

Figure 9.12 Williams-Sonoma operates over 250 retail stores in the United States and Canada.
....

a hardware store owner) for some of the cooking pots, pans, and other equipment used by Child. Soon Williams converted his hardware store into a cooking supply store for chefs, and Williams-Sonoma came into being.

Before long, the store relocated to San Francisco in an exclusive shopping area near prosperous establishments such as the Elizabeth Arden beauty salon and exclusive women's clubs. Clients of the salon would stop to browse and buy the imported cutlery and cookware featured at Williams-Sonoma. This good fortune taught Williams the importance of the right retail location. One day, a customer who was in the advertising business told Chuck Williams that the store needed a catalog. He took her advice and soon the first Williams-Sonoma catalog appeared. The business grew, incorporated, opened branch stores in Los Angeles and the San Francisco suburbs, began to expand in other areas, and went public. Gardeners' Eden, a catalog business selling plants and gardening tools, was bought and later sold. The next project, Hold Everything—a business offering storage supplies and containers—started out selling goods through catalogs and later expanded to stores. Williams-Sonoma then purchased Pottery Barn, an eastern chain of stores known for its dinner ware and furniture. Williams' next venture was a cookbook and guide to using Williams-Sonoma utensils. A new and compatible acquisition was Chambers catalog, featuring fine European linens and towels. Bridal registries for Williams-Sonoma and Pottery Barn soon followed. Three catalog centers and expanded retail stores added to the company's sales.

Web sites for Williams-Sonoma, Pottery Barn, and the bridal registries were a logical step into the twenty-first century. Pottery Barn Kids catalog was inaugurated, featuring home furnishings and furniture, such as sleigh beds, scaled to younger consumers. The success of the catalog led to the first retail stores in Canada as well as in the states. In 2001 the company opened Williams-Sonoma, Pottery Barn, and Pottery Barn Kids in Toronto. Other stores followed in Vancouver and Calgary, to serve Canadian customers, many of whom had shopped these stores in the United States. Soon a moderately-priced furniture catalog, West Elm, appeared. Then Pottery Barn created a catalog specifically for teenage customers. PBteen catalog features furniture for consumers older than Pottery Barn Kids, whose lifestyle demands its own bedroom and study furniture, lighting, rugs, and accessories. Williams-Sonoma-Home was the company's next major venture with stores and Web sites. While product-line expansion has been the focus of Williams-Sonoma, physical presence in other countries and Web sites providing a global reach are a vital part of its business as international consumers become increasingly familiar with its goods.[27]

Figure 9.13 Calvin Klein fashions appeal to consumers throughout the world.
. . . .

Figure 9.14 Customers for Carolina Herrera's fashions in the U.S. and overseas seek the chic look of her designs.
....

Figure 9.15 One of the newest Ralph Lauren stores sits on Avenue Montaigne in Paris, amidst other world-renowned fashion organizations.

....

EXPORTING BY DESIGNERS

Many established American fashion designers are well known overseas. A few of these include: Calvin Klein, Carolina Herrera, Marc Jacobs, and Ralph Lauren.

Calvin Klein

One of the most popular designers among Americans and Europeans is Calvin Klein. Known for the elite Calvin Klein Collection, cK apparel and accessories, and cK Jeans brands, among the company's major products are: apparel, accessories, shoes, underwear and sleepwear, hosiery, eyewear, watches, coats, fragrances, and home products.[28] Much of the fashion merchandise the company produces is through licensing agreements with two major American manufacturers: Phillips Van Heusen Corporation (PVH) and Warnaco. PVH also includes manufacturing agreements with Kenneth Cole, Michael Kors, Sean Jean, and Tommy Hilfiger, among others. Warnaco owns the largest licenses, those for the Calvin Klein jeans and underwear. PVH plans for its Calvin Klein agreements include 500 stores added throughout Europe, Asia, and South America in 2008.[29]

Carolina Herrera

Born in Caracas, Venezuela, applying herself to the fashion field for 27 years, receiving the Council of Fashion Designers of America (CFDA) Lifetime Achievement Award, mother of four, grandmother of 10, with fashion goods marketed in the Western Hemisphere, Europe, and the Middle East, nevertheless, Carolina Herrera manages to maintain a low-key demeanor. Her **signature line**, or highest priced CH Carolina Herrera collection, is intended for consumers with a fashionable lifestyle with minimum fuss. Garments include evening gowns to T-shirts, plus jackets, shawls, shirts, caftans, windbreakers, menswear, fragrances for men and women, and items for the home such as blankets.

Of some 40 stores offering Herrera merchandise, 19 of these are in Spain. Stores opened recently are located in Kuwait, Jeddah, Qatar, Bahrain, and Saudi Arabia, with additional stores planned for home town Caracas, Venezuela, Riyadh, Saudi Arabia, and Abu Dhabi, United Arab Emirates. Herrera also maintains a factory in Spain which she visits twice a year. Her **diffusion lines**, lower priced adaptations of her signature line, are manufactured there. About her life and work, Herrera says, "I love the idea that I was brought up with so much discipline. It made me organized, and it made me understand how important it is to be on time and to have my own life . . . The discipline was always there. Fashion is always on deadlines. But first of all, I have to say I enjoy my work. The important thing is I love what I do and I am also able to have another life. It's important to have your own life and your own time. That's good for your work, too." [30]

Marc Jacobs

The youngest designer ever to win an award from the Council of Fashion Designers of America, Marc Jacobs' life is filled with fashion designs and enterprises. After graduating from the

Parsons School of Design in New York, he went to work for the Perry Ellis organization and later moved on to Louis Vuitton where he is still creative director, in addition to handling his own merchandise lines. Those include: his top collection line for women and men; Marc, a diffusion line for men, women and children, plus accessories, home ware, and special items such as union jack surfboards, beach and bath towels, and colorful London T-shirts. Well-known in the States, Marc Jacobs opened his first European store in Paris. His biggest markets are in Japan (Tokyo, Kyoto, and Osaka among other cities); the United States (where his lines are found with multiple retailers such as Neiman Marcus); China, and the United Kingdom. Jacobs' lines are also found in other Asian locations including Korea, Indonesia, and Thailand and in the Middle East. The recent opening of his London flagship store served as a dramatic finale to the city's fashion week. In addition, a Marc Jacobs store in Moscow is owned by an investor. Offering the Marc Jacobs collection and Marc labels as well as children's wear and accessories, the store is located in an upscale shopping area of Moscow, across from Louis Vuitton, and claims as neighbors Dior, Chanel, and Burberry. Plans include another store in St. Petersburg.[31, 32, and 33]

Ralph Lauren

Perhaps the best known American designer today, Ralph Lauren is credited with being the first to think of fashion as a lifestyle concept. His creations, emulating upper-class British style, began to call out for compatible surroundings, and so Ralph Lauren home furnishings and accessories—table top linens and china, towels and bedding, draperies, furniture, and paints for the wall—became part of the company's product line.

An international presence is important to the organization, and through franchise agreements with local investors, Ralph Lauren stores are an integral part of upscale shopping from Australia to Venezuela, including Belgium, France, Germany, Japan, New Zealand, Panama, Russia, and the United Kingdom, among others. Some stores overseas market jeans exclusively, while others are Ralph Lauren, Polo Ralph Lauren, or outlet stores. One of the most recent Ralph Lauren stores to open, the second in Paris, is on fashionable Avenue Montaigne, home to other world-renowned design organizations such as Christian Dior, Nina Ricci, Prada, and, yes, Calvin Klein. To be truly global, the company also maintains an international Web site.[34, 35]

SUMMARY

Since the demand for fashion goods is global, designers and marketers from very small to gigantic are participating in international marketing. A company does not have to be large to take part. Small bricks-and-mortar and virtual fashion businesses such as Kathryn Kerrigan's, are finding that international customers seek them out through their Web sites. Young designers such as Tory Burch and Phillip Lim are among the first to understand the importance of global marketing and are building overseas connections into their organizations.

With the exception of Wal-Mart which is located throughout the world, and Saks, which has had an international presence for some time, the large department and specialty stores such as Macy's and Bloomingdale's are proceeding gingerly into overseas markets. Realizing domestic markets are mature, and that a potentially profitable way to increase market share is through international marketing, they are investigating potential opportunities.

Some fashion marketing organizations such as Abercrombie & Fitch, GUESS, and Levi Strauss have long known the importance of global marketing and are reaping some rewards for their efforts. Others, such as Williams-Sonoma are expanding conservatively into nearby international sites. Fashion designers with established names such as Calvin Klein and Carolina Herrera know the demand for their goods is international and they are continuing to maintain and expand positions in the global fashion arena.

Key Terms

> Bricks-and-mortar store
> Diffusion lines
> Fashion marketing organization

> Flagship store
> Markup
> Signature line
> Sourcing office
> Vertically integrated

Review Questions

1. What is the advantage of a Web site to a fashion goods retailer interested in global marketing?

2. Why are domestic department stores such as Macy's and Bloomingdale's now beginning to consider expanding overseas?

3. What made Saks' entry into foreign markets relatively easy?

4. How do Abercrombie & Fitch and Guess account for their acceptance overseas?

5. What did the research done by the Estée Lauder organization reveal about the customers for cosmetics and fragrances in India, and what did the company do to satisfy customer preferences there?

Discussion Questions and Activities

1. Interview one or two local fashion goods retailers who maintain Web sites to determine their interest in global marketing and ascertain the extent to which they receive merchandise orders from customers overseas. Report your findings to the class.

2. In light of the mature domestic market of large department and specialty stores, how do you account for their comparative slowness in deciding to enter into global marketing, particularly when fashion goods marketers like Guess and Nike are so internationally successful?

3. Why do you suppose a home furnishings company such as Williams- Sonoma is expanding its catalog offerings extensively, yet to date has limited its retail store openings to Canada?

4. What are two or three factors that account for the ability of iconic design organizations such as Calvin Klein and Ralph Lauren to have an international presence in major fashion goods markets throughout the world?

5. Prepare a brief report on some of the ideas you gathered from this chapter that could be useful to you in planning your own entry into global marketing.

References

1. Sharon Edelson, "Tommy Hilfiger to Open Fifth Avenue Shop in November, *Women's Wear Daily*, March 12, 2008, p.10.

2. Debra Bass, "Fashion Communicates across the Globe," *St. Louis Post-Dispatch*, August 17, 2006.

3. Kalya Foreman, "Retail Lifts Off at Europe's Airports," *Women's Wear Daily*, May 5, 2008, p. 24.

4. John Zarocostas, "U.S. Faces Growing Competition in Global Market, Report Finds," *Women's Wear Daily*, May 15, 2008, p.15.

5. Email to author from Kathryn Kerrigan, kathryn@ kathrynKerrigan.com, April 18, 2008.

6. Rebecca Little, "Boutiques set up shops online," *Chicago Tribune*, March 20, Sec. 5A, p. 4.

7. Booth Moore, "Tory Burch has turned her line of classics into a must-have lifestyle brand," *Los Angeles Times*, June 1, 2008. Retrieved on June 6, 2008, from www .newsday.com/features/ lifestyle/.

8. Amanda Kaiser, "Phillip Lim Begins Japan Push with Tokyo Flagship," *Women's Wear Daily*, April 26, 2008, p.3.

9. Michael Barbaro, "Lord & Taylor Considers Stores Outside the U.S.," *New York Times*, April 30, 2008. Electronic edition. Retrieved on June 9, 2008 from www.nytimes .com/2008/04/30/business.

10. David Moin and Whitney Beckett, "L & T's Aggressive Plans: Eyes Growth in Home and Expansion Abroad," *Women's Wear Daily*, April 30, 2008, pp. 1 and 10.

11. David Moin, "Macy's Taps Edelman to Foster International Growth," *Women's Wear Daily*, May 9, 2008, p. 4.

12. Luisa Zargani, "Bloomingdale's Said in Talks for Mideast Partner," *Women's Wear Daily*, March 17, 2008, p. 3.

13. Saks Fifth Avenue, www .Saks, Inc./Investor Relations/ News release/November 28, 2007. Retrieved on June 10, 2008.

14. Brenda Lloyd, "Saks Looking Overseas for Growth, Opens Men's Boutiquein Dubai," *Women's Wear Daily*, June 5, 2008, p. 6.

15. Mark Landler and Michael Barbaro, "Wal-Mart overseas push can be lost in translation," *International New York Herald Tribune*, Online, August 2, 2006. Retrieved on June 14, 2008.

16. Sharon Edelson, "Wal-Mart Lauds Winning Model as May Sales Rise 9.8%," *Women's Wear Daily*, June 9, 2008, p. 15.

17. Alastair Goa, "Russia Appears Ripe for Wal-Mart," *Women's Wear Daily*, May 8, 2008, p. 16.

18. Heather Burke, "Abercrombie Buoys Stock as Male Models Woo Shoppers, (Update Two)," *Bloomberg.com.* Updated June 16, 2008; retrieved the same date.

19. David Moin, "Building Tall in Tokyo: A & F Latest to Join Megastore Stampede," *Women's Wear Daily*, August 6, 2007, pp. 1 and 34.

20. Guess, GUESS, Inc. Annual Report, 2008.

21. Vicki M. Young, "Global Reach Propels Guess," *Women's Wear Daily*, June 4, 2008, p. 2.

22. Mahlia S. Lone, "Lauder Brand Opens First Store in India," *Women's Wear Daily*, June 27, 2008, p. 27.

23. Pete Born, "Estée Lauder Buys Stake in India Firm," *Women's Wear Daily*, July 18, 2008, p. 5.

24. David Lipke, "Levi's Bets on Premium Positioning," *DNR*, April 4, 2008, p. 9.

25. Nike, www.nike.com. Retrieved on July 8, 2008.

26. Kathleen E. McLaughlin, "Nike Designs Olympic Uniforms, Stays Out of Fray," *Women's Wear Daily*, May 15, 2008, p. 6.

27. Williams-Sonoma, www .williams-sonoma.com/ companyoverview. Retrieved on April 17, 2009.

28. Calvin Klein, www .calvinklein.com. Retrieved on June 3, 2008.

29. Marc Karimzadeh, "PVH Sees Acquisitions Opportunities, *Women's Wear Daily*, June 20, 2008, p. 2.

30. Rosemary Feitelberg, "CH Carolina Herrera Spanning the Globe," *Women's Wear Daily*, May 6, 2008, p. 10.

31. Olga Zaretskaya, "Marc in Moscow," *Women's Wear Daily*, May 5, 2008, p. 22.

32. Marc Jacobs, www .marcjacobs.com. Retrieved on May 8, 2009.

33. Bridget Foley, *Marc Jacobs*, New York: Assouline Publishing, 2007.

34. Polo.com Ralph Lauren, "About Us," History: http:// aboutpolo.com/history/history .asp. Retrieved on August 12, 2008.

35. Ralph Lauren, *Ralph Lauren*, New York, Rizzoli, 2008.

Chapter 10

Getting Paid
or Paying
for Exports
or Imports

Figure 10.1 Negotiating purchase terms suitable both to the exporter and to the client is an essential part of building successful international trade.

. . . .

10

GETTING PAID OR PAYING FOR EXPORTS OR IMPORTS In order to turn international marketing opportunities into actual sales, exporters and importers need to learn the basic fundamentals of international trade finance so that their sales transactions will lead to the ultimate goal of getting paid in full and on time. This chapter presents the fundamentals of getting paid for export sales, and how to pay for imports that ultimately will be sold to consumers domestically. For a detailed presentation of this topic, see the Trade Finance Guide, which is available online at Export. gov, the U.S. government's export portal.[1]

uccess in the global marketplace often depends on negotiating sales terms and credit as well as appropriate payment methods. Whether exporting or importing goods or services, this information is useful in selecting the method of payment most appropriate to the transaction.[1]

Even an experienced exporting firm extends credit very cautiously. You need to evaluate new customers with care and continuously monitor ongoing accounts. An exporter may decline a customer's request for open account credit if the risk level is too great. Instead, the exporter may propose payment on any of the following delivery terms: cash payment in advance of delivery; through a letter of credit; documentary collections; or ultimately agree to an open account or even consignment sale. During—or before—contract negotiations the seller (exporter) should consider which payment option affords the needed level of security while also minimizing the cost and inconvenience to the buyer (foreign importer). Long-term international trade relationships are built upon mutually beneficial payment methods and terms. The primary methods will be detailed in this chapter.

For a fully creditworthy international customer, exporters should consider **extended terms**, meaning they can pay invoices later than the traditional 30 days, which domestically is considered the same as cash. In this situation, the exporter needs to remember that, according to law, any export is a gift until payment is received. From the importer's perspective, any payment is a donation until the goods are received. In some countries, cash terms are the business custom, extending credit on open account for 90 or even 120 days, without interest penalties is frequently the case in Asian countries, such as Japan. Some exporters will be unable to manage their cash flow and inventory control profitably within this arrangement and therefore may have to arrange special financing or just walk away from long-term credit sales.

Credit terms usually depend upon the quality of the business relationship, the economic strength of each party, and the payment terms competitors are offering. Getting paid in full and on time is the ultimate goal for every export transaction.

One way to reduce credit risks is to collect up-to-date credit information for potential or current business partners. This can be difficult when dealing with customers in countries where private financial information is only available from the business itself—which means having to rely on their honesty and integrity, and the solidity of the relationship.

If customers are established firms, or located in more advanced countries, private credit companies—such as Dun & Bradstreet (D&B), which offers both its *International Comprehensive Report* and the *International Business Information Report* and Graydon International—provide, for a fee, useful credit information. Some of the reports may cite U.S. companies that conduct business with the firm the exporter is checking out. By con-

Figure 10.2 Dun & Bradstreet (D&B) and Graydon International are two companies offering international credit reports that may help determine the importers ability to pay for goods or services, or the probability (not a guarantee) of an exporter to ship the goods or provide the services described in the contract of sale.

....

tacting these U.S. firms, an exporter may be able to find out the payment practices of a foreign prospect.

Companies new to export may first wish to check out what the U.S. Department of Commerce offers. It features the *International Company Profile (ICP)*, a customized report that can be used in evaluating potential affiliates as well as clients.[2]

Developed by the U.S. government's overseas posts, the profile includes a company's background information, standing in the local business community, plus bank references, and overall reliability and suitability. There are fees for this program as well, but at a much lower rate than private companies charge.

With the recent volatility in global trade, good credit practices include being aware of any unfavorable changes in a customer's payment patterns, refraining from going beyond normal commercial terms, and consulting with a U.S. Department of Commerce trade specialist.

INTERNATIONAL COMPANY PROFILE REPORT
Report prepared on: XXX
Country: Australia
Date: April 23, 2005

REPORT GENERATED BY:

Contact: John Kanawati, Commercial Specialist
Organization: U.S. Commercial Service, Sydney
Telephone: 61-2-9373 9207
Fax: 61-2-9221 0573
Email: John.Kanawati@mail.doc.gov

REQUESTING COMPANY INFORMATION:

Contact: Mr XXX, Government Legal Counsel
Organization: XXX
Address: XXX
Phone: XXX
Fax: XXX
Email: XXX

REPORT PREPARED ON THE FOLLOWING COMPANY:

Contact: Ms XXX
Organization: XXX
Address: XXX
Telephone: XXX
Fax: XXX
End of report.

Figure 10.3 The U.S Commercial Service's *International Company Profile (ICP)* provides exporters with credit checks and financial reports on companies in over 80 countries. Its worldwide network of specialists can investigate the financial strength of selected companies, using foreign press, industry contacts, and other sources. These reports are required by many export financing organizations.

. . . .

SPOTLIGHT ON GLOBAL TRADE 10.1:
The SWIFT Operating Center

An international wire transfer is commonly used and is almost immediate payment for goods—often before they are shipped. The exporter needs to provide bank routing instructions to the importer's bank, including the receiving bank's name and address, SWIFT (Society for Worldwide Interbank Financial Telecommunication) address and ABA (American Banking Association) number, as well as the seller's name and address, bank account title, and account number. Wire transfers are more costly to the importer than other cash-in-advance options, since the banks charge a fee for the transfer that is usually paid for by the sender.

SWIFT is solely a carrier of messages. It does not hold funds nor does it manage accounts on behalf of customers, nor does it store financial information on an ongoing basis. As a data carrier, SWIFT transports messages between two financial institutions. This activity involves the secure exchange of proprietary data while ensuring its confidentiality and integrity.

METHODS OF PAYMENT

There are several ways in which exporters can receive payment when selling their products abroad. Typically with domestic sales, if the buyer has good credit, sales are made on **open account**. Goods are shipped first and paid for within a specific amount of time, usually 30 days, or with finance charges assessed for balances due beyond the terms. A typical example would be a bill bearing the terms 2/10, net 30 that is a 2 percent discount for paying within 10 days of receipt of an invoice, with the balance due within 30 days. If the buyer's ability to pay is in question, **cash-in-advance** or payment prior to shipment is required.

For export sales or import purchases, however, these are not the most common methods. From the exporter's (seller's) perspective, the basic international payment terms, listed in descending order from the most secure to the most risky are:

> cash-in-advance;
> letter of credit;
> documentary collections (draft at sight or time);
> open account, and
> other payment mechanisms, such as consignment sales.[3]

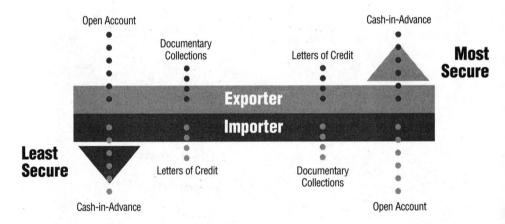

Figure 10.4 **Methods of Payment in International Trade.**

......

Source: U. S. Government Publications, retrieved on July 1, 2008, from www.trade.gov/media/publications/pdf/tfg2008.pdf.

Cash-in-Advance

Receiving cash-in-advance of a shipment might seem ideal, but you may insult your customer if you insist on this method. Although you may be relieved of collection problems and you get immediate use of the money, it could be the least attractive option for the buyer and it doesn't help to build a long-term, trusting relationship. Not as common internationally as in the United States, this method seems to be acceptable only when the exporter's product is unique, not available from other suppliers or is in strong demand, such as a designer original wedding gown or formal wear.[4]

Exporters just getting started in the export-import business may explain to customers that they need the advance payment in order to get them the best pricing, as **early-pay programs**—full payment to a manufacturer before shipment, or sometimes even prior to production—are an incentive for manufacturers to charge lower prices. A possible barrier to this method is the buyer's concern that the goods may not be sent if payment is made in advance. From an importer's perspective, advance payments also could create cash flow problems, as well as increased risk. They will, however, expect payment terms as soon as the trade relationship is established.

Electronic Transfer of Funds

Cash-in-advance payments should be processed through the international **electronic transfer of funds (ETF)**, when money is transferred from one bank to another, electronically, whether domestically or internationally. Also referred to as a **wire transfer**, it has the advantage of almost immediate, bank-to-bank payment.

Credit Cards

Many traders involved in exporting or importing directly with foreign buyers or sellers accept credit cards in payment for consumer and other products, generally of a low dollar value, purchased by end users, especially on the Internet and in other e-commerce exchanges. Since domestic and international rules governing international credit card transactions can differ, exporters and importers should contact their processor or bank for current procedures. These transactions are typically done by telephone, fax or e-mail, so sellers, as well as buyers, should be aware of possible fraud and take steps to protect their business. Even though exporters have to pay fees to the credit card companies and assume the risk of disputed charges, the convenience credit cards offer customers on a global basis will help this type of payment method—and exports—grow.[5]

Payment by Check

Advance payment by check can result in a collection delay of several weeks, which defeats the original intention of the seller receiving payment before shipment. If the importer's check is in U.S. dollars and drawn on a U.S. bank, the collection process is the same as for any U.S. check. But funds deposited by non-local checks, especially those totaling more than

$5,000 on any one day, may not become available for withdrawal for up to 10 business days, according to the Federal Reserve code.[6] The process becomes even more complicated if the check is in a foreign currency or drawn on a foreign bank.

If shipment is made before the check is collected, the exporter is at risk that the check may be returned due to insufficient funds in the buyer's account or due to a stop-payment order.

Letters of Credit

Since cash-in-advance is the most secure payment method for exporters, but least secure for importers, a compromise of sorts is the use of a **letter of credit (LC)**—which is a contractual agreement whereby an importer's bank, acting on behalf of its customer, authorizes the exporter's bank to make payment to the exporter upon the receipt of documents stipulated in the letter of credit. The issuing of a letter of credit alone is not a guarantee that the seller will be paid. The seller must comply with all the terms and conditions stated in the LC before funds will be transferred.[7]

INTERNATIONAL BANKING GROUP

ORIGINAL

Megabank Corporation
P.O. BOX 1000, ATLANTA, GEORGIA 30302-1000
CABLE ADDRESS: MegaB
TELEX NO. 1234567
SWIFT NO. MBBABC 72

OUR ADVICE NUMBER: EA00000091
ADVICE DATE: 08MAR97
ISSUE BANK REF: 3312/HBI/22341
EXPIRY DATE: 23JUN97

****AMOUNT****
USD****25,000.00

BENEFICIARY:
THE WALTON SUPPLY CO.
2356 SOUTH N.W. STREET
ATLANTA, GEORGIA 30345

APPLICANT:
HHB HONG KONG
34 INDUSTRIAL DRIVE
CENTRAL, HONG KONG

WE HAVE BEEN REQUESTED TO ADVISE TO YOU THE FOLLOWING LETTER OF CREDIT AS ISSUED BY:
THIRD HONG KONG BANK
1 CENTRAL TOWER
HONG KONG

PLEASE BE GUIDED BY ITS TERMS AND CONDITIONS AND BY THE FOLLOWING:
CREDIT IS AVAILABLE BY NEGOTIATION OF YOUR DRAFT(S) IN DUPLICATE AT SIGHT FOR 100 PERCENT OF INVOICE VALUE DRAWN ON US ACCOMPANIED BY THE FOLLOWING DOCUMENTS:

1. SIGNED COMMERCIAL INVOICE IN 1 ORIGINAL AND 3 COPIES.

2. FULL SET 3/3 OCEAN BILLS OF LADING CONSIGNED TO THE ORDER OF THIRD HONG KONG BANK, HONG KONG NOTIFY APPLICANT AND MARKED FREIGHT COLLECT.

3. PACKING LIST IN 2 COPIES.

EVIDENCING SHIPMENT OF: 5000 PINE LOGS – WHOLE – 8 TO 12 FEET
FOB SAVANNAH, GEORGIA

SHIPMENT FROM: SAVANNAH, GEORGIA   TO: HONG KONG
LATEST SHIPPING DATE: 02JUN97

PARTIAL SHIPMENTS NOT ALLOWED   TRANSHIPMENT NOT ALLOWED

ALL BANKING CHARGES OUTSIDE HONG KONG ARE FOR BENEFICIARYS ACCOUNT.
DOCUMENTS MUST BE PRESENTED WITHIN 21 DAYS FROM B/L DATE.

AT THE REQUEST OF OUR CORRESPONDENT, WE CONFIRM THIS CREDIT AND ALSO ENGAGE WITH YOU THAT ALL DRAFTS DRAWN UNDER AND IN COMPLIANCE WITH THE TERMS OF THIS CREDIT WILL BE DULY HONORED BY US.

PLEASE EXAMINE THIS INSTRUMENT CAREFULLY. IF YOU ARE UNABLE TO COMPLY WITH THE TERMS OR CONDITIONS, PLEASE COMMUNICATE WITH YOUR BUYER TO ARRANGE FOR AN AMENDMENT.

Figure 10.5 This sample international letter of credit indicates a bank's commitment to pay, on behalf of the importer, the exact amount of credit—provided the terms of credit are met by the exporter.

....

Banks issue LCs, at the request of their customers (buyers) in an international trade transaction, based upon their current account or line of credit. In this process, the bank—rather than the customer—assumes the promise to pay the seller. Payment must be for the exact amount of the credit. The buyer pays his or her bank a fee—a percent usually based on the value of the transaction—for this service.[8]

The involvement of established banks is important, since it lowers risk levels and protects the interests of both the exporter and the importer in an international trade transaction. LCs require that banks process payment based on the presentation of documents verifying the transfer of title and that specific steps have been taken, primarily by the exporter. Exporters request LCs when reliable credit information about a foreign buyer is difficult to obtain, but they are satisfied with the creditworthiness of the buyer's foreign bank. Buyers are also protected in the sense that no payment obligation kicks in until the goods have been shipped or delivered as promised in the credit. In the LC, the importer or buyer is called the **applicant**; while the exporter or seller is called the **beneficiary** to the LC.[9]

The LC is a separate contract from the sales contract on which it is based, so the banks are not concerned whether each party fulfills the terms of the sales contract. For example, if a letter of credit is the agreed upon payment method for an order for 10,000 100-percent-silk scarves to be shipped from China to a midwestern U.S. department store chain, payment will be made as soon as the stipulated documents, as described in the LC, have been received by the U.S. importer's bank. Even if the shipment contains 10,000 polyester scarves (instead of silk), payment will still be made. When using an LC, the buyer's bank's obligation to pay is solely conditioned upon the seller's compliance with the terms and conditions of the LC. The banks deal only in documents—not goods—when using an LC. Shipping errors, as in the example above, whether accidental or intentional, must be resolved outside the arena of the letter of credit.

Buyers paying for imported goods with a letter of credit need to remember that an LC is never intended to be a substitute for the seller's honesty or competence. The working relationship and level of confidence in a seller's ability or willingness to ship exactly what the customer ordered, is outside the function of the LC. Using D&B or Graydon International (cited earlier) will give an importer some idea of a supplier's reputation for paying its bills—but not on the delivery of the right goods and on time. Of course, most sellers interested in long-term, profitable relationships will not substitute lower quality merchandise or the wrong orders—but the occasional crooked firm has been known to take the customer's money and run![10]

The buyers' recourses are few, as international law suits to recover the cost of mistakes or intentionally fraudulent transactions would most likely be much more costly than the actual value of the goods in dispute. Also, just shipping the wrong goods back is not the answer, as two-way transportation costs could be more than the value of the shipment.

The letter of credit specifies the required documents the exporter must present, such as an **ocean bill of lading** or **air waybill** (if shipped by air), **consular invoice** (if the importer's country requires one) and an insurance policy, if the terms of sale require one be purchased by the exporter. The LC states an expiration date that all parties to the credit must adhere to or the credit is considered void. Before payment is made, the issuing bank will verify that all documents received from the exporter's bank conform to the LC's requirements. If not, the discrepancy must be resolved before payment can be made and before the expiration date.[11]

Confirmed Letter of Credit

A higher degree of security is available to the exporter when a **confirmed letter of credit**, an LC issued by a foreign bank (the importer's issuing bank) is confirmed by a U.S. bank, is required to comply with the terms of sale. The customer instructs the issuing bank to authorize a bank in the exporter's country to confirm the advising bank. The advising bank, which becomes the confirming bank, becomes obligated to pay the exporter, according to the terms of the credit—even if the buyer (or buyer's bank) defaults on the purchase. Remember, the banks are charging fees for their services, so they are happy to oblige.[12]

If a letter of credit is not confirmed, but still advised through a U.S. bank, it is referred to as an **advised letter of credit**, without the extra protection of confirmation. U.S. exporters should confirm letters of credit issued by foreign banks if they are unfamiliar with the foreign bank or concerned about the political or economic risk associated with the country in which the bank is located. Exporters need to check with the *U.S. Dept. of Commerce Export Assistance Center* for notice of any current foreign bank fraud or warnings regarding fake, worthless LCs—not uncommon in Africa and parts of Asia. Warnings may also be listed on the Web sites of U.S. government offices involved in trade, such as the U.S. Department of State, office of the Special Trade Representative (STR) and the Bureau of Industry and Security (BIS).[13]

Any change to a letter of credit after it has been issued is called an **amendment**. Banks charge fees for this service, even if just to extend the payment due date. It should be specified in the amendment if the exporter or the buyer will pay these fees. Every effort should

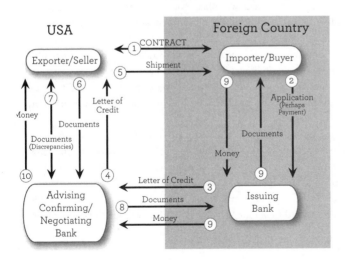

**Figure 10.6
Typical flow of a
Letter of Credit**

. . . .

Source: Figure recreated from *The Global Entrepreneur*, Second Edition, by James Foley, Jamric Press International, 2004.

be made to get the letter of credit right the first time, since these changes can be time-consuming as well as expensive.

Types of Letters of Credit

There are two basic types of LCs:

> Revocable
> Irrevocable

A **revocable letter of credit (LC)** can be withdrawn or modified at any time without notice to or consent from the seller. Employing a revocable letter of credit is inadvisable, as it carries too many risks for the exporter. Companies or individuals new to export should not use this payment form, unless they are doing an internal sale or transfer of goods between different branches of the same company. For example, General Motors U.S.A. may consign American-made autos to its subsidiary company in Spain. General Motors U.S.A. can feel pretty confident it will get paid through a revocable letter of credit, although payment may take place after the initial sales contract deadline and that of the letter of agreement.[14]

An **irrevocable letter of credit (LC)** is a legally-binding document that can't be changed by any of the parties to a credit (seller-exporter, buyer-importer, issuing or applicant bank, and the beneficiary bank), unless all parties agree to and sign off on an amendment.[15]

A **confirmed irrevocable letter of credit** is opened by an issuing bank whose authenticity has been confirmed by the advising bank and where the advising bank has added its confirmation to the credit. The words "we confirm the credit and hereby undertake..." are usually included in the confirmed LC.[16]

An exporter whose terms of payment call for a confirmed, irrevocable LC can expect on-time payment—as long as the requirements of the LC are met. The confirmed, irrevocable LC is particularly important from buyers in countries that are economically or politically unstable. The exporter or importer will have to pay an extra charge, called the **confirmation fee**, which may vary from bank to bank. New or inexperienced exporters or those dealing with unfamiliar customers should use only confirmed, irrevocable letters of credit.

Lower Risks

One reason for the popularity of LCs is that they help reduce risk for both the buyer and the seller, [when goods or payments are exchanged during exporting or importing] in the following ways:

> The seller's risk is reduced because a bank has promised to pay for the goods—providing the seller has met all the terms of the credit.
> The buyer/importer's risk is also reduced, knowing the seller won't get paid unless the importer's bank has received the proper documents—proving the terms as stated in the credit—have been met.

Key Points to Remember

> First, the LC does not guarantee payment to the seller. It only allows payment if the seller complies exactly with the terms of the credit.
> Second, the LC does not guarantee the buyer will receive goods that are the expected quality, color, style or other specification as described in the bill of sale.

Sellers do make honest mistakes, however, and should immediately replace the wrong order—shipping by air, if necessary. To maintain an on-going relationship, the seller may offer the buyer the option of purchasing the cheaper or erroneous goods at a very low price (to cover shipping costs) or at no cost if the buyer objects and the seller wants to rebuild trust and reliability—good customer relations.

Glossary of Letters of Credit Terms

> **Applicant:** The party applying for the letter of credit, usually the buyer/importer in a transaction.
> **Issuing Bank:** The bank that issues the letter of credit and assumes the obligation to make payment to the beneficiary, usually the seller/exporter.
> **Beneficiary:** The party in whose favor the letter of credit is issued, usually the exporter.
> **Advising or Negotiating Bank:** The bank that "negotiates, or approves" the letter of credit and receives payment and documentation from the issuing bank, on behalf of the beneficiary.
> **Amount:** The sum of money, usually expressed as a maximum amount, of the credit defined in a specific currency.
> **Terms:** The requirements, including documents that must be met for the collection of the credit.
> **Expiration date:** The final date for the beneficiary to present against the credit.[17]

A Typical Letter of Credit Transaction

Here are the basic steps of an irrevocable letter of credit that has been confirmed by a U.S. bank:

1. After the exporter and buyer agree on an LC as the payment method for an international sales transaction, the buyer arranges for its bank to open a confirmed irrevocable letter of credit in favor of the exporter (seller). It specifies the documents needed for payment, including the commercial invoice and letter of credit. The exporter can request that a particular U.S. bank be the confirming bank, or the foreign bank may select a U.S. correspondent bank.

2. The buyer's bank electronically transmits the LC to the seller's bank, which forwards it to the exporter, usually a manufacturer or distributor. It includes all details relating to the purchase and payment with the LC.

3. The exporter forwards the goods—and documents—to a freight forwarder —the service provider who prepares the goods who prepares the goods for transit and who presents the export documentation necessary for exiting the United States and entering the buyer's country.

4. Once the forwarder receives the goods it provides the exporter with a receipt from the shipper, a bill of lading (B/L) if by ship, train, or truck, or an air waybill if by air cargo. The B/L or air waybill is a contract between the exporter and the shipping company, not with the buyer.

5. The exporter's freight forwarder will ship the goods and submit the B/L or air waybill, along with any other required documents called for in the original terms of sale and the LC, to their own bank. The U.S. bank checks the documents for compliance with the LC and presents them to the buyer's bank for payment.

6. The importer's bank will review the documents and, if compliant, will pay the seller's bank; the importer's account will be debited the amount of the credit and the seller's bank will credit that account for the sale.

7. The importer's bank will forward the documents to the importer allowing them to claim the goods from the carrier and to clear them at customs.[18]

Documentary Drafts

A **documentary draft**, sometimes also called a bill of exchange, is analogous to a foreign buyer's check. Like checks used in domestic commerce, drafts carry the risk that they will be dishonored. However, in international commerce, title does not transfer to the buyer until they pay the draft, or at least engages a legal undertaking that the draft will be paid when due.[19]

Sight Drafts

A **sight draft** is used when the exporter wishes to retain title to the shipment until it reaches its destination and payment is made. Before the shipment can be released to the buyer, the original ocean bill of lading (the document that evidences title) must be properly endorsed by the buyer and surrendered to the carrier. It is important to note that air waybills of lading, do not need to be presented in order for the buyer to claim the goods. As such, risk increases when a sight draft is being used with an air shipment.

In actual practice, the ocean bill of lading is endorsed by the exporter and sent via the exporter's bank to the buyer's bank. It is accompanied by the sight draft, invoices, and other supporting documents that are specified by either the buyer or the buyer's country (packing lists, consular invoices, and insurance certificates). The foreign bank notifies the buyer when it has received these documents. As soon as the draft is paid, the foreign bank turns over the bill of lading thereby enabling the buyer to obtain the shipment.

There is still some risk when a sight draft is used to control transferring the title of a shipment. The buyer's ability or willingness to pay might change from the time the goods are shipped until the time the drafts are presented for payment; there is no bank promise to pay standing behind the buyer's obligation. Additionally, the policies of the importing country could also change. If the buyer cannot or will not pay for and claim the goods, returning or disposing of the products becomes a big problem for the exporter.

Time Drafts and Date Drafts

A **time draft** is used when the exporter extends credit to the buyer. The draft states that payment is due by a specific time after the buyer accepts the time draft and receives the goods (e.g., 30 days after acceptance). By signing and writing "accepted" on the draft, the buyer is formally obligated to pay within the stated time. When this is done the time draft is then called a trade acceptance. It can be kept by the exporter until maturity or sold to a bank at a discount for immediate payment.

A **date draft** differs slightly from a time draft in that it specifies a date on which payment is due, rather than a time period after the draft is accepted. When either a sight draft or time draft is used, a buyer can delay payment by delaying acceptance of the draft. A date draft can prevent this delay in payment though it still must be accepted.

When a bank accepts a draft, it becomes an obligation of the bank and thus, a negotiable investment known as a **banker's acceptance**. A banker's acceptance may also be sold to a bank at a discount for immediate payment.[20]

Open Account

In a foreign transaction, an open account means that when the exporter ships the goods and the bills, the customer is expected to pay by a certain date in the future, or a finance charge will be assessed on the balance due. This can be a convenient method of payment—if the buyer is well established, has a long and favorable payment record, or has been thoroughly checked for creditworthiness. Some of the largest firms abroad make purchases only on open account, but it's a risky method for those new to exporting.[21]

The fact that official documents are not used and a bank is not guaranteeing payment, make it difficult to pursue the legal enforcement of claims. It is just too costly and time consuming for an exporter to collect overdue accounts abroad. There are several ways to reduce credit risk, through such means as export credit insurance.

Consignment

Although not recommended for international sales, **consignment**, or the transfer of possession of a seller's goods to a buyer without any formal commitment to pay for the goods if they are not sold, is sometimes used in specific industries, the diamond trade being one of them.

Figure 10.7 Diamonds are among the fashion goods sold on consignment.

....

The great risk is that the buyer is not really a buyer, just a repository for the exporter's goods until they are sold. At that time, the buyer is expected to pay the seller the agreed upon price. This is very risky for export trade, as the costs of recovering any unsold—or unpaid for goods—is usually prohibitive. This method is not recommended unless it's a standard practice in a given industry because the buyer is not getting credit until the goods are sold.

Exporters thinking about any open sales terms should be completely aware of current political, economic, and commercial risks. Although it is up to sellers to decide on the payment method, they will weigh the amount of protection they desire against the inconvenience caused the buyer. The following factors may influence the payment method required by the seller:

1. The value of the transaction.
2. Type of merchandise exported.
3. Market conditions; a buyer's market or a seller's market.
4. Credit standing of the buyer.
5. Political conditions, exchange controls, currency fluctuations in country of destination.
6. Customs in the trade.
7. Payment terms of competitors.

Of course, buyers want a payment method that is most convenient for them, one that gives them the most advantage over the use of their money. So, if the buyer wants time payment delay, the exporter has the right to charge interest.

Payment terms, as well as prices, are important factors when marketing price-competitive products in global markets. Both exporters and importers should consult with their bankers if financing will be needed for the transaction before agreement on an international sales contract or issuing a pro forma invoice to a buyer.

SPOTLIGHT ON GLOBAL TRADE 10.2:
Where in the World Will Consumers Pay More?

Customers willing to pay for high-priced fashion populate not just New York, Paris, London, or Tokyo; they are from all over the world. Recently, The Nielsen Company, as part of a Global Designer Brand Survey, asked some 25,000 consumers in 48 countries if, when shopping, they sought out designer brands. The countries and their locations may seem unusual, but each of the 10 countries below has its own shopping areas and boutiques, and many feature fashion weeks. Entrepreneurs interested in expanding their fashion businesses might give these locales the once-over. The top 10 countries, ranked by the percentage of respondents stating they buy designer brands, are:

1. **Greece.** Forty-six percent of the consumers surveyed responded "yes." Grecian designs have influenced fashion throughout the centuries, and fashion consumers who can afford designer looks buy them. Emanuel Ungaro and Anna Molinaro for Bluemarine, and Greek designer Sophia Kokosalaki are among the well-known names here.

2. **Hong Kong.** Thirty-eight percent of those surveyed look for designer brands. Current research here says designer goods indicate not only wealth but social class. Popular brands here include Esprit Holdings, Giordano, and Coach.

3. **India.** Thirty-five percent shop for designer brands, leading designer Stella McCartney to open six stores in India, and Hermès and Fendi to open boutiques in Delhi.

4. **Hungary.** Thirty-two percent expressed interest in designer brands. Hungarians appreciate designs and brands because they are seen to present a better image.

5. **United Arab Emirates.** Thirty-one percent expressed interest. The cities here are mushrooming, particularly Abu Dhabi (now cited as the wealthiest city in the world) and Dubai. The Dubai Mall opening in 2009, the largest in the world, is Bloomingdale's first overseas venue. An Armani Hotel will occupy the lower floors of the world's tallest building here.

6. **Poland.** Twenty-seven percent. The Warsaw shopping mall, Arkadia, is home to 180 shops (Tommy Hilfiger and Pierre Cardin among others) and restaurants. In Krakow, the Galeria Krakowska is home to fashion retailers such as MaxMara, Versace, H & M, Zara, and more. Poland also holds its own fashion week.

7. **South Africa.** Twenty-seven percent. Johannesburg contains a number of stores offering brands such as Chloé, Miu Miu, Missoni, Prada Sport, and Kate Spade.

8. **Philippines.** Twenty-six percent. Greenbelt Mall, in Manila, claims as tenants Balenciaga, Banana Republic, Marc by Marc Jacobs, and Paul Smith.

9. **Netherlands.** Twenty-three percent. The street considered the Fifth Avenue of Amsterdam contains designer houses such as Chanel, Hermès, and Louis Vuitton. A street for pedestrians only is the base of retailers such as H & M, Mexx, and Zara. The jeans companies Levi Strauss & Company and Acne have plans for stores here, too.

10. **Ireland.** Twenty-two percent. Dublin offers retailers Marks & Spencer and Brown Thomas. Popular Irish designer Daryl Kerrigan shows her two collections—Daryl K and Kerrigan—in New York as well.

Source: Cecily Hall, "The WWD List. Fashion World: The Top 10 countries ranked by the percentage of residents surveyed who say they buy designer brands," *Women's Wear Daily*, April 3, 2008, p. 20.

SELECTING YOUR BANKER

Since banks make money on international trade finance, even your neighborhood bankers will try to get your business. They may not be experienced in letters of credit or other financing options, but local bankers will use an international bank in larger cities as a correspondent bank to handle their transactions.

Figure 10.8 **Large international banks can give advice on export financing methods.**

....

The practice should work out fine for the very small exporter who is only dealing with basic letters of credit. But if your business is on a larger scale, or you anticipate the need for more sophisticated international trade finance, you should consider going directly to banks experienced in this area. For exporters, the selection of an international bank can be crucial to their success. Banks can play a major role in expediting export sales transactions—or may be a major contributor to a failure. Consider a prospective bank's experience in the country where the majority of sales are expected. What are the legal lending limits? Is it full-service with respect to trade finance and letters of credit? Do bankers listen carefully to your needs and wants, not only concerning financial services, but also foreign market research and business contacts?

The larger international banks often have research departments and experts to give advice on more non-traditional financing methods. Their fees may be higher, but not as much as extra fees to a local bank that uses one of the bigger banks for its transactions. In times of global economic concerns, it is critical to seek out international bankers who have a better pulse on global financial risks, rewards, and methods for reducing risk.

Figure 10.9 **When selecting a banker, many exporters find that large international banks are able to offer advice on financing methods.**

....

SUMMARY

Success in today's global marketplace depends on having a competitive edge over not only foreign firms but also other U.S. companies engaged in export-import trade. One strategy is to offer prospective customers attractive sales terms, supported by appropriate payment methods. Although getting paid in full and on time for each sale is the ultimate goal for exporters, they should understand that a time payment delay will allow their importer customer the best use of their financial resources. Of course, the best payment method is one that minimizes risk for both the exporter and the importer.

Exporters, as sellers, must also accommodate the needs of their customers. For them, any sale is a gift until they are paid. Importers are often sellers as well, after importing goods or services for resale to the end user. But for them, any payment is a donation until the goods are received in good condition and matching their specifications.

Agreement on payment terms takes the guesswork out of a transaction. The guidelines should be clearly spelled out in the original terms of sale contract. All parties to the exchange should take care to know when payment must be made and how the funds will be transferred.

Exporters want to get paid as soon as possible, preferably as soon as an order is placed or even before the goods are sent to the importer. Therefore, the most secure payment method for exporters is to receive cash-in-advance. In this method, the exporter can avoid credit risk because payment is received before the ownership of the goods is transferred. Wire transfers and credit cards are the most commonly used cash-in-advance options. However, insisting on cash-in-advance may lose business to competitors who offer more attractive payment terms. Foreign buyers may be concerned that the goods may not be sent if payment is made in advance and that also can create cash-flow problems.

Importers want to receive the goods shortly after an order is placed, but would like to delay payment as long as possible. They want the chance, if possible, to inspect the arrived shipments for both the right quantity and quality and condition of the goods prior to making payment. Since they usually resell the goods, they would like to delay payment until they collect funds from their customers.

A compromise payment method, acceptable to both exporters and importers, is the letter of credit (LC), which reduces risk levels for both parties. The other common payment methods are: cash-in-advance; documentary collections; open account, and consignment. Both exporters and importers will negotiate a transaction's terms of sale to obtain the most advantageous payment method—in much the same way price is part of any sales transaction.

While most of the basic payment methods can be initiated by most local banks, firms anticipating the need for more sophisticated international trade finance should consider going directly to banks experienced in this area.

Key Terms

- Advised letter of credit
- Advising or negotiating bank
- Air waybill
- Amendment
- Amount
- Applicant
- Banker's acceptance
- Beneficiary
- Cash-in-advance
- Confirmation fee
- Confirmed letter of credit
- Confirmed irrevocable letter of credit
- Consignment
- Date draft
- Documentary draft
- Early-pay program
- Electronic transfer of funds (ETF)
- Expiration date
- Extended terms
- Freight forwarder
- Irrevocable letter of credit (LC)
- Issuing bank
- Letters of credit (LCs)
- Ocean bill of lading
- Open account
- Revocable letter of credit (LC)
- Sight draft
- Terms
- Time draft
- Wire transfer

Review Questions

1. How does use of the letter of credit reduce risk levels for the exporter? For the importer?

2. Which of the standard methods of payment are most risky for the exporter? Which are most risky for the importer?

3. Does the use of a letter of credit guarantee payment to the seller?

4. Is there any way to guarantee delivery of exactly what is ordered from a foreign source? What is your recourse if the wrong goods are received?

5. In what situations is a revocable letter of credit deemed acceptable?

6. Why should those firms new-to-export insist upon using a confirmed, irrevocable letter of credit in international transactions?

Discussion Questions and Activities

1. Interview one or two local bankers, starting with your own, for recommendations about locating a banking source with international trade finance experience. Your goal is to obtain advice on payment procedures and credit sources for your specific export-import activities.

2. Identify local international freight forwarders and Customs brokers and plan a class visit to one of their facilities, if approved by your school. Ask them to provide an International Order Flow Chart, tracing an international sale from the sales contract to the delivery of the merchandise of service.

3. Contact an international trade lawyer and ask what recourse an importer may have if goods paid for with a letter of credit arrive damaged or are intentionally switched with lesser quality or other specs that were not according to the original sales agreement. Report to your class the lawyer's suggestions on how to protect your rights in an international sales transaction.

References

1. "Trade Finance Guide: A Quick Reference for U.S. Exporters," April, 2008, by The International Trade Administration, U.S. Department of Commerce. Retrieved on July 1, 2008, from www.trade.gov/media/publications/pdf/tfg2008.pdf.

2. "International Company Profile," U.S. Commercial Service, U.S. Department of Commerce. Retrieved on February 9, 2009, from www.export.gov/salesandmarketing/ICP.asp.

3. First National Bank-International Trade Services, Omaha, NE, "Methods of Payment." Retrieved on July 23, 2008, from www.firsttradenet.com/its/methods/.

4. Op .cit. Trade Finance Guide, p. 5.

5. Ibid. p. 6.

6. "Regulation CC of the Federal Reserve-229.13(ii)," as stated in the Federal Reserve Code.

7. "Letters of Credit—An Introduction," *SITPRO Trading Advice: Letters of Credit—An Introduction*, December 15, 2008. Retrieved on December 28, 2008, fromwww.sitpro.org.uk/trade/lettcredintro.html.

8. Op. cit. Trade Finance Guide, p. 7.

9. Ibid. p. 7.

10. "Methods of Payment for International Sales," Encyclopedia of Credit, p.6. Retrieved on January 10, 2009 from www.encyclopediaofcredit.com.

11. Ibid. p. 9.

12. Op. cit. Trade Finance Guide, p. 7.

13. "L/C Fraud—that's how it works," Alibaba.com, posted November 27, 2007. Retrieved on February 9, 2009 from http://resources.alibaba.com/topic/230661/L_C_Fraud_that-s_how_it_works.htm.

14. Op. cit., SITPRO, p.3.

15. Ibid. p. 3.

16. Ibid. p. 3.

17. "What are letters of credit in international trade?" by WORLDLawDirect, July 3, 2008. Retrieved on July 30, 2008, from www.worldlawdirect.com/printerfriendly.php?id=530 .

18. "Letter of Credit Cycle," *Encyclopedia of Credit*. Retrieved on February 9, 2009, from www.encyclopediaofcredit.com/WebHelp/international_credit/letter_of_credit_graphical.htm.

19. Op. cit. Trade Finance Guide, p. 4.

20. "Banker's Acceptance," Risk Glossary.com., p. 1. Retrieved on February 9, 2009, from www.riskglossary.com/articles/bankers_acceptance.htm.

21. Op. cit. Trade FinanceGuide, p. 11.

Glossary

A

ABSOLUTE QUOTAS (7): Specific quantities of products that may enter the country during a given time period.

ACQUISITIONS (1): Occur when one company buys another.

AD VALOREM RATE (7): A duty percentage added to imported goods based on their value.

ADVISED LETTER OF CREDIT (10): An unconfirmed letter of credit.

ADVISING OR NEGOTIATING BANK (10): A bank that advises or negotiates a letter of credit and receives payment on behalf of a beneficiary.

AESDIRECT (5): U.S. Census Bureau's free, Internet-based system for filing shipment export declaration forms.

AGREEMENT ON TEXTILES AND CLOTHING (ATC) (3): Agreement to phase out the multifibre agreement and its quota system.

AIR WAYBILL (5): A non-negotiable type of bill of lading that serves as a receipt of goods shipped by an airline; a contract of carriage between the shipper and the carrier.

AMENDMENT (10): Any change that is made to a letter of credit.

AMOUNT (10): The sum of credit allowed as stated in a specific currency.

ANDEAN COUNTRIES (3): These include the textile- and apparel-producing nations of Bolivia, Colombia, Ecuador, and Peru.

ANTI-DUMPING DUTIES (6): Taxes on imported goods priced to sell at less than in the country of origin.

APPLICANT (10): The term used for buyer in a letter of credit.

ASSOCIATION OF SOUTHEAST ASIAN NATIONS (ASEAN) (3): A regional trade group that includes the countries of Brunei Darussalam, Cambodia, Indonesia, Laos, Malaysia, Philippines, Thailand and Vietnam.

AUTOMATED BROKER INTERFACE (ABI) (7): An integrated part of the Automated Commercial System (ACS), used by U.S. Customs to track, control, and process commercial goods imported into the United States.

AUTOMATED COMMERCIAL ENVIRONMENT (ACE) (8): An online access point connecting the Customs and Border Protection agency and the international trade community, increasing the effectiveness of trade enforcement, by preventing cargo from becoming tools of terrorism.

B

BALANCE OF PAYMENTS (1): A record of all export-import trade and other financial transactions, including investments and gold, flowing in and out of each country.

BALANCE OF TRADE (1): The difference between a country's total imports and its exports over a set time period. Should exports exceed imports, a favorable balance of trade, or a *surplus*, occurs; if imports are greater than exports, the country experiences an unfavorable trade balance, or a *deficit*.

BANKER'S ACCEPTANCE (10): A time draft accepted by a bank which then may be sold at a discount for immediate payment.

BENEFICIARY (10): The term for exporter in a letter of credit.

BILATERAL ALLIANCES (2): Agreements between two sovereign nations.

BILL OF LADING (B/L) (4, 10): A document issued by a carrier (ship, rail, truck) to a shipper (exporter) verifying specific goods have been received for delivery to a named place, to a certain consignee.

BRETTON WOODS CONFERENCE (2): The name given to the United Nations Monetary and Financial Conference held at Bretton Woods, New Hampshire, July, 1944.

BRICKS-AND-MORTAR STORE (9): A retail organization's physical store, as opposed to an Internet virtual store.

BUREAU OF INDUSTRY AND SECURITY (BIS) (5): An agency of the U.S. Department of Commerce, the Bureau's mission is to protect the national, economic, cyber, and homeland security of the United States through a law enforcement program focused on: sensitive exports to hostile entities or those that engage in onward proliferation; prohibited foreign boycotts; and related public safety laws.

C

CASH-IN-ADVANCE (10): Payment prior to shipment.

CE MARKING (2): A mandatory conformity mark on many products placed on the single market in the European Union (EU). It certifies that a product has met EU consumer safety, health, and environmental requirements for selling to any EU member country.

CENTRAL AMERICAN-DOMINICAN REPUBLIC-UNITED STATES FREE TRADE AGREEMENT (CAFTA-DR) (3): Agreement among the United States, Costa Rica, the Dominican Republic, El Salvador, Guatemala, Honduras, and Nicaragua to lower tariffs and other trade barriers.

CIA WORLD FACTBOOK (3): Contains U.S. government profiles of countries and territories around the world, including information on geography, government, business, economy, and communication.

COMMERCE CONTROL LIST (CCL) (5): Primary listing of export items subject to licensing

COMMERCE COUNTRY CHART (CCC) (5): Identifies reasons for U.S. export controls, by country.

COMMERCIAL INVOICE (5, 8): A bill for goods from the seller to the buyer showing the value and description of the merchandise plus payment terms.

COMPLIANCE ASSESSMENT (8): The systematic evaluation of importers' systems supporting their Customs and Border Patrol-related activities.

COMPONENTS (6): Materials and parts that go into finished goods.

COMPOUND RATE (7): A combination of ad valorem and specific duty rates.

CONFIRMATION FEE (10): Paid by an importer or exporter to obtain a bank's confirmed letter of credit.

CONFIRMED IRREVOCABLE LETTER OF CREDIT (10): An irrevocable letter of credit whose payment is guaranteed by a bank.

CONFIRMED LETTER OF CREDIT (10): An L/C that adds the endorsement of a seller's bank (the accepting bank) to that of the buyer's bank (the issuing bank). It provides the highest level of protection to the seller because the L/C cannot be canceled or changed unilaterally by the buyer or any other party to the credit without the consent of all parties involved.

CONSIGNMENT (10): A method of paying the seller only after the goods are sold.

CONSULAR INVOICE (5): Required by certain importing countries, this describes the goods to be shipped and their value, and it designates the buyer and seller—usually in the language of the importer's country and obtained from the Consulate of that country.

CONSUMER DEMAND (4): The amount consumers are willing to buy.

CONSUMPTION ENTRY (8): Usually for perishable goods; the importer indicates the tariff classification and pays estimated duties and processing fees.

CONTAINER SECURITY INITIATIVE (CSI) (6): A U.S. Customs control mechanism intended to avert terrorists' use of maritime containers to deliver a weapon into the United States.

COST, INSURANCE, AND FREIGHT (CIF) (7) term of sale indicating the cost of the goods, insurance, and freight

COUNTERVAILING DUTIES (3): Special taxes on imported goods from countries that unfairly subsidize these exports.

COUNTRY COMMERCIAL GUIDES (CCGS) (3): Free government reports that present a comprehensive look at a given nation's commercial environment, using economic, political, and market analysis.

CURRENCY REVALUATION (6): The government initiated, official changes in the value of a country's currency relative to other currencies.

CUSTOMS: See U.S. Customs and Border Protection.

CUSTOMS AUTOMATED COMMERCIAL SYSTEM (ACS) (7): See Automated Commercial System.

CUSTOMS BROKER (7): An independent business licensed by the Treasury Department and engaged in clearing goods through U.S. Customs.

CUSTOMS DUTIES (7): Government-imposed taxes on certain goods or services brought into a country from a foreign source; also known as *duties*.

CUSTOMS MODERNIZATION ACT (THE MOD ACT) (7): Declares that it is the importer's responsibility to use reasonable care in classifying imported goods and estimated values to enable Customs to accurately assess duties and ascertain that other legal requirements have been met.

CUSTOMS UNIONS (2): Nations agree to impose a common tariff wall on imports from nonmember countries (example: EU).

D

DATA WAREHOUSE CONCEPT (1, 3): Monitoring retail sales in order to fill in-store inventory swiftly.

DATE DRAFT (10): Specifies the date a payment for goods or services is due.

DESTINATION CONTROL STATEMENT (5): Appears on a commercial invoice and bill of lading and states that the shipment may go only to the specified destination.

DIFFUSION LINES (9): Lower-priced adaptations of a designer's signature line.

DOCK AND WAREHOUSE RECEIPTS (5): Documents used to transfer accountability when moving goods from the exporter to the port of embarkation.

DOCUMENTARY DRAFT (10): Analogous to a foreign buyer's check.

DOHA DEVELOPMENT AGENDA (2): The fourth ministerial conference of the WTO, held in Doha, Qatar, that presented mandates for regulators on a variety of subjects, including agriculture and services, but ended in failure as the early exit of China and India caused the talks to collapse. A serious blow to free world trade, the resumption of the Doha talks was uncertain at the time of publication.

DOHA TRADE TALKS (2): The fourth ministerial conference of the WTO, held in Doha, Qatar, provided mandates for regulations on a variety of subjects, including agriculture and services.

DUAL-USE ITEMS (5): Items with commercial and military applications.

DUMPING (6): The practice of selling products in foreign countries at less than wholesale price in the originating country in an attempt to dominate regional markets for certain targeted industries.

DUTIABLE VALUE (7): The value of the shipment subject to import duties.

DUTIES (7): See Customs duties.

E

E-COMMERCE (6): The buying and selling of products over electronic systems such as the Internet and other computer networks.

E-TAILERS (6): Retailers operating their own Web sites.

EAR 99 (5): An export control classification number for items that are subject to the Export Administration Regulations (EAR), but not specifically described by an Export Control Classification Number (ECCN) on the Commerce Control List (CCL).

EARLY- PAY PROGRAM (10): Full payment to a manufacturer before shipment and sometimes before production.

ELECTRONIC TRANSFER OF FUNDS (ETF) (10): Payments are transferred by computer, from one bank to another, such as a wire transfer, to pay for the international exchange of goods or services.

END-USERS (6): The final consumers of a product.

ENTITY LIST (5): Informs the public of parties whose activities imposed a risk of diverting exported and re-exported items into programs related to weapons of mass destruction.

ENTRY (7): The presentation of all documents necessary to clear the U.S. Customs, allowing foreign goods to enter the United States.

EQUITY (1): Ownership.

EURO (2): The official currency of the Eurozone.

EUROPEAN UNION (EU) (2): An organization of most of the nations of Western Europe, the EU was set up in the aftermath of World War II to bring peace, stability, and prosperity to Europe. The EU encompasses 493 million people in 27 countries.

EUROZONE (2): Includes the European states of Austria, Belgium, Finland, France, Germany, Greece, Ireland, Italy, Luxembourg, the Netherlands, Portugal, Slovenia, and Spain, plus the islands of Cyprus and Malta.

EVERYTHING INTERNATIONAL (3): A university-sponsored collection of resource links to many aspects of international trade relations found on the Web.

EXPIRATION DATE (10): The final date for the beneficiary to present documents against a letter of credit in international trade finance transactions.

EXPORT ADMINISTRATION REGULATIONS (EARs) (4): Regulate the export and re-export of most commercial items. Usually refers to regulation of "dual use" items—those that have both commercial and military or proliferation applications—but purely commercial items without an obvious military use are also subject to the EAR.

EXPORT CONTROL CLARIFICATION NUMBER (ECCN) (5): The code identifying the level of export control on the Commerce Control list.

EXPORT ENFORCEMENT ARM (EEA) (5): That part of the Bureau of Industry and Security (BIS) which protects national security by intercepting illegal exports and prosecutes export violations.

EXPORT-IMPORT TRADE (1): The marketing and physical distribution of goods, services, and technologies or ideas to countries other than that of their origin.

EXPORT LICENSE (5): A transaction-based requirement for an exporter to obtain a license from the U.S. Department of Commerce, Bureau of Industry and Security, if there is no assumed grant of authority to export goods, services, or other specific "items," under No License Required or License Exception. There is no License designated as an "Exporter's License"; each transaction will be judged by BIS to determine export requirements.

EXPORT MANAGEMENT COMPANY (EMC) (4): An independent firm which acts as the exclusive export sales department for non-competing manufacturers. An EMC functions in foreign markets in a way similar to how a sales representative or exclusive wholesaler functions for a manufacturer in the U.S. EMCs should not be confused with Export Trading Companies (ETCs), which are organizations that specialize in procurement on behalf of foreign clients. An ETC has no "loyalty" to a particular manufacturer. They are just looking for the best terms for their clients.

EXPORT PACKING LIST (5): Itemizes the contents of each shipment.

EXPORTER'S BILL OF LADING (B/L) (5): A contract between the exporter and a commercial carrier—ship, train, or truck—unless the goods ship by air, which is called an air waybill. B/Ls are either negotiable or non-negotiable.

EXPORTING (4): The distribution of a product, service, technology, or idea beyond the originating country's borders for the purpose of re-selling it.

EXPORTS (1): Sales of goods that flow out of the country.

EXTENDED TERMS (10): Allowing payments for goods and services to be made later than the traditional 30 days as in domestic sales.

F

FAIR TRADE (3): a system of exchange that creates greater equity and partnership in international trade.

FASHION MARKETING ORGANIZATIONS (9): Fashion businesses that have control over the design, manufacturing, and distribution of consumer goods.

FIRST PRICE (6): The manufacturer's selling price in the factory showroom.

FLAGSHIP STORE (9): A large company retail presence in a busy major city.

FOREIGN DIRECT INVESTMENT (1): Occurs when an investor, an individual, company, or even a government organization gains an equity (ownership) interest in a foreign operation.

FOREIGN INVESTMENT (1): Financial transactions involving loans or ownership of international enterprises and institutions.

FORMAL ENTRY (8): Imports of commercial or non-commercial (personal) shipments that exceed $2,000 in value; usually require a surety bond to guarantee payment of government-imposed duties.

FREE TRADE (3): A government trade policy that allows importers and exporters to interact without interference from government laws or protectionist policies. Under such policies, prices for international trade transactions are primarily based on market forces—supply and demand—and are not subjected to import tariffs or non-tariff barriers to trade.

FREE TRADE AGREEMENTS (3): Agreements eliminating almost all trade restrictions and subsidies.

FREE TRADE AREA (2): Geographic region without trade barriers. Member countries reduce tariffs on goods from each other but allow each nation to set its own duties for nonmembers (example: NAFTA).

FREIGHT FORWARDER (10): An independent, third-party international logistics specialist offering exporters transportation, documentation, and, in some cases, financial services, for a fee. Forwarders are usually licensed by the Federal Maritime Commission if they are involved in ocean transportation, and by the International Air Transport Association (IATA) if they act as an air cargo agent.

G

GENERAL AGREEMENT ON TARIFFS AND TRADE (GATT) (2): An international agreement to encourage free trade among members by regulating and reducing barriers to trade and by providing a common mechanism to dissolve trading disputes. Its duties were later assumed by the World Trade Organization (WTO).

GLOBAL BUSINESS (1): All commercial transactions—private and governmental—between individuals or enterprises of more than two countries.

GLOBAL SOURCING (6): The process of purchasing imports from markets throughout the world.

GLOBALIZATION (1): The increasing interdependency and interaction of nations, economies, and businesses all over the world.

GROSS DOMESTIC PRODUCT (GDP) (1): A nation's total output of domestically-produced goods, typically within a one-year period.

GROUP OF EIGHT (G8) (2): An international forum for promoting trade liberalization and economic cooperation. Current members are: Canada, France, Germany, Italy, Japan, the United Kingdom, the United States, and Russia.

GUANXI (1): Connections usually referring to government contacts and influence (Chinese term).

H

HAMILTON TARIFF ACT (8): In 1789, the second statute of the U.S. government authorized the collection of duties on imported goods.

HARMONIZED TARIFF SCHEDULE OF THE UNITED STATES (HTSUS) (7): A classification system to determine the amount of duties, or tariffs, U.S. Customs will assess imports into the United States, as proscribed by law. The importer must determine the classification number of the merchandise being imported, as a prerequisite to the entry process, but Customs makes the final determination of the correct rate of duty.

I

IMPORT LICENSE (5): Documentation required for certain foreign goods.

IMPORT QUOTAS (7): A quantity limit on imported merchandise for a specific period of time.

IMPORT TRADERS (6): Business people who import goods for resale.

IMPORTS (1, 3): Purchases of foreign goods or services that enter a country in various forms, including raw materials, component parts, and finished goods. Imports into the United States are generally controlled by the U.S. Customs and Border Protection agency of Homeland Security.

IN-BOND ENTRY (8): Arrangements made by exporter permitting duties to be paid upon arrival of the goods at the final port.

INFORMAL ENTRY (8): A process covering personal, commercial, and mail shipments entering to be consumed; in most cases the value is under $2,000.

INFRASTRUCTURE (8): A nation's bridges, highways, communications, and transportation systems.

INSPECTION CERTIFICATE (5): Required by some purchasers and countries in order to guarantee the goods shipped are the same as ordered.

INSURANCE CERTIFICATE (5): Used to assure the buyer that insurance will cover the loss of or damage to the cargo in transit.

INTELLECTUAL PROPERTY RIGHTS (2): The rights to creative works that may be protected by patents, trademarks, or copyrights.

INTERNATIONAL MONETARY FUND (IMF) (2, 8): An organization of 185 countries, working to foster global monetary cooperation, secure financial stability, and facilitate trade by providing temporary financial aid to countries with balance-of-payment problems.

INTERNATIONAL TRADE (1): Trade between businesses or governments in two or more countries.

IRREVOCABLE LETTER OF CREDIT (10): A legally binding document that can't be changed by any parties unless all agree.

ISOLATIONISM (6): Limiting international trade.

ISSUING BANK (10): The bank that issues the letter of credit and assumes the obligation to make the payment.

J

JOINT VENTURE (1): A direct investment in which two or more partners share specific percentages of ownership.

L

LANDED COST (6): The cost of goods at the final port-of-entry; includes shipping and entry costs, and duty charges to the foreign port of entry.

LEAD TIME (6): The amount of time between ordering goods and receiving shipments.

LESS DEVELOPED COUNTRIES (LDCS) (2): Economically impoverished countries, the poorest countries in the world.

LETTER OF CREDIT (L/C) (10): A bank's commitment to pay, on behalf of the buyer (importer), a specific sum of money, in a stated currency, within a fixed time period, to the seller (manufacturer/exporter), provided that the seller meets the terms as stated in the L/C and presents all required documents. L/Cs are common in international trade as they reduce the risk levels for both the seller and the buyer, since established banks are negotiating the documents and facilitating payments.

LICENSE EXCEPTION (5): An export item that normally would require a license, but is exempted due to special circumstances. Do not require written export control approval.

LICENSING AGREEMENT (1): An arrangement between a company with a well-known name and a manufacturer who pays a royalty to create goods using that name.

LIQUIDATION (8): The final step of the customs entry process, liquidation signifies the settlement of accounts between importer and the Government, and the importer's taking possession of the goods.

M

MANAGEMENT INFORMATION SYSTEMS (MIS) (1, 3): A combination of customized computer technologies and processes that provide information for management decision-making.

MARKET (6): A concept or place where producers of goods or services can offer their wares to buyers willing to pay the negotiated prices for those goods or services. International trade markets now include electronic venues such as eBay, Amazon, and Yahoo.

MARKET RESEARCH (4): Primary or secondary data collection and analysis to determine the needs or wants of a target market participant, including manufacturers, distributors, retailers or consumers.

MARKUP (9): The amount of increase in purchase cost between the various levels of the supply-chain, including the raw materials supplier, the manufacturer, the distributor, and the retailer to the final end user.

MERGERS AND ACQUISITIONS (M & As) (1): A merger occurs when two or more firms join together for a specific purpose, with each participant retaining a portion of ownership or control over the new entity; an acquisition takes place when one firm buys another.

MIXED VENTURE (1): A commercial operation in which ownership is shared by a government and a business.

MULTIFIBER ARRANGEMENT (3): A general legal framework for developing the conditions for controlling the textile and apparel trades.

MULTINATIONAL AGREEMENT (2): Agreement among more than two independent countries.

N

NATIONAL ASSOCIATION OF SECURITIES DEALERS AUTOMATED QUOTATIONS (NASDAQ) (3): The automated over-the-counter securities exchange, generally consisting of medium-sized firms.

NON-TARIFF BARRIERS TO TRADE (NTBs) (3): All international trade barriers that do not involve the assessment of duties, or taxes, in order to manage trade. Included are quotas, standards, and special certifications, such as Underwriters Lab listings and French language labeling requirements for exports to Canada's Quebec Province.

NORMAL TRADE RELATIONS (7): Relationships with the countries with whom we trade regularly and maintain the lowest duty rates.

NORTH AMERICAN FREE TRADE AGREEMENT (NAFTA) (2): An agreement among Canada, Mexico, and the United States, establishing a free trade area consisting of these countries.

NTIS EAR MARKETPLACE (5): Web site that offers EAR database and files that may be viewed and downloaded.

O

OFF-SHORE PRODUCTION (6): Goods produced in another country.

OFFICE OF FOREIGN ASSETS CONTROL (OFAC) (5): That part of the U.S. Treasury Department that administers and enforces economic and trade sanctions based on U.S. foreign policy and security goals.

OFFICE OF TEXTILES AND APPAREL (OTEXA) (3): A part of the U.S. Department of Commerce that develops programs and strategies to improve the competitiveness of the U.S. textile, apparel, footwear, and travel goods industries. It is a resource for current trade data and industry news.

OPEN ACCOUNT (10): Goods are shipped first and paid for within a predetermined specified time, typically 30 days.

ORGANISATION FOR ECONOMIC CO-OPERATION AND DEVELOPMENT (OECD) (3): An international establishment, created after World War II under the Marshall Plan, to help rebuild and promote social and economic growth among war torn countries.

OUTSOURCING (1): Shifting factory production, or services, such as call centers, to less-developed, cheaper labor countries.

P

PACKING LISTS (7): Documents that include information needed for transport such as the number and kinds of items in the shipment.

PIGGYBACKING (4): Seeking out and tying in with other non-competing, complementary product line exporters to achieve overseas distribution.

PORTFOLIO INVESTMENT (1): A non-controlling interest in a venture made in the form of either debt or equity.

PREFERENTIAL TRADE AGREEMENTS (PTAs) (3): Agreements between two countries to lower or eliminate trade barriers that have taken precedence over multilateral trade negotiations.

PRIMARY DATA (4): Original data collected for a specific research project.

PRIVATE LABEL (3): Brand name created by a retailer or wholesaler.

PRO FORMA INVOICE (4): An exporting form describing the merchandise, its specifications, packaging, per unit price, and payment terms.

PROTECTIONISM (6): Restraining trade between nations through tariffs, quotas, and other government restrictions.

PROTECTIONIST POLICIES (3): Government-imposed barriers to imports into a country, usually in the form of tariffs.

PROTEST (8): An importer's right to contest a Customs decision concerning the admissibility of a given shipment.

Q

QUICK RESPONSE (3, 6): The computerized replenishment system of popular items while in demand.

QUOTAS (1): Limits on the amount of certain categories of goods allowed to be imported from specific countries over a period of time, usually one year.

R

REVOCABLE LETTER OF CREDIT (10): A letter of credit that can be withdrawn or modified at any time without notice to the seller.

RULES OF ORIGIN (3): The rules that determine the country where an imported product was originally manufactured.

S

SECONDARY DATA (4): Research data previously compiled by various sources.

SHIPPER'S EXPORT DECLARATION (SED) (5): A document required by the U.S. government for any single export item valued over $2,500.

SIGHT DRAFT (10): Enables the exporter to retain title to a shipment until it reaches its destination and payment is made.

SIGNATURE LINE (9): Usually the highest priced items in a designer's collection. sourcing office (9): A buying office devoted to finding regional suppliers for fashion goods marketers.

SPECIFIC RATE (7): Duties set at a measurable rate such as per piece, liter, or kilo.

SPECIFICATION BUYING (6): A domestic retailer designs the product and has it produced overseas according to the buyer's directions.

STOCKING DISTRIBUTOR (4): Overseas intermediary who purchases products in quantity and maintains staff and facilities for international marketing.

SUPPLY-CHAIN MANAGEMENT (3): Coordinating supply sources with market demands to ensure production and delivery meet customer needs.

SURETY BOND (8): Required for all formal entries as a guarantee of payment duties posted with Customs.

S.W.O.T. ANALYSIS (6): An assessment of an organization's strengths, weaknesses, opportunities, and threats.

SYSTEM FOR TRACKING EXPORT LICENSE APPLICATIONS (STELA) (5): An automated voice response system that will provide the up-to-the minute status on any pending license application or commodity classification.

T

TARIFF PREFERENCE LEVELS (TPL) (7): Under NAFTA, administered like tariff-rate quotas.

TARIFF RATE QUOTAS (7): Provide for the entry of a specified quantity of quota products during a given time period.

TARIFFS (1): Tariffs are taxes imposed by governments on imports that may compete unfairly with domestically-produced goods, usually due to cheap labor, as a way of controlling the number of foreign products that can enter a domestic market.

TERMS (10): The requirements that must be met for the collection of the credit.

TEXTILE VISA (7): An endorsement in the form of a stamp on an invoice or export control license which is executed by a foreign government. It is used to control the exportation of textiles and textile products to the United States and to prohibit the unauthorized entry of the merchandise into this country.

TIME DRAFT (10): When the exporter extends credit to the buyer, the draft states when the payment is due (e.g., 30 days after acceptance).

TRADE DEFICIT (1): When a country's imports are higher than its exports.

TRADE DIVERSION (2): When a business in one country set up facilities in another country to supply material components to the original company.

TRADE SHOWS (4): Periodic wholesale markets for buyers and sellers in related fields, e.g., the MAGIC Apparel show in Las Vegas.

TRADE SURPLUS (1): When a country's exports are higher than its imports.

TRANSACTION VALUE (7): The price actually paid or payable by the buyer to the seller for goods sold for export to the U.S.

U

URUGUAY ROUND OF GATT (2): Member nation meetings (from 1986 to 1994) where among its negotiations, GATT was transformed into the WTO.

U.S. BILATERAL INVESTMENT TREATY (BIT) (3): A program that helps protect private investment, develop market-oriented policies in partner countries, and promote U.S. exports.

U.S. CUSTOMS AND BORDER PROTECTION (CBP) (7): The government agency responsible for the legal movement of goods into the U.S.; a name given the U.S. Customs Service as a result of the merger of Customs with other government agencies.

U.S. CUSTOMS AND BORDER PROTECTION DECLARATION FORM (8): A full and accurate description of imported merchandise that must be attached to the outside of each shipment.

V

VERTICAL INTEGRATION (9): An organization that controls the entire manufacturing and distribution processes of its products, (e.g., Nike, International).

VOLUNTARY SELF-DISCLOSURES (VSD) (5): When individuals and companies admit to violating export laws.

W

WAREHOUSE RECEIPTS (5): See dock and warehouse receipts.

WIRE TRANSFER (10): See electronic transfer of funds (ETF).

WORLD BANK (2): A specialized agency of the U.N. consisting of 184 countries whose goals are to give long-term financial assistance to middle-income nations and to poorer countries to alleviate poverty and encourage economic development.

WORLD CUSTOMS ORGANIZATION (WCO) (7): A global organization of some 171 Customs administrations that in total processes 98 percent of the world's trade.

WORLD TRADE ORGANIZATION (WTO) (2): The only global organization providing a forum for governments to negotiate trade agreements and a place for them to settle trade disputes.

Credits

Chapter 1

1.1   © Dave Yoder/Polaris
Table 1.1 Recreated by Alisha Neumaier
1.2   Courtesy of U.S. Customs and Border Protection
1.3   ACDI/VOCA
1.4   Courtesy of Fairchild Publications, Inc.
1.5   Recreated by Alisha Neumaier
1.6   Courtesy of Fairchild Publications, Inc.
1.7   Courtesy of Fairchild Publications, Inc.
1.8   Courtesy of Fairchild Publications, Inc.
1.9   Courtesy of Fairchild Publications, Inc.
1.10 Courtesy of Zappos
1.11 Courtesy of the U.S. Capitol
1.12 © Jackson Lowen/epa/Corbis

Chapter 2

2.1   Courtesy of Fairchild Publications, Inc.
2.2   Courtesy of the International Monetary Fund
2.3   Courtesy of the International Monetary Fund
2.4   Courtesy of the International Monetary Fund
2.5   © World Bank
2.6   Courtesy of WTO
2.7   Tomohiro Ohsumi-Pool/Getty Images
2.8   iStockPhoto
2.9   iStockPhoto
2.10 iStockPhoto

Chapter 3

3.1   Courtesy of Fairchild Publications, Inc.
3.2   Port of Los Angeles
3.3   Recreated by Alisha Neumaier
3.4   Mary Knox Merrill/Christian Science Monitor via Getty Images
3.5   © SCPhotos/Alamy
3.6   Courtesy of U.S. Customs and Border Protection
3.8   © EVERETT KENNEDY BROWN/epa/Corbis
3.9   Sean Gallup/Getty Images
3.10 © Robert Harding World Imagery/Corbis
3.11 Eamonn McCormack/WireImage
3.12 AP Images
3.13 REUTERS/Amit Dave/Landov
3.14 Jasper Juinen/Getty Images
3.15 ChinaFotoPress/Getty Images
3.16 Recreated by Alisha Neumaier

Chapter 4
4.1   Boston Globe/Pat Greenhouse /Landov
4.2   Courtesy of Fairchild Publications, Inc.
4.3   Courtesy of Fairchild Publications, Inc.
4.4   Courtesy of Central Intelligence Agency
4.5   Courtesy of Fairchild Publications, Inc.

Chapter 5
5.1   Courtesy of the Bureau of Industry and Security, U.S. Department of Commerce
5.2   Recreated by Susan Ramundo
Table 5.3 Recreated by Alisha Neumaier

Chapter 6
6.1   Courtesy of Sierra Trading Post
6.2   Courtesy of Fairchild Publications, Inc.
6.3a
and b   Courtesy of U.S. Customs and Border Protection. Recreated by Alisha Neumaier.
6.4   Courtesy of U.S. Customs and Border Protection. Recreated by Alisha Neumaier.
6.5   Courtesy of John Robinson
6.6   Recreated by Alisha Neumaier
6.7   Copyright 2008 Columbia Books, Inc. www.associationexecs.com, www.columbiabooks.com
6.8   REUTERS/Zainal Abd Halim
6.9   Courtesy of Metropolitan Pier and Exportation Authority
6.10   Courtesy of WTO. Recreated by Susan Ramundo.
6.11   REUTERS/Reinhard Krause
6.12   REUTERS/Aly Song

Chapter 7
7.1   Courtesy of U.S. Customs and Border Protection
7.2   Courtesy of U.S. Customs and Border Protection
7.3   Courtesy of U.S. Customs and Border Protection
7.4   Courtesy of www.usitc.gov
7.5   Courtesy of Fairchild Publications, Inc.
7.6   Photo by James Tourtellotte/Courtesy of U.S. Customs and Border Protection

Chapter 8
8.1   Copyright © The Granger Collection, New York / The Granger Collection
8.2   Courtesy of U.S. Customs and Border Protection
8.3   Courtesy of Fairchild Publications, Inc.
8.4   © nick baylis/Alamy
8.5   Courtesy of U.S. Customs and Border Protection
8.6   Courtesy of U.S. Customs and Border Protection
8.7   Courtesy of U.S. Customs and Border Protection
8.8   Courtesy of U.S. Customs and Border Protection
8.9   Courtesy of U.S. Customs and Border Protection
8.10   Courtesy of U.S. Customs and Border Protection
8.11   Courtesy of U.S. Customs and Border Protection

Chapter 9

9.1 Courtesy of Fairchild Publications, Inc.
9.2 Courtesy of Fairchild Publications, Inc.
9.3 Courtesy of Fairchild Publications, Inc.
9.4 Courtesy of Fairchild Publications, Inc.
9.5 Courtesy of Fairchild Publications, Inc.
9.6 Courtesy of Fairchild Publications, Inc.
9.7 Courtesy of Wal-Mart Stores, Inc.
9.8 Courtesy of Fairchild Publications, Inc.
9.9 Courtesy of Guess? Inc.
9.10 Courtesy of Fairchild Publications, Inc.
9.11 Courtesy of Levi Strauss & Co.
9.12 AP Images
9.13 Courtesy of Fairchild Publications, Inc.
9.14 Courtesy of Fairchild Publications, Inc.
9.15 AP Images

Chapter 10

10.1 © Rob Wilkinson/Alamy
10.2 iStockPhoto
10.3 Courtesy of Department of Commerce/International Trade Administration
10.4 Recreated by Susan Ramundo
10.6 Recreated by Erin Fitzsimmons
10.7 iStockPhoto
10.8 Courtesy of Fairchild Publications, Inc.
10.9 iStockPhoto
Page 289 Courtesy of Swift

Index

Page numbers in italics refer to figures or tables.